The COMPLETE IDIOT'S GUIDE TO

Word for Windows® 95

by Dan Bobola

D0123852

que®

A Division of Macmillan Computer Publishing
201 W. 103rd Street, Indianapolis, IN 46290

To my parents, who taught me the value of hard work and persistence.

©1995 Que Corporation

International Standard Book Number: 0-7897-0378-5

Library of Congress Catalog Card Number: 94-73411

97 96 95   8 7 6 5 4 3 2

Interpretation of the printing code: the rightmost number of the first series of numbers is the year of the book's printing; the rightmost number of the second series of numbers is the number of the book's printing. For example, a printing code of 95-1 shows that the first printing of the book occurred in 1995.

Printed in the United States of America.

Publisher
Roland Elgey

Vice-President and Publisher
Marie Butler-Knight

Editorial Services Director
Elizabeth Keaffaber

Publishing Manager
Barry Pruett

Development Editor
Melanie Palaisa

Technical Editor
Discovery Computing, Inc.

Production Editor
Phil Kitchel

Copy Editor
Anne Owen

Cover Designers
Dan Armstrong
Barbara Kordesh

Book Designer
Kim Scott

Illustrator
Judd Winick

Indexer
Kathy Venable

Production Team
Angela D. Bannan, Amy Cornwell, Chad Dressler
Joan Evan, Barry Jorden, Damon Jordan, Kaylene Riemen,
Bobbi Satterfield, Michael Thomas, Jody York

Contents at a Glance

Contents

7 Making Your ABCs Look Better: It's Called Formatting 75

8 Formatting Bigger Things: Sentences and Paragraphs 85

xiii

18 Start Your Own Newspaper: Desktop Publishing Techniques   213

22 Managing Your Documents and Your Health 267

Part 5: Troubleshooting Word for Windows 95 279

23 Finding Lost Things (Documents, Toolbars, and Your Mind) 281

Introduction

You're certainly not an idiot, but if Word for Windows 95 Version 7.0 makes you feel like one, then you need a book that can help. You don't need a book that assumes you are, or want to become, a Word *geek*. You also don't need anyone telling you that Word is one of the most sophisticated and complex word processors in the world, because you've probably already learned that the hard way. You are a busy person working hard in a busy world, and you just want to get your document written, printed, and available for you to use in the future.

Why Do You Need This Book?

With so many computer books on the market, why do you need this one? Because it focuses on getting your work done. This book is different because it won't assume that you know anything at all about how to use Word for Windows 95, or Windows 95, for that matter.

The most common tasks are broken down into easy reading chapters that you can finish in a short period of time. Simply open the book when you have a question or a problem, find the answer, solve your problem, and then get on with life.

How Do I Use This Book?

For starters, this isn't a novel you can take to the beach and read from cover to cover. I suppose you could, but people would talk. Rather, it's a book to guide you through tough times while you're at work or home. When you need a quick answer, use the Table of Contents or the Index to find the right section. Each section of the book is self-contained with exactly what you need to know to solve your problem or to answer your question.

Part 1: Creating a Masterpiece is especially for beginners. This section describes what Word is all about, how to get into it, and how to get out of it. Best of all, it describes how to get help while you are inside of Word. Along the way, you'll pick up some interesting tips about using the mouse, trying out those menus and buttons on the screen, and, oh yes, even create a document while you're at it.

Part 2: Enhancing Your Work takes Word a step further. Would you like your document to be noticed? Sure, you could print it on flourescent pink paper and paste it on the car windshields of your audience, but I'm thinking of something more subtle but still effective (and legal). You can make your text **bold**, *italic*, or <u>underlined</u> so key parts stand out from the rest. Or build a classy table and stick your words in it. And why stop at words?

Stick pictures in your documents (including borders and captions) and you're sure to create a stir. You can even learn what a header and footer are, and decide if and how they can help your document.

In **Part 3: Final Touches: Pampering, Proofing and Printing**, we fix all our mistakes and add our finishing touches *before* we print. How many times have you printed a document, only to trash it because a word was misspelled, or a caption was missing, or it just plain didn't look very good? It's always a good idea to take a final (quick) peek at the whole thing first, to catch simple errors. This section will cover all the hints and tips you need to know to apply those last minute touches that improve the appearance and contents of your document. You'll even learn how to quickly and easily replace one word with another throughout the whole document. And you can also experiment with the way it looks by using some fancy desktop publishing techniques (like using multiple columns, bigger first letters, fancy borders, and so on) to really impress that special someone in your life, even if it's only your boss.

In **Part 4: Customizing Word to Work for You**, we'll show you how to save time with Word's timesaving features. No one has to remind you that your time is valuable, so why not take shortcuts when they are available? Word is packed with things called templates that are terrific-looking documents just waiting for your words. No muss or fuss with any formatting or margins; just type and go! And you can learn how to create your own templates if you don't like any from Microsoft. This section will also point out some hints at managing the many documents you create, from storing them in the computerized version of the manilla folder to taking them home with you at night.

Finally, in **Part 5: Troubleshooting Word for Windows 95**, we'll help you find answers to some of Word's common problems. They say computers are really dumb, but mine knows precisely when to break down at the moment that causes me the most pain. The printer will jam when I'm already late for a meeting. A document that I swear was there yesterday mysteriously disappears. The mouse has gone bonkers and it's selecting text all over the darned screen. If you have similar problems you can either scream for help or else review these chapters on troubleshooting the most common problems encountered using Word.

You can follow along with any example in the book. If you are supposed to press a particular key on your keyboard, that key will appear in bold, as in:

Press **Enter** to continue.

The names of the keys, tabs, and boxes within dialog boxes are set apart in a special font:

Click on the General tab in the Options dialog box.

And buttons or tabs you work with in dialog boxes are bold:

Click **OK** when you're finished in the Save As box.

Sometimes you will be asked to press two keys at the same time. This is called a *key combination*. Key combinations appear in this book with a plus sign between them. The plus means you should hold down the first key while you press the second key listed. Here's an example:

Press **Alt+F** to open the **File** menu.

In this case, you should hold the **Alt** key down and then press the letter **F**, and something will happen on your screen. Then you can let both letters back up, the order doesn't matter. The **Alt** key is popular; it's used with practically all the letters on the keyboard to do one thing or another. These key combinations are explained throughout the book chapters and also on the Tear-Out card.

These boxes contain helpful hints, definitions, and shortcuts for clarifying some subjects and getting your work done even faster.

Also included throughout this book are special boxed notes that will help you learn more of the basics, and some of the advanced stuff, too:

These contain more of the advanced material that you can safely ignore if you don't have the time or the interest.

Acknowledgments

Thanks to everyone at Que who made this book possible. Melanie, Phil, Anne, and many others who were always there to help, including holidays and the middle of the night. I still wonder when they sleep. A very special thanks goes to Barry and Martha for considering me for this project, and for their guidance and professionalism.

Experienced users of Word 6 or Word 2 will benefit from discovering these completely new features in Word 7.

Trademarks

All terms mentioned in this book that are known to be trademarks or service marks are listed below. In addition, terms suspected of being trademarks or service marks have been appropriately capitalized. Que cannot attest to the accuracy of this information. Use of a term in this book should not be regarded as affecting the validity of any trademark or service mark.

Microsoft Word for Windows 95 Version 7.0, Windows 95, Windows, Microsoft Graph, Windows NT, and Microsoft Word are registered trademarks and Word for Windows 95 is a trademark of Microsoft Corporation.

WordPerfect is a registered trademark of Novell Corporation.

CorelDRAW! is a trademark of Corel Systems.

PC Paintbrush is a registered trademark of Zsoft Corporation.

Ventura Publisher is a registered trademark of Xerox Corporation.

Part 1
Creating a Masterpiece

Great! You paid a couple thousand dollars for a bundle of technological debris to help you write reports, and the thing takes up more space, time, and energy than your old typewriter ever did. But could that old clunker ever give you as much enjoyment as battling starships, blasting away doomed demons, or wandering through the myst? Certainly not!

And, oh yeah, it can also do word processing. I'm not here to tell you that the new Word for Windows 95 will be as exciting as all that. But maybe together we can make the basics of creating documents less of a chore, so you can get back to the finer things in life. Whatever they may be.

Chapter 1

Top Ten Things You Need to Know About Word for Windows 95

Word for Windows 95 *may* be easier than previous versions of Word, but you need a friend to show you the secret shortcuts. When you don't have time to search the rest of this book, you can check this chapter for the major steps in creating a document.

1. You can open Word for Windows 95 from the Taskbar.

Press the **Start** button on the Windows 95 Taskbar. Slide up to the **Programs** menu and watch it open up with a list of all the programs installed and ready to run on your computer. Now slide the mouse cursor over to this list and find **Microsoft Word** and click on it. Word for Windows 95 will start.

If you want to get fancy, you can also open Word a different way. Click the right mouse button over any empty space on your Windows 95 desktop. A menu will pop-up, and you can move the mouse arrow down to the command **New**, opening a second menu. Click on New Microsoft Word Document, and a new icon will appear on your desktop. It's a Word document! Just double-click on it and Word will open, ready to edit this new document.

You can close Word for Windows 95 by pressing the **Close** button at the top right corner of your screen. The **Close** button is a small square button labeled with an **X**, living in the Title bar.

2. Finding and opening your documents

To locate any document, open the **File** menu and choose the **Open** command. You can also press the **Open** button on the **Standard** toolbar.

The list of documents will appear in the Name box on the Open dialog box. You can open any document by clicking on it once to select it, and then pressing the **Open** button (or the **Enter** key). You can also open documents from this list by double-clicking on the document name.

The Open dialog box provides a way to search, preview, and open your documents. Documents show up in the Name box on the left. If your document isn't there, you have several features to choose from to help you look. You can press the **Look in Favorites** button to check the contents of a commonly used folder. You can put out a search for the document using any of the four text boxes at the bottom. These are used to search for files based on name, type, property, or even when you last worked on it, and pressing the **Find Now** button starts the search.

You can even perform more sophisticated searches for your documents, and all the details you'll need can be found in Chapter 23.

3. If you think the mouse is faster, use it.

I'm sure there are plenty of professional touch-typists out there who can run circles around even the best mouse person and can't stand to take their hands off the keyboard. No problem! Absolutely every feature in Word for Windows 95 can be performed using either the keyboard or the mouse. So choose your weapon. Or use them both inter-changeably.

Most beginners to word processing find their threshold of pain has already been ex-ceeded, so it doesn't hurt much more to also learn the mouse. It's a good idea. Word for Windows 95 includes lots of shortcut tasks that are completed at the click of a mouse button. It is the recommended way of moving around in Windows programs. Learn more about your friendly mouse in Chapter 3.

4. Wizards and templates make it easier to create documents.

When starting a new document, open the **File** menu and choose the **New** command. You will be able to choose from over 35 preconstructed and professionally formatted docu-ment templates that can save you all the time that's normally spent making your docu-ment look better.

You can create standard business letters or faxes without wasting time on deciding where the date should go or how much space should be between paragraphs. You can focus on the content of your document.

Not interested in focusing on content? Okay, I'll let you in on a tip. There are prewritten letters stored inside of Word for Windows 95! These are genuine letters ready for you to plagiarize without penalty or guilt. Just change a few words, and it may serve a needed purpose for you. Okay, maybe there will be some guilt if you actually send the *Letter To Mom* to your mother without customizing a single word. Or at least there should be. Learn more of the magic of using wizards in Chapter 21.

5. If you want to change something, you must first select it.

Word for Windows 95 uses the term *select* to describe the action you must perform to choose the text (or graphics) you want to manipulate. You can practice selecting text by clicking and dragging with the left mouse button anywhere inside your document. When text is selected, it will look different on the screen. If your normal background color is white, the selected portion will be black.

You can select a single letter of a word (a character) or a whole word, a sentence, a paragraph, a page, or the whole stinking document. (You get the idea.) Anyway, the reason you select something is to prepare it for the onslaught of a Word feature, like **bold** or *italic*. Click those buttons on selected text, and it will change before your eyes. To learn more of this selecting thing, check out Chapter 6, an entire chapter dedicated to this important method of manipulation.

6. You can change the view if you don't like what you see.

You have choices available for how to view your document. The default screen view of your document is called the Normal View. It is the best view to use for performance reasons—Word reacts quickest to your commands in this view. The down side is that you don't see everything that might be printed, like headers, footers, page numbers, and so on. You also may see things that won't be printed, like dotted lines and paragraph symbols.

You can change your view quickly by opening the **View** menu and choosing either the **Normal** or the **Page Layout** view. In Page Layout view, you actually see the representation of a sheet of paper on your screen. That's helpful when you are trying to balance text and graphics on the screen, and also to see what might be stored in your margins (like page numbers or footnotes).

If you need more help on changing your view, be sure to check out Chapter 19.

7. Save time and effort by importing things into your document.

All you need to import text or graphics from almost any other Windows program in your Word document is available at your fingertips. You can even import a lot of stuff from your old DOS programs! So don't throw away anything you've created in the last ten years if you think you could benefit from re-using it. If it can fit inside of your computer, there's a good chance you can import it into a new document in Word for Windows 95. Of course, if you've created nothing worth keeping in the last ten years, then get rid of it and make room for the new furniture.

Almost everything you're likely to need to know about importing files can be found in Chapter 13.

8. Ask for help when you need it!

If you aren't sure how to do something in Word, ask for help. Press the **F1** key. Press that light bulb button and start the Tip Wizard. Or press that button next to it (the one with the pointer-question mark combo) and then click on top of the thing you need help with. Open the **Help** menu and choose either the help topics or the **Answer Wizard**. In fact, if you open the Answer Wizard, you can type your questions in plain English and get common sense answers in reply.

And help isn't limited to problems—let Word for Windows 95 help keep your documents accurate with proofing tools like the spell checker, thesaurus, and grammar checker. They're all available from the Tools menu, but the spell checker is running all the time automatically. Any misspelled words are underlined with a red wavy line. Just click on the misspelled word using the right mouse button and a pop-up menu will provide correctly spelled alternatives to choose from. Chapter 4 explains all of Words' help features to you.

9. Printing your document doesn't have to be painful.

Just press the **Printer** button on the Standard toolbar to print a copy of your document. You can also open the **File** menu and choose the **Print** command and use the Print dialog box, where you can choose options like a different printer, making multiple copies, and collating. You can even choose to print a document without opening it. Just click the document name with the right mouse button in the File Open dialog box and choose **Print** from the pop-up menu. Learn more about printing in Chapter 17.

If you are frustrated because your document is not printing, check the obvious things first (printer turned on, cable attached, and so on) and then refer to Chapter 25.

10. Save your work often, and wear clean underwear.

You never know when you may have an accident and find that it's too late to do anything about it. In Word for Windows 95, you've got lots of choices. The nimble-fingered may prefer **Ctrl+S** to save the last changes to a document. Mousers can click on the **Save** button (the picture of a diskette) found in the standard toolbar at the top of the screen. Geniuses can figure out how to get Word to automatically save your work every five minutes. You can, too, by turning to Chapter 5 and learning about the Autosave feature.

What's New in Word 7.0 for Windows 95?

Here are some of my favorite new features of Word for Windows 95. Some of them can be addictive, like typing crazy questions—and getting answers—with the Answer Wizard, and others work so quietly that you almost forget they are running—like the automatic spell checker. But they're all so helpful that you will wonder how you ever got along without them. Oh, by the way, throughout the book, I'll sometimes call Word for Windows 95 Word 7, Word 7.0, or just Word. It's all the same thing.

The Answer Wizard

An entertaining new feature is included with the help provided by Word called the Answer Wizard. It's a dialog box where you can type your question in plain English and get real answers in reply. For instance, you can type *What button do I press to get this stupid thing to print?* And the Answer Wizard will politely respond with the correct answer and provide even more helpful information specific to printing and toolbar buttons. And one of the most important words you can feed it is *troubleshoot*, which is the key word for providing step-by-step solutions to dozens of the most common problems you are likely to run into.

Learn more about the Answer Wizard in Chapter 4.

Automatic Spell Checker

You'll never have to run the spell checker again. That's because it's always running, in the background, waiting to pounce on your misspelled words and wave the red flag—actually, a wavy red line that appears as an underline for any misspelling. When you feel like correcting them, just click on the word with the right mouse button and a pop-up menu will provide the closest correct spelling choices. Just click on the one you want and it replaces your mistake instantly.

By the way, you can still run the old familiar spell checker in the dialog box if you want. You will notice that it's significantly faster, though, because all the words in your document will have already been looked up. All you have to do is decide on a replacement for each one.

Find out more about the nifty new spell checker, along with other helpful proofing tools, in Chapter 16.

Instant Numbered or Bulleted Lists

No more messing around with that Style box to create your numbered or bulleted lists. You don't have to do anything more than type a number, followed by a space or period, then some text, and press Enter. Before you can bat an eyelash, the next number pops out of nowhere and your cursor is lined up in a nicely formatted auto-numbering style. You just keep typing the text, and the numbers will keep appearing. And you just have to press Enter twice to turn off the numbers. That's easy numbering.

You can do the same with bulleted lists by using the asterisk key, or the small letter 'O'. The bullets will keep flying until you turn them off. If you're interested in learning more about instant numbering and bullets, turn to Chapter 8.

Quick Borders

In the same spirit as instant numbered and bulleted lists, you can create a quick border in less than a second, depending on how long it takes you to tap a key three times. Just place your cursor wherever you'd like a border to appear and press the hyphen key three times (you can also chant "there's no place like Word" and maybe a vision of Bill Gates will appear on your screen). Anyway, pressing the hyphen key three times creates a thin border automatically. You can also press three equals symbols and create a double border. Find out more about borders in Chapter 18.

Managing Your Documents Easier

Where's the best place to manage your documents? Anywhere you can find them, I say. And I can always find them in the Open dialog box, listed with dozens of others, just waiting for me to decide to open or not. Well, it happens that you've been given much more power inside this Open dialog box, and it's all in your right mouse button. Click any document in the list with the right mouse button and a shortcut menu will appear. You'll see just about every command you will need to manage that document at your fingertips, including renaming it, deleting it, even printing it, and you never have to open it up.

You can learn more document management techniques in Chapter 22.

Use a Yellow Highlighter for What's Important

I can't live without using my yellow highlighter to mark up documents and call attention to important passages. Believe it or not, they found a way to put this same function into

Word for Windows 95. But before you take a yellow marker to your computer screen, let me point out that it's easier to press the **Highlight** button on the Formatting toolbar. You can apply it to any text in your document just as you would Bold, Italic, or Underline. They even made it so the edges aren't as smooth, as though you drew the line by hand.

Obviously, this is a feature intended to be used while viewing documents on your screen. You could print them, I suppose, but you'd need a color printer. If you are interested in other character formatting techniques, turn to Chapter 7.

Find and Replace in the Past, Present, and Future

Here's a big improvement guaranteed to save you lots of editing time and keep you grammatically correct at the same time. The old Find and Replace feature has been improved to include different forms of a word. You know, the past, present, and future effect that tends to change words slightly, causing most Find and Replace features to miss them. So now you can decide to replace every instance of the word *purchase* with the word *buy*, for example, and automatically have the other forms of the word replaced correctly (*purchasing* will become *buying*, and *purchased* becomes *bought*). This stuff is so good that it got its own chapter in this book, and it's called Chapter 14.

Your Guardian Tip Wizard

Microsoft packed a little helper in each copy of Word for Windows 95. It's called the Tip Wizard, and you can think of it as sort of a mentor that constantly watches over you (at least while you're typing in Word). The Tip Wizard is designed to watch and track your actions and suggest better ways to complete your tasks. For instance, start creating a numbered list the old fashioned way and the Tip Wizard will bring you up to speed with the latest shortcuts on completing the task. There's even a Show Me button you can press if you want to sit back and let the Tip Wizard demonstrate a particular technique right inside your document. Yes, you might expect to pay millions of dollars for such a helper, but it's yours free. All of the help topics are covered in detail in Chapter 4.

Printing Is Better, and You Deserve It

They say printing is now a fully independent 32-bit task, but they can say anything they want. What it really means for you is that printing is faster. Your work comes out faster, and you can move on to your next document faster—which means you can get home faster to do the things you'd much rather be doing. Chapter 17 tells you all about printing your Word documents.

Your Document Can Be Named Whatever You Want

Instead of cramming all the important identifying thoughts about a document into eight letters, you can now use whole words, and even spaces between the words! Sure, there is a limit to the total length of the name, and you still can't use some symbols found on the keyboard, but hey, this is about as good as it gets for old DOS die-hards! Wake up now and have some fun naming that document. Refer to Chapter 5 if you need more help.

Chapter 2

Fast Start: Creating a Letter

In This Chapter

➤ A method for quickly creating a new document

➤ Where is Word hiding in Windows 95?

➤ Typing and printing a simple letter in Word

➤ Sampling a Wizard to create an attractive memo

But I Want to Go Home

It's 4:45 on a Friday afternoon. Your boss is demanding that report from you before you leave for the weekend. Your throat is dry and your palms are sweaty. The company typewriter was hauled away two days ago when a misplaced Twinkie gummed up its guts. That machine was your lifeline. No one's around to help. What do you do?

Windows 95 at Your Service

Look at that new computer on your desk. Someone has loaded Windows 95 and a "food processor" called Word. Your boss is expecting you to use these to finish your report. You've got 15 minutes to write and print a simple one-page status report or else scrap the weekend plans for the trip to the beach.

Don't panic. You've got this book, and it's opened to the right chapter. Nothing more here than typing a document and printing it out. If you need to do more than just create and print the report, you can refer to the remaining chapters. They go into much more detail. Good luck! (By the way, Word is a *word* processor!)

Turn on the computer. If you don't know how, check the computer's user's manual or ask someone for help. Look at the display screen. Pretty Windows 95! A few pretty little pictures on a vast, empty, blue screen. You're doing well.

Don't Kill the Mouse That's Wearing Buttons!

Look for the mouse. No, not the one in the pantry, the one connected to this computer. It looks like a soap on a rope. It has two or more buttons on it. A healthy mouse lies with its buttons up. Grasp the mouse and glide it back and forth across the desk, but away from the doughnut crumbs. Now stop looking at the mouse and look at the screen. You should see a little arrow moving around at the same time you roll the mouse. Hold the mouse a different way if the arrow movement doesn't match your hand movement. Back and forth… now try circles… Great job! You're communicating with the computer.

It's time to tell the computer that you want to write that report. Move the mouse arrow on your screen to a clear spot on the vast, open, blue screen. Look closely at the mouse. It's time to try the buttons—there's nothing to fear. You'll be using both buttons (they do different jobs), so we'll call them left and right mouse buttons. If you have a middle button, you can ignore it.

The mouse helps you communicate with your computer.

Meet Your Mouse

The real trick in learning how to use the mouse is to get comfortable with it. Keep your index finger on one button and your middle finger on the other. Ignore any middle buttons if you have them. Now try clicking each button on an empty background spot of the Windows 95 desktop. The right mouse button will cause a square box to appear. You can change the left and right buttons by pressing the Windows 95 **Start** button on the Taskbar, opening the **Settings** menu, and choosing **Control Panel**. Double-click the Mouse icon and click the left-handed option in the Mouse Properties dialog box.

Giving Birth to a New Document

Press and release the right (not the left) mouse button. This action is called a *click*. In computer terminology, you have just *clicked* the right mouse button. Look at the screen to see what you've created.

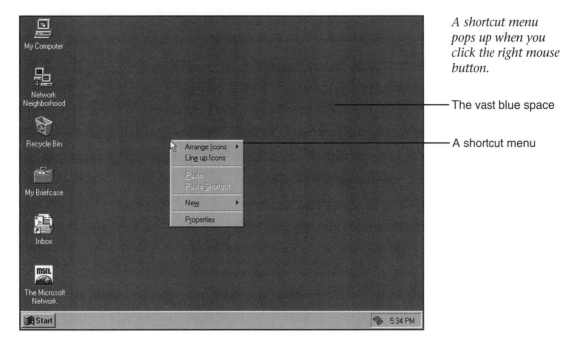

A shortcut menu pops up when you click the right mouse button.

The vast blue space

A shortcut menu

No, it's not your report, but it's a start. You've opened a shortcut menu, and now the computer is asking if you want to do something. Slowly move the arrow down to the word **New**. We want to create a new report. If you startle easily, be forewarned that another box is about to pop up. When the arrow lands on the word New, you'll see the following:

The start of something great.

Cascading menus may appear on either side.

Gently move that mouse arrow left or right so it can land on this new box. Now slide it down to where it says Microsoft Word Document. Holding the mouse real steady (so it stays on Microsoft Word Document), click the left mouse button. Either button will work, but the left button is technically correct for purists.

These mysterious boxes disappear into the vast blue again, and you are left with something new on your display screen. See it? Look closely to find the little picture with the title New Microsoft Word Document. You made this—you should be proud!

Now slide the mouse arrow anywhere on top of this new little picture. Steady the mouse again because we're going to try something fancy. Try to click the left button twice, right in a row, quickly. This is called *double-clicking* on the new little thing you just created. Having trouble double-clicking? It's just a shortcut—you don't have to master the skill. Instead, you can click once and then press the **Enter** key on the computer keyboard. Most keyboards label this key to help you find it.

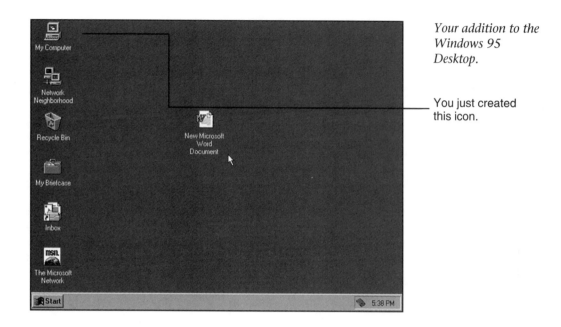

Your addition to the Windows 95 Desktop.

You just created this icon.

After either double-clicking or pressing the Enter key, you'll be rewarded with a complete change of scenery.

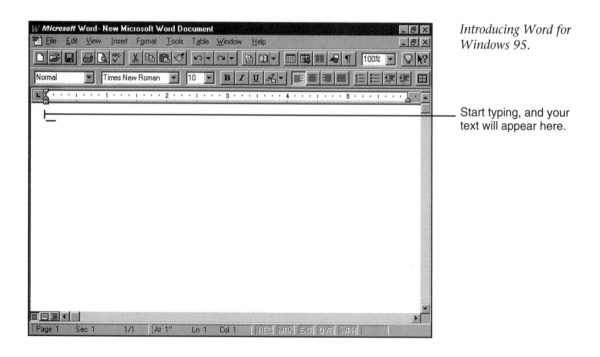

Introducing Word for Windows 95.

Start typing, and your text will appear here.

Welcome to Word 7

You see a large, white background. Think of this as a sheet of paper. Look again at the computer keyboard. Think of it as your old typewriter. However you were able to manage before, try it now. No need to use the mouse for awhile, just the keyboard. Now type. If this is a report for your boss, start by typing the date. That way the archaeologists will be able to accurately identify when you died in case of a disaster.

If you're very careful typing, you won't have to look through the rest of this book to find things like backing up and changing things (Chapter 3), skipping backwards to adjust a previous sentence (Chapter 14), or making sure things are spelled correctly (Chapter 16).

After typing the date, try pressing the **Enter** key once. Press the **Enter** key once again. Now type something like "Dear boss" and press the **Enter** key again. Get the idea? Now type your report the best you can. You don't have to press the Enter key at the end of each line (like with your old typewriter)—just keep typing and see what happens. Your words automatically flow to the next line.

Keep Typing

Before long, you'll have a report that looks something like the following:

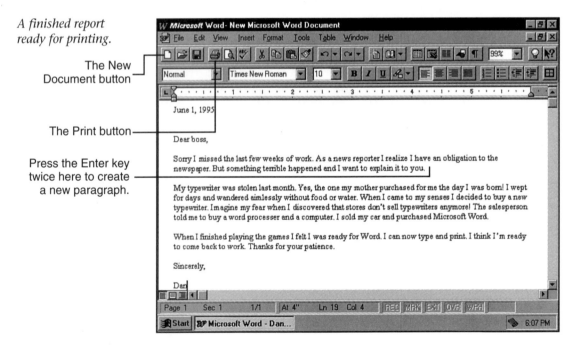

A finished report ready for printing.

The New Document button

The Print button

Press the Enter key twice here to create a new paragraph.

If it's good enough for you, it should be good enough for your boss. Now you can just leave it on your computer and hope your boss comes by to read it. Better yet, why not get this thing printed on real paper and actually hand it to your boss?

Now it's mouse time. Move it around again to see that it has been there all the time. Look at the preceding figure again and notice the little pictures near the top. Little computer pictures are called *icons*. These icons happen to be plastered on *buttons*. Buttons are gathered together in rows known as *toolbars*. With your mouse, you can actually press these buttons, and the computer will do something. The figure identifies an important button that looks like a printer. Yes, pressing this button will print your report.

If you can't see the Print button, your toolbar may be hidden. Be sure to check Chapter 23 to learn ways to bring back the standard toolbar.

It's a Print!

Gently move the mouse around until it lands directly on top of the **Print** button. Holding the mouse steady, click the left mouse button. That's it. Seriously, that's it! If you want another copy, press the button again. If you've been blessed with good fortune, this computer is connected to a printer, your report is already finished, and you are happy.

If, on the other hand, nothing happened, you are probably feeling rage, anger, and hatred. That's normal with computers. Call your spouse or significant other and tell him or her you'll be a few minutes late. Then turn to Chapter 17 to get help with printing, or Chapter 25 if you *really* need help printing.

Assuming you're happy with the results and you've given your boss the report, you can go home now. You've accomplished what previously required a typewriter, paper, and ribbon. You've done something very productive—you've made technology work for you.

The memo you just created can be stashed away on your computer and *saved* if you think you'll need to use it in the future. For help on how to do this, turn to Chapter 5.

Something Better

Feeling brave? Reasonably comfortable with the mouse? Want to create a professional-looking report for your boss without straining your cranium? A wizard will show you how.

Move the mouse arrow up to the Word File button on the top left of your screen. This row is called the Menu bar and File menu. Click the **File** menu to reveal its commands, then click the **New** command. Click it once with the left mouse button, and you'll see something similar to this:

A selection of prepared memos to choose from.

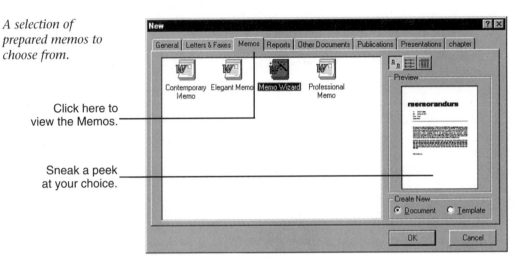

Click here to view the Memos.

Sneak a peek at your choice.

Just above the largest white space on your display screen you'll see words like Letters, General, Faxes, and others. Find the one that says Memos and move the mouse arrow so it's right on top of the word **Memos**. Now click the left mouse button once. When you see a bunch of Memo icons in the large white space, you'll know that you're looking at the choices for creating a new memo.

The Wizard of Word

Move the mouse arrow so it rests on top of the icon labeled **Memo Wizard**. Click the left mouse button twice in rapid succession (double-click). If you can't manage the double-click thing, then just click once and press the **Enter** key, or click it once and then click the **OK** button.

Now the wizard will come to life. You'll be asked some questions about how you want your memo to appear. You don't have to do anything except press the **Next** button. Press the **Next** button six times and you've completed all of the questions. Then press the **Finish** button at the checkered flag.

This looks like magic, doesn't it? Nice big letters and lines already painted on the page. The parts of the memo are easy to figure out. Someone already stuck the date in for you. They even put your name in the **From:** part! At least I hope it's your name; it actually inserts the name of the licensed owner of Word 7 automatically. All you have to do is tell the computer who this memo is intended for.

Look at what's written next to the **To:** line. Inside the brackets is the suggestion to **Click here and type names**. Try it. Move the mouse arrow until it rests on any word between the brackets. Then click the left mouse button once. The sentence changes in appearance, turning light gray in color, anticipating activity from you. Now type your boss's name—or your dog's name if you're just practicing. They may even be the same, for all I know. The typed name will appear and replace the brackets and sentence. You're ready to move on.

Similarly, you can click on the **CC:** area and type a name for the carbon copy, or click on the **RE:** area and type something regarding what this memo's about.

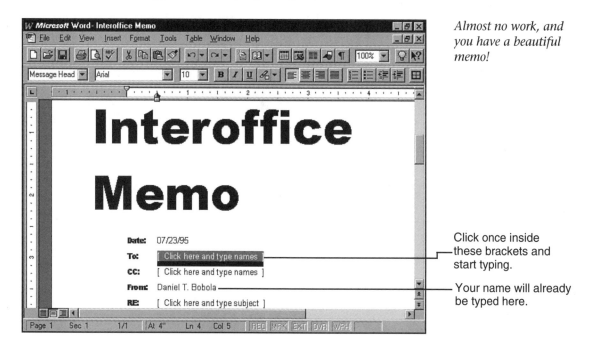

Almost no work, and you have a beautiful memo!

Click once inside these brackets and start typing.

Your name will already be typed here.

Now move the mouse arrow down to the part that says **Click here and type your memo text**. This is the main body of the memo. Go ahead and type the memo to your boss. As you did earlier, don't worry about reaching the end of the line. Keep on typing; the computer will take care of moving to the next line as needed.

Printing Again

Good enough? Time to print. Just as in the previous example, move the mouse arrow until it rests on top of the Print button with the hardly recognizable printer icon. Now click the left button once. Your document will be on the way to the printer, and you'll soon be on your way home.

You might want to stay around and celebrate. After all, the memo you just created probably looks better than professionally manufactured memo forms that your company pays lots of money for. Avoid the urge to celebrate with your computer. Go home and celebrate with your significant other or your dog.

If you're interested in learning more about these automatic wizards, try reviewing Chapter 21. You actually have many letters, forms, reports, calendars, and other things already built-in and, in some cases, already filled out! Like a letter to your mother that's ready to send! Or a monthly calendar personalized with your name already on it!

Welcome to the world of computing.

The Least You Need to Know

You don't have to know much about Word for Windows 95 to get some productive work out of it. In this chapter, you learned that:

➤ You can create a new Word document by clicking the right mouse button anywhere on empty space on the Windows 95 desktop.

➤ Although it's easy to just start typing, it's even easier to use a wizard, like Memo Wizard.

➤ Printing in Word for Windows 95 is as easy as clicking the Print button on the toolbar.

Word Basics: Do You Do Windows?

If you come from the world of DOS (or even Windows 3.1) and are ashamed to admit that you don't remember very much, I have some good news for you. You don't have to remember much. And for those of you who have previously cursed the mouse, perhaps going so far as to swing the critter by the tail right into a wall, we hope you feel better. Now it's time to give your mouse a second chance.

Windows Basics 101

For those of you who don't do windows, swallow your pride, pick up a squeegee, and join me for a brief lesson in Windows. Or you can find someone who knows the basics and pay them to stay by your side at all times. Let's start with the mouse, open and close some windows, and get started by typing something into Word for Windows 95.

Using the Mouse

Your mouse is linked with a graphic on the screen called the *pointer* (also referred to as the *cursor*). Move the mouse, and your pointer moves. The trick is to get the two in synch, and make the pointer go where you want it to. By carefully moving the pointer and clicking the buttons on your mouse, you can accomplish some real work.

Get acquainted with your mouse.

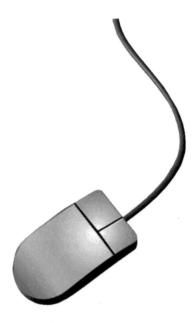

All basic mouse actions in Word for Windows 95 use either the left or right mouse button. Lay the beast flat on the mouse pad, with the ball down. The cord should come out of the top, going away from you. The left mouse button is used to select or activate something. The right mouse button is used to provide additional information about an object or to display menus. Windows 95 allows you to swap the mapping of the buttons if you are left-handed.

22

Quick Mouse Tips

To get to know your mouse quickly, here are some easy tips:

➤ Place the mouse in the middle of the mouse pad, with its cord extending away from you.

➤ Rest your hand on the mouse, with your palm at the base. Grip the mouse comfortably with your thumb and ring finger. When curled, your fingers should rest lightly on the buttons at the top of the mouse. Rest your index finger on the left mouse button and your middle finger on the right button. If your mouse has a middle button, ignore it.

> **Three Button Mice** For a mouse that supports three buttons, well, forget about the middle button. It's pretty much ignored in Word for Windows 95.

➤ Move the mouse around. Slowly at first, then gain some speed. Watch the screen and observe how the mouse pointer moves as you move the mouse.

➤ If the mouse reaches the end of the mouse pad, but you still have farther to go on the screen, then lift up the mouse, put it back in the middle of the mouse pad, and continue where you left off. It's like using your hand to keep a spinning wheel spinning.

➤ Practice until your eyes can tell your hand to move the mouse up, or a little to the left, and so on. When you are confident with who's in charge, and it's not the mouse, you win!

Once you can move the mouse around, what's next? Try the act of *clicking* and *double-clicking*. These terms usually apply to the left mouse button, but Windows 95 has included some functions with a click on the right button.

There are basically three actions you can take with your mouse (I'm sure you can think of more, but these are the *productive* things you can do). First, there's *clicking*, and you can do this by pressing either the right or left button once. Next, there's *double-clicking*, performed only with the left button by clicking it twice in rapid succession. Finally, there's *dragging*, which is kind of like walking and chewing gum at the same time. Click on an object (like an icon, or a box) with the left button and hold it down, and continue to hold it down while you move the mouse around. You are now dragging. Also, when you release the left mouse button, it's known as *dropping*.

Now it's time to put these skills together. Move your mouse pointer to an icon and practice clicking and double-clicking it. You can't hurt anything by doing this. You'll find that a single-click selects something, while a double-click actually starts or runs something. When you single-click the right mouse button, a helpful menu appears.

Mouse Pointers You're Likely to See

As you move the mouse pointer across the screen, its appearance can change to provide feedback about a particular location, operation, or state of mind. This table lists common pointer shapes and their uses.

The Changing Mouse Pointer

Looks Like	Where You See It	What It's Used For
⌖	Over most objects	Pointing, selecting, moving, resizing
I	Over text	Selecting a position or text
⧗	Over object or location	Wait! Your computer is busy!
⌖⧗	Over any screen location	Computer is busy, but the pointer is still active
⌖?	Over most objects	Contextual Help (point and learn)
Q	Inside a window	Zooming a view (point and zoom)
←∣→	Along column gridlines	Resizing a column
↕	Along row gridlines	Resizing a row
←∣∣→	Over split box in vertical scroll bar	Splitting a window (or adjusting a split) horizontally
≑	Over split box in horizontal scroll bar	Splitting a window (or adjusting a split) vertically
⃠	Over any object	Not available. Can't do. Don't try.
☞	Over text list	Choosing item from list

Exploring a Window

When you double-click on an icon like My Computer on the Windows 95 desktop, you'll open the window called My Computer. Once you've opened one window, you've opened them all. All the windows in Windows 95 and all Windows applications, such as Word, have several elements that are the same: title bars, title bar buttons, toolbars, menu bars, and borders. It makes it easy for you, and easy for me, because I only have to explain all this once!

You'll also notice that when you open a window on the desktop, a "depressed" button with the name of the open window on it appears in the Taskbar at the bottom of the screen.

Minimize, Maximize, Restore, and Close

The basic component of Windows is, well, *windows*. Windows are boxes on your screen that you can open, close, move, and resize, and they usually contain folders or programs that open up new windows. Where should you start?

You should become familiar with the three buttons in the top right corner of all windows in Windows 95. They are officially called the *title bar buttons*. The middle title bar button can change, by the way, depending on how you are viewing your window. The figure shows the different choices—in this case, the left set of buttons is for the program window and the right set is for the document window.

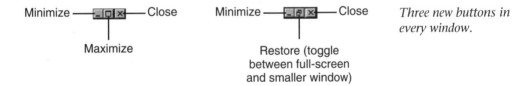

Three new buttons in every window.

Following is a list of the title bar buttons:

Minimize   This button shrinks the window and makes it a button on the Taskbar.

Maximize, or Restore   If your window is not taking up the entire screen, this button will force it to. It's also a toggle button, so if the current window is already full screen, it will change it to a smaller window that shares the desktop space with other windows.

Close   This button will close the current window. This is a new concept in Windows 95 and Word for Windows 95. It's another way (and the recommended way) to close programs from now on.

Moving and Resizing Windows

Sometimes you'll have two programs visible on the screen at the same time, like when you're writing a report in Word and want to see figures found in an Excel worksheet. You'll want to resize and move the program windows around so you can clearly see the contents of both. Try this with your Word screen. Click the middle title bar button (**Restore**) to toggle from full-screen to a smaller window. Everything is still there; it's just smaller. Try to change the size of the window. Using your mouse pointer, move it to any of the four edges of the Word window (top, bottom, right, or left). The pointer will change in appearance to a two-headed arrow. If you click and drag the edge, you can shrink or expand the width or height of the window. If you click and drag from the corner of the window, both the width and height resize simultaneously. Practice your window sizing technique—it may come in handy someday.

Click, then drag-and-drop the
top or bottom to change its size.

*Word in a window,
but not full screen.*

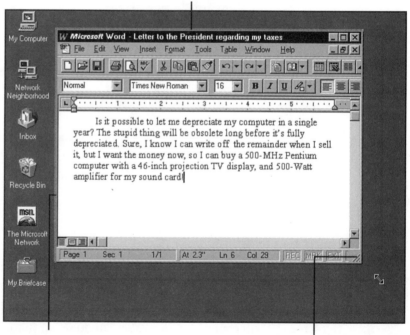

Click, then drag-and-drop the side
of a window to change its size.

Click, then drag-and-drop a window
corner to do both at the same time.

You may have to move a window out of the way. You move windows by clicking and dragging the title bar at the top of the window. You can move a window so it hangs off of your visible screen. Windows 95 won't let you move a window completely off the screen; there's always a tiny piece of the title bar that you can grab with the mouse and drag back into view.

Working with Folders and Files

When you double-click on the My Computer icon, the window displays more icons. Here are two important icons you'll see:

　　　　Diskette Drive

　　　　Hard Drive

You may have other icons for the Control Panel and printer, and perhaps for additional drives. The Hard

> **Folders and Documents** If you come from the DOS world, you'll recognize that *directories* are now called *folders*. And *files* are now called *documents*; at least the ones you create in Word.

Drive icon is the starting point for finding a file or folder. *Files* are what you create; *folders* are where you store your creations; and the documents you create in Word are also known as files. You can create folders to organize your documents. You can easily browse through the files and folders on your computer just by double-clicking on the Hard Drive icon with the left mouse button.

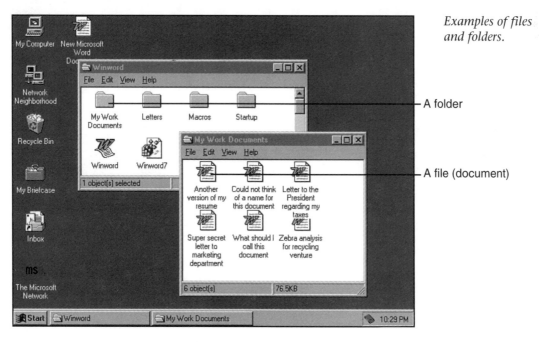

Examples of files and folders.

A folder

A file (document)

Starting Word for Windows 95

In Chapter 2, I showed you the quickest way to open a new Word document. But there are more traditional ways to open Word. You can start Word by clicking on the **Start** button, selecting **Programs**, and clicking the **Microsoft Word** menu command. The following figure shows which menus to open.

Starting Word the old-fashioned way—from the menu.

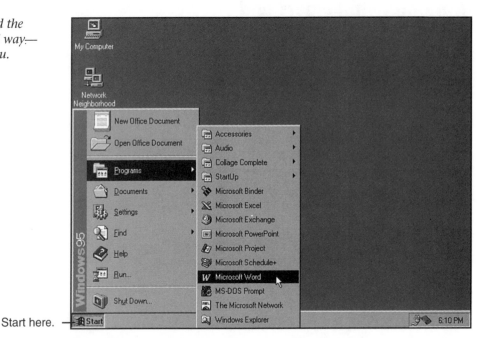

Start here. ──

Check This Out...

Get Your Programs to Show Up If you installed all of your Microsoft Office programs using the Start/Remove Programs feature of the Control Panel (found by selecting Settings from the Main menu), they will show up in the Programs menu.

The following figure shows what the majority of users see when they open Word. Nothing has been created yet. The largest part of the display screen is white with nothing in it. It represents a blank sheet of paper ready for you to type on. You will be using the computer keyboard to type words onto this simulated sheet of paper. That's easy enough to understand. But what are all these gadgets on the screen?

Think of this as your visual index for finding help about the Word screen as you read this book.

Insertion point (text cursor)

Title bar   Menu bar   Standard toolbar   Formatting toolbar   Ruler

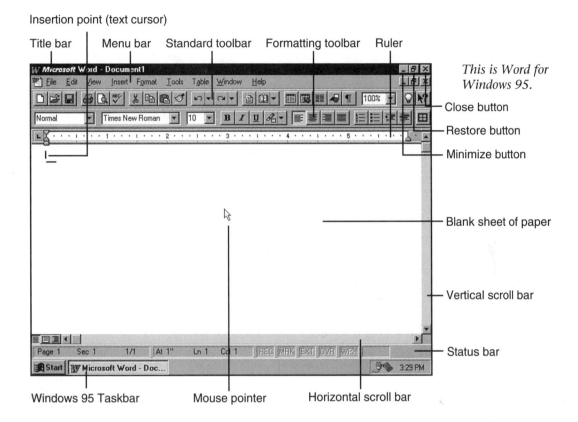

*This is Word for
Windows 95.*

Close button

Restore button

Minimize button

Blank sheet of paper

Vertical scroll bar

Status bar

Windows 95 Taskbar   Mouse pointer   Horizontal scroll bar

Title Bar

The *title bar* is always visible at the top of your screen. Besides identifying Microsoft Word itself in the title bar, Word now shows the name of the document on which you're currently working.

Menu Bar

Take a look at the row of words near the top of your screen. See the words File, Edit, View, and so on? These words make up the *menu bar*. It's called the menu bar because it holds a bunch of menus. You use a menu when you want Word to do something for you, like print or add in footnotes. Of course, you don't see *print* or *add in footnotes* because only the names of the main menus are visible. To read the menus, you have to open them. To open a menu, move your mouse on top of the menu item you want and click the left mouse button once.

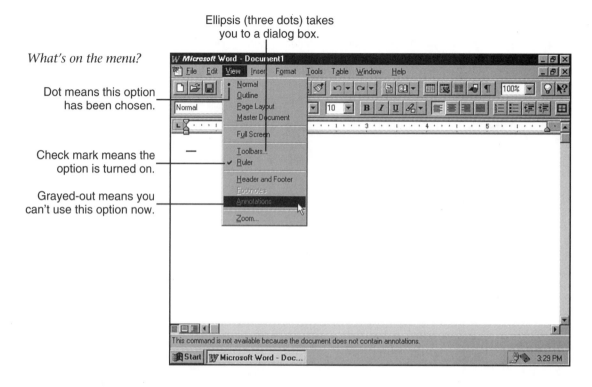

What's on the menu?

Ellipsis (three dots) takes you to a dialog box.

Dot means this option has been chosen.

Check mark means the option is turned on.

Grayed-out means you can't use this option now.

So clicking the left mouse button opens each menu and makes the commands visible, but watch what happens as you move your mouse across the menu bar! Slide it over to **View** or **Insert** and see what happens. The menu pops down! Slide the mouse down each command in the menu to practice highlighting each selection. You can execute any of the commands that are selectable (not grayed out) by clicking the left mouse button.

If you look closely at the View menu, you'll see that some commands are plain, like Full Screen, and do simply what they say. When you click on the Full Screen command, all the toolbars and menu bars disappear, leaving you with much more room for typing your document. Try it! You can always press the Escape key to bring back all of the toolbars, menu bars, and everything else.

Some commands, however, have other symbols attached at the beginning or the end.

➤ The dot in front of some commands tells you that this mode (or method of doing something) is currently selected. Other choices are seen immediately above or below.

➤ The check mark is a standard way of letting you know that an option is "on." For example, the Ruler command is a toggle that can be turned on or off. Select such a command when the check mark is displayed, and you'll turn it "off." When the Ruler command is on, the ruler appears on your screen below the formatting toolbar. When it's off, the ruler is hidden.

➤ An ellipsis (three dots) at the end of a command will bring up big and hairy dialog boxes that you'll learn about shortly.

Standard Toolbar

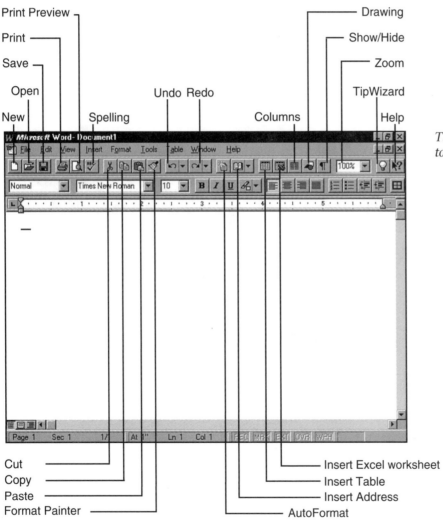

The Standard toolbar buttons.

The *Standard toolbar* contains icons (little pictures) of the tasks the average user is most likely to use. That's the average user according to Microsoft, of course. (I'd like to meet the average person that needs to insert Microsoft Excel worksheets into their Word document so often that they earned their own button on the standard toolbar.) You can change the order of buttons you see, or even add new ones. But that's going beyond the scope of this book. Leave them where they are and you'll always have them when you need them.

Formatting Toolbar

Here are the buttons you will likely use to spiffy-up the way your words look on the page. These buttons help you select fonts and font sizes, make text bold or italic, and perhaps center your words in the middle of the page. All of Part 2 of this book is dedicated to these functions. Once again, Microsoft took a stab at what they thought the average user would want on this toolbar.

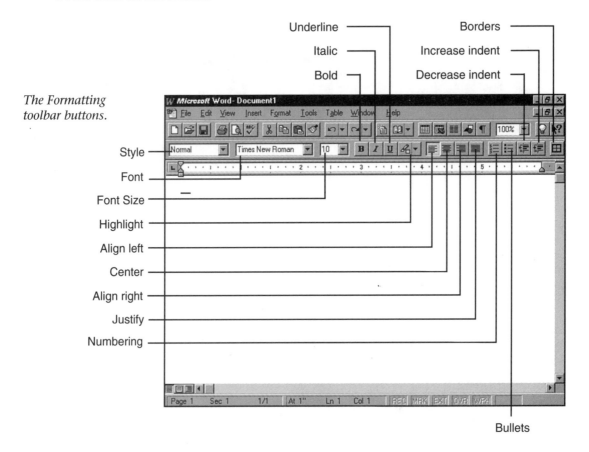

The Formatting toolbar buttons.

Ruler

This ruler is not your average ruler. If you hold a six-inch ruler up to your screen, you may discover that the two rulers don't match and you may have the urge to return your copy of Word as defective. Resist that urge. Word is fine, and so is the ruler. This *ruler* is used to set and display tabs. The ruler is also accurate in size, but the measurement you see is for the future printed page, not the page you see on your screen. What you see is usually larger, and that's helpful for your eyes. You can learn more about setting tabs by using the ruler in Chapter 8. If you don't care to see this ruler (most beginners don't need the extra distraction), you can get rid of it by following the steps in Chapter 23.

Minimize, Maximize, Restore, and Close

You've already learned about these title bar buttons. Click **Minimize** to remove the current program from the screen, but still keep it running and open. You'll see that this program is still running and active on the Windows 95 Taskbar. Click **Restore** to toggle between the full-screen view and a smaller window. This button will then toggle to the **Maximize** button to reverse the operation. Finally, when you're tired of using Word, you can click the **Close** button and Word will go away. If you have documents open at the time, don't worry—Word won't close until you are given the chance to save your changes to those documents.

The Scroll Bars

The horizontal and vertical *scroll bars* are used to travel throughout your document. The most helpful of the two available is called the *vertical scroll bar*, but you can recognize it as the thing on the right. The vertical scroll bar in Word represents the length of the document. The top arrow represents the top of the document, and the bottom arrow represents the bottom of the document. The area in between the two arrows represents all of the pages, but the most important part of the scroll bar is that small square. That square represents the current spot you are viewing on the screen. As you move up or down the screen (or page), the square moves too, showing you where you are in the document.

> ➤ To scroll your document up one line of text, click the mouse on the up scroll arrow at the top of the scroll bar.

> ➤ To scroll down one line of text, click the mouse on the down scroll arrow at the bottom of the scroll bar.

Proportional Scroll Bars These are more helpful in Word for Windows 95 than in previous versions of Word for Windows because you quickly see how large a document is by the size of the scroll bar marker. Clicking the left mouse button on the proportional scroll bar marker will quickly display the current page number.

➤ Somewhere inside the scroll bar is the proportional scroll bar marker. It gives you an idea of which part of your document you're looking at (if the marker is near the top of the scroll bar, you are near the top of your document). Drag the scroll marker up or down to move quickly through the pages of your document. Click on the marker to see the current page number.

Near the bottom of your screen, you'll find the horizontal positioning bar, with arrow buttons on each end and a scroll box (or marker) somewhere in between. You can position your view by clicking on the bar or the arrows in the direction you want to go; this will move the page left or right on your screen.

Status Bar

You can find interesting information about your document in the area called the *status bar*. Most helpful is probably the page number. If you have nothing else to do, you can click in different parts of the screen and watch the numbers in the status bar change. These changing numbers are the coordinates of your whereabouts, or text cursor position, on the page. Isn't it useful to know you are 5.8 inches from the top of your printed page, at line 28 and column 13? We thought so.

Windows 95 Taskbar

Although the Windows 95 Taskbar is not part of Word, it is visible and provides an easy way to get in and out of any open program on your computer. Click the **Start** button to open the Start menu. By sliding the mouse over the commands, you can choose from a variety of activities, from starting programs, to opening documents, and even searching for things or finding help.

Blank Sheet of Paper

The blank sheet of paper is where you see the words you type. Sometimes you may want to see more of this area. You can increase this white area by getting rid of, or hiding, the other parts of the Word screen, like the toolbars or scroll bars. Another way is to temporarily maximize this area so it's the only thing you see. If you are interested, you can find complete details about changing the view of your document in Chapter 19.

How to Enter Text into a Word Document

When you start Word for Windows 95, it places your cursor automatically at the top of an empty document window so you're ready to start entering text. To enter text into a document, simply start typing. As you type, your words will appear on the screen, like words from a typewriter. Unlike using a typewriter, however, *you should not press Enter when you reach the edge of the screen.* Just keep typing. Word for Windows 95 will automatically move your words to the next line as needed. This is called *word wrap*, and it's the most basic feature of any word processor. When you get to the end of a complete paragraph, you press **Enter**. Here are some hints on entering text in a Word document:

➤ **Press Enter only when you reach the end of a paragraph or to insert a blank line.** If you want to divide an existing paragraph into two, move the cursor to the dividing point (between sentences) and press **Enter**. To put two paragraphs back together, move to the first letter of the second paragraph and press **Backspace**.

➤ **Use the spacebar to insert a single space between words or sentences.** Do not use the spacebar to indent or center text.

➤ **Press Tab (not the spacebar) to indent the first line of a paragraph.** Spaces are not just blank holes on the page; they are real characters. Depending on the size of the characters used throughout your document, your paragraphs can look uneven if you use the spacebar to align them. Using the Tab key allows Word for Windows 95 to line things up for you.

➤ **A dotted line marks the end of a page.** Just ignore the dotted line when you see it; it's there to tell Word for Windows 95 where one page ends and another begins. If you add text above a dotted line, the excess text will flow to the top of the next page automatically. You can also force the end of a page (before it's full) by pressing **Ctrl+Enter**. When you do this, the dots multiply (get more dense) to show that this is a *forced page break*.

> *Check This Out...*
>
> **Word Wrap**
> With word wrapping, words are automatically advanced to the next line of a paragraph when they "bump" into the right margin. Likewise, you can insert words into the middle of a paragraph, and the rest of the paragraph will be adjusted downward automatically. If you change the margins, paragraphs will adjust automatically.

But What If I Make a Mistake?

Correcting typing mistakes in Word for Windows 95 is easy. Simply press the **Backspace** key to back up and erase text to the left of the insertion point, or press the **Delete** key to erase text to the right of the insertion point.

Check This Out...

Making a Mistake If you delete something by mistake and want to undo the deletion (get the text back), simply press the **Ctrl+Z** keys.

How do you correct a mistake found in the middle of a paragraph? You simply move the insertion point (that skinny blinking cursor) by clicking on the spot where you want it to go. Now you can use the **Delete** key or the **Backspace** key to remove the unwanted text.

You can quickly get rid of entire words by placing the cursor at the beginning of a word and pressing the **Ctrl+Delete** keys. Or you can back up over a word with the **Ctrl+Backspace** keys.

Dialog Boxes

Sometimes Word has the urge to talk to you. You may have pressed a key or hit a button that Word just can't figure out at the moment. It happens. When it does, Word wants nothing more than to clarify the situation with you. Because Word can't actually talk yet (and that's probably good) it uses messages in boxes. These are called *dialog boxes*. Following is an example:

Talking to Word: the dialog box.

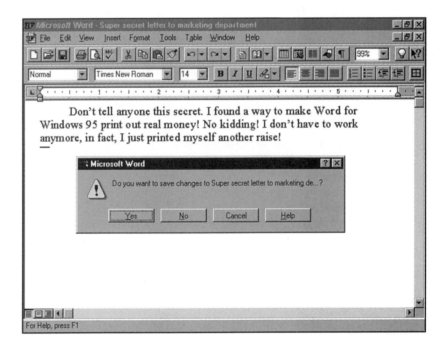

This dialog box asks a question and gives you four ways to respond. Those are the most *options* you are likely to see. The good news is that once you learn these buttons, they will apply to any dialog box you see.

➤ Yes means you really want to do what you have started. It may sound strange, but Word may be trying to warn you about something else that might change.

➤ No means you are answering no to the question in the dialog box. When in doubt, choose Cancel over No.

➤ Cancel means let's just forget the whole thing. I don't like Yes and I don't like No. Always the safest choice.

➤ Help is getting better. It may even explain what to do in this dialog box.

You can click the buttons with your mouse, or you can use your keyboard. Word prepares the most likely button you are to choose with a dark border line around it. Pressing the Enter key is the same as clicking this button. The Tab key can be used to move to each button if you prefer not to use the mouse at all. The Escape key makes the dialog box go away (it's the same as pressing Cancel).

Larger Dialog Boxes

When you select a menu command followed by an ellipsis, as in the File Print... command, a large dialog box appears.

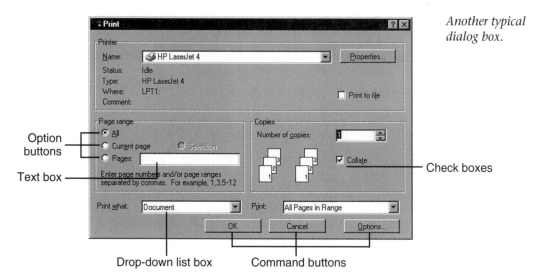

Another typical dialog box.

Option buttons

Text box

Drop-down list box

Command buttons

Check boxes

Dialog boxes are made up of lots of different parts. Here's a look at just a few of them:

List box   Presents a list of items to choose from, such as a list of files.

Drop-down list box   This is like a normal list box, except that the list is not displayed until activated. The list is displayed and the selection will appear in the box.

Text box   Allows you to type information, such as the name of a document, or a range of pages to print.

Check box   Indicates options that can be turned on or off, such as Collate Copies. When a check box is selected, an X or check mark appears inside of it.

Option buttons   Lets you select mutually exclusive options (only one can be picked), such as All, Current Page, or Pages. When an option button is selected, a dot appears inside it.

Command buttons   Performs some specific command, such as OK or Cancel. To make things interesting for you, some commands (containing ellipses) actually bring up another dialog box for you to deal with.

To move around inside a dialog box, click on any item to activate it. If you prefer to use the keyboard, press **Tab** until you get to the area you want. The Tab key will cycle through every option available in the dialog box and return to the beginning and start over. If you zip past it, just keep going and it will eventually get back through again. You can also press the key combination **Shift+Tab** to move backwards.

To display additional options in a list, click on the up or down arrow to scroll one item at a time and click on an item to select it. If you're using the keyboard, use the arrow keys to scroll through the list and press **Enter** to select an item.

To open a drop-down list box, click on the arrow to the right of the box. Click on an item to select it. With the keyboard, use the down-arrow key to open the list box and to highlight an item.

To select an option button or check box, click on it to toggle the option on or off. With the keyboard, press **Tab** (as explained earlier) to move to the option button or check box area. Then use the down arrow to move to the option button or check box you desire. Finally, use the spacebar to toggle an option on or off.

To exit a dialog box, use either OK, Cancel, or Close. Cancel will ignore the changes you've made in the dialog box and take you back to your work. OK will perform the activity you have selected with your choices in this dialog box. Close simply saves the choices you've just made and closes the dialog box without executing your choices right now. Be careful using the Enter key while in any dialog box, because it can sometimes select an unwanted button, or close the dialog box.

Really Big and Hairy Dialog Boxes

Nothing to be afraid of. When you select a menu command followed by an ellipsis, as in the Tools, Options... command, a really scary dialog box appears. But it's only scary if you can't figure out that these are tabbed folders that each contain information about a particular topic. Want to change topics? Click on a different tab, and that topic will move to the front. These dialog boxes were created to include an enormous amount of information in a small area.

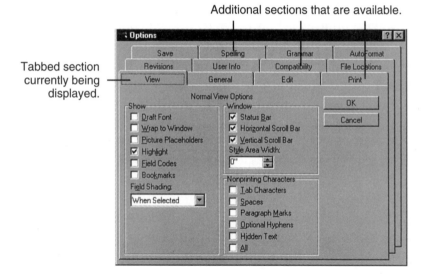

Additional sections that are available.

Tabbed section currently being displayed.

Don't be intimidated by Word's dialog boxes.

The Least You Need to Know

Word for Windows 95 brings many happy things to your table, like mice and other things:

➤ You can click the left mouse button to select something or double-click to open or run something. The right mouse button now brings up helpful menus with a single-click.

➤ To move a window, drag it by its title bar.

➤ To manipulate windows, use one of the three title bar buttons in the top right corner of the window. The first button will **Minimize** it, the second will toggle between **Restore** and **Maximize**, and the third button (the X) will **Close** that window.

➤ You can open menus to reveal their commands.

➤ Dialog boxes are used to communicate information between you and your Windows program. To select an item in a dialog box with the mouse, just click on it. Click on the down arrow to open a drop-down list box, and click on an item to select it. Clicking on an option button or a check box toggles it on or off.

➤ To select an item in a dialog box with the keyboard, use the **Tab** key. To move between tabbed topics of a dialog box, use **Ctrl+Tab**. Use the arrow keys to select an item from a list. Use the **spacebar** to toggle option buttons and check boxes on or off.

Chapter 4

Help! Using Word for Windows' Awesome Help

In This Chapter

➤ Getting good help fast

➤ Using the Help Contents, Index, and Find features

➤ Searching for help on something specific

➤ Understanding the Tip Wizard

Good help is hard to find, but relax—you've found this chapter. It's dedicated to helping you help yourself with Word for Windows 95. Word is an incredibly sophisticated program, so it's no wonder that we sometimes slow down when using a new feature or remembering an old one. Word provides help for absolutely every function and feature inside of Word. Most of it is pretty good. Some of it is so complex that you'll even find help for the help. You'll also discover the three basic ways to get help. You may find that you like all of them.

Lazy Help

Especially helpful for nonaggressive types, Word offers several flavors of help that require no thought on your part. You don't even have to look very hard to find these helpful hints.

Magic Pop-Up Name Tags

Don't knock it—especially those of you looking for your car keys. Just look at the Word toolbars. Can you remember which button is which? Sometimes the pictures just don't cut it. A paintbrush? Light bulb? A bent arrow? Word provides a simple way to remember what the heck any button is used for on any toolbar, and it requires minimal effort. Simply let your mouse arrow float over the button. Don't press any mouse buttons; just wait a moment. Magically, the name of the button will appear just below the button. In addition, if you look near the bottom of the screen, a short description of what the button does will appear in the status bar.

Tip of the Day (Now Inside the Tip Wizard)

When you first start Word for Windows 95, you can be greeted with helpful hints from the folks who wrote the product. These helpful hints are called the Tip of the Day (assuming you start Word once a day), and they're a painless way to learn the features of Word. It can be helpful to read the tip and think, "Have I ever needed to do this? Is this a better way?" To see these helpful tips, just click the **Tip Wizard** button on the Standard toolbar. The Tip Wizard box will appear below any other visible toolbars. The next time you start Word, you'll be greeted with a Tip of the Day in the Tip Wizard box.

Tip Wizard

Tip Wizard will automatically suggest ways to use Word more quickly and efficiently. For example, if you mistype or misspell a word, Tip Wizard will underline it with a red wavy line. Simply click the right mouse button on the word, and it will be corrected automatically. If you type the number 1, add a space, type some text, and press Enter, the Tip Wizard will jump into action. The Tip Wizard box will explain that Word has automatically converted what you typed into a numbered list, and that the Tip Wizard can help you further, by showing you how to Undo this activity, or by showing you more information with the Show Me button. The Tip Wizard is a great way to get a lot of information about what's going on with some of the new features in Word for Windows 95.

Sometimes it's great to have an expert looking over your shoulder giving tips at the right moment. It's even better if these tips are available at no cost. Word for Windows 95 gives you these tips with the Tip Wizard. Click on the **Light Bulb** button in your standard toolbar, and the Tip Wizard toolbar will appear. Watch the contents from time to time because they will change based on your activity. For instance, when you're building a table, you'll see one of many table tips appear in this box. And it will appear at the appropriate time to help you. For instance, you won't

Tip Wizard   Word 7 has changed the way you see the Tip of the Day. It's now viewed in the Tip Wizard toolbar.

be bothered with help in placing a table across multiple pages until your table starts growing across multiple pages.

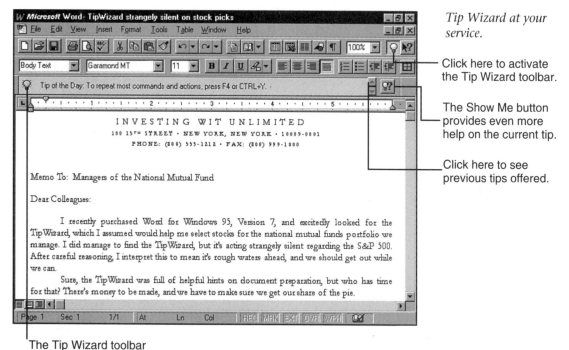

Tip Wizard at your service.

Click here to activate the Tip Wizard toolbar.

The Show Me button provides even more help on the current tip.

Click here to see previous tips offered.

The Tip Wizard toolbar

Looking for Better Help

You want help now, and you want it fast. And it better be accurate, or look out. Well, Word for Windows 95 is good, but it can't read your mind. When you want help, you should ask for it. Here are some tips on ways to obtain specific help for what your current problem is.

Getting Good Help Fast with F1

Help for Word for Windows is available 24 hours a day by pressing the F1 key (that's short for Function Key #1). This is no ordinary help function—it's called *context-sensitive* help, which means that Help pays attention to what you're doing and provides help specific to your task. For example, if you're trying to print and can't figure out what the collate box does, press the **F1** key. Instead of seeing a generic "getting started" help screen, you'll find help already opened right to printing, and Collate will be an option to view. You'll find the details you need quickly without having to search for them.

Click the Help Button to Point and Learn

You can use the Help button on the standard toolbar to figure out what a button on a toolbar really does, or what kind of formatting codes are applied to existing text in the document window. The Help button is the button with the combined picture of an arrow and question mark. Click it and see what happens. The button sinks as if it's depressed, and your mouse cursor changes from an arrow to an arrow-question-mark thing. When you move your mouse, the button follows you across the screen and you can't seem to get rid of it. What possible good can come of this?

Well, the Help pointer is great for pinpoint selection of what you want help with on the Word for Windows 95 screen. Just land the Help pointer directly on top of a button you need help with, or a menu you don't understand, or anything else you can find, and click either mouse button. You receive detailed help for that feature. That includes getting help with your own work! The figure shows an example of placing the Help pointer directly on your composition to see what kind of formatting is actively at work.

Click here again to return the cursor to normal.

Discovering useful information with the Help pointer.

You can also click this pointer on Toolbar buttons to see a more detailed description of its function.

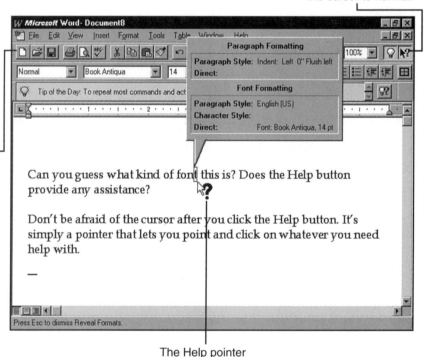

The Help pointer

If you change your mind and want to get rid of the Help pointer and return to your normal mouse arrow, simply move back up to the Help Pointer button and click it again. This action returns you safe and sound to normal operation.

Keyboard lovers (and mouse haters) will appreciate being able to select the Help pointer by holding down the **Shift** key and pressing the **F1** key. This same **Shift+F1** key combination will get rid of the Help pointer if you no longer need it.

The Help Menu: Welcome to the Major Leagues

You may recognize that all Windows programs have, or should have, a Help menu listed as the rightmost entry on the menu bar. This Help menu has changed slightly in Word for Windows 95—it's shorter. All you have to choose is the first command, **Microsoft Word Help Topics**, to get help on all the features of Word.

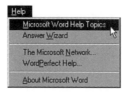

Looking for some good help?

The Answer Wizard takes you right into a dialog box where you can ask a question in plain English and get back a few appropriate answers (some of the answers may even solve your problem!).

The third item on the Help menu is the Microsoft Network.... It's listed here if you have installed the Microsoft Network, the online service provided by Microsoft and Windows 95. It's included here because the Microsoft Network is a good place to look for current information on Help topics, which you can find in the zillions of forums available.

If you happen to know WordPerfect but are new to Word, try the **WordPerfect Help** command. It's a great way to put your previous knowledge to productive use. You'll find a great cross-reference guide of the commands you're familiar with, and demos of how this task is accomplished in Word. And if you are a WordPerfect user who really hates Word but has to use it, you can always use the combination keys you remember from WordPerfect, and they will function correctly in Word! How the heck did that happen?

The remaining command is the **About Microsoft Word** command. If you have time to waste, you can read the licensing information for your copy of Word. But the dialog box that appears does provide some helpful, although very technical, information on your computer and programs if you click on the **System Info...** button. You might be asked to peek in here someday to get some information to help solve a problem you're having. Technical support people love this kind of information to help debug a problem.

The Little Help Books

Click on the **Help** menu and then select **Microsoft Word Help Topics**. Click on the **Contents** tab to bring it to the front. You'll be treated to a collection of little Help books arranged by category. There are literally thousands of pages of Help available in all these little books. You just have to decide which little book to look in. Let's say you want your text to spread out closer to the edges of the paper. Which book might help? You can give **Insert the date and time in a document** a try. Double-click on the book, and you'll see it open and display more little books and some question marks that represent specific answers.

The little Help books.

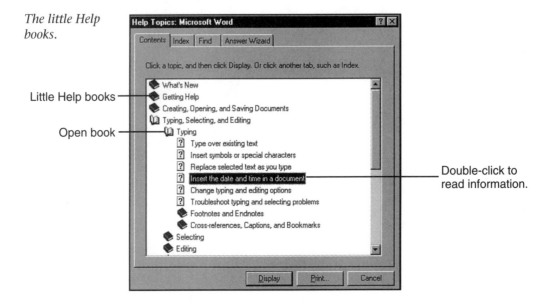

Little Help books

Open book

Double-click to read information.

Print it! You can also print any of these helpful screens by clicking the **Options** menu in the Help screen and choosing the **Print Topic** command.

You'll find big improvements in Help compared with earlier versions of Word for Windows. The numbered steps are complete and easy to follow, and the help topic stays on top of the screen automatically while you execute the instructions. Some of the topics even have "show me" buttons that let you sit back and watch as Microsoft Word for Windows 95 shows you how to do something.

To return to the Help Topics once you're inside one of the Help guides, simply click the **Help Topic** button at the top of each Help dialog box.

Browsing the Help Index

To use the Help Index, open the **Help** menu and choose the **Microsoft Word Help Topics** command. Now click the **Index** tab on the Help Topics dialog box to bring it to the front. In the Find text box under number 1, just type the first few letters of the word you want help with, and the text box below it will fill with the closest matches. Then you can click or use the arrow keys to browse around in the list until you find what you're looking for. Click the **Display** button on selected items to see the same help you found in the little Help books.

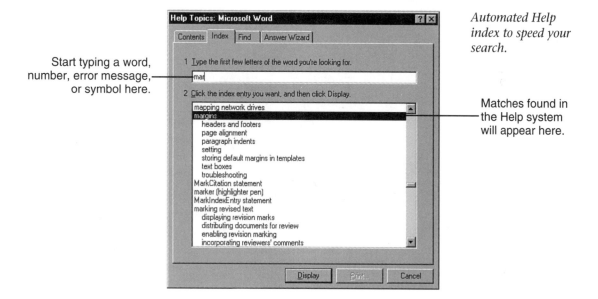

Start typing a word, number, error message, or symbol here.

Automated Help index to speed your search.

Matches found in the Help system will appear here.

Using the Find Feature of Help

When you start to play with the new Find feature of Help in Word for Windows 95, you'll wish you had a more powerful computer. The Find feature can become addictive; however, it can be slow. You can search for help by using any combination of words that explain your problem. Even if you aren't sure of what words to use, you can set an option to use similar forms of a word. For example, if you're having problems printing because text is getting chopped off the page, you could try to enter **text cut print** in the Find text box. Word will do its best to figure out what you're asking for and will provide a variety of answers. The correct solution is found and displayed in the following figure. Be creative and test the range of words you can work with.

Finally someone understands me.

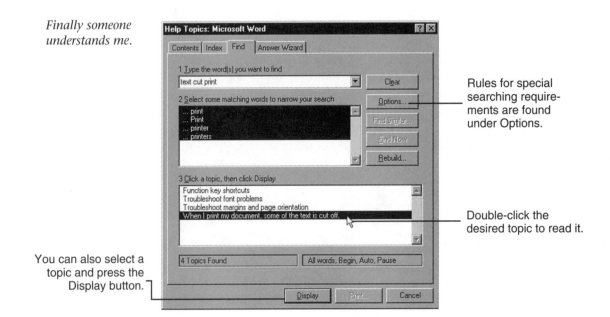

Rules for special searching require-ments are found under Options.

Double-click the desired topic to read it.

You can also select a topic and press the Display button.

Using the Answer Wizard

Have some fun. Microsoft packed some real intelligence into this function that actually draws you into the process of asking questions. You can now ask for information by using plain English, and you'll get the help you need—also in plain English. For example, click the Answer Wizard and type **Where did my stinking toolbar go?**. In response, the wizard will take you right to the dialog box for displaying or hiding toolbars and give you a tip for completing the task. Be as creative or bold as you dare—it's a great stress-reliever, and it may even help answer your questions.

Type your question
here in plain English.

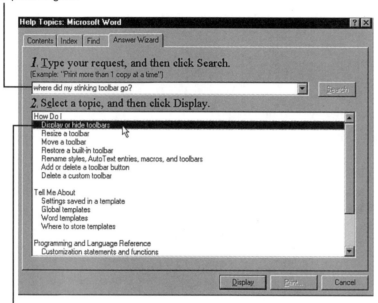

*Tell your sorrows to
the Answer Wizard
for help.*

Choose a topic from
among the responses and
double-click to read it.

Troubleshooting with Help

What's the best thing to do if something is not working as planned? A good suggestion is to try searching on the word *Troubleshoot*. That's the word that Word uses to explain how to fix something that's broken. You'll find more than 20 general topics covering everything from bookmarks to tables, and each entry contains up to 10 different problems relating to that topic. Active buttons on the help screen reveal the actions to take to resolve the problem, easiest ones first. The help screen stays on top so you can see it. When you

Troubleshooting has been made easier in Word 7. Just enter the word **trouble-shoot** in the Index or Find portions of Word Help Topics, and you'll find dozens of step-by-step procedures to guide you through the problem.

finish doing what Help suggests, it will ask you if the problem is fixed. If not, the Help screen will provide the next logical steps to take. This is a mild form of entertainment. It sure beats the alternative of shouting angrily at your machine.

The Least You Need to Know

Getting help in Word for Windows 95 does not require a call to 911. It's much easier to use the built-in Help features described in this chapter. Here are some of the more important ones:

➤ Some forms of help may be staring you in the face, like Tip of the Day found in the Tip Wizard.

➤ Use the **F1** key when you need help fast.

➤ Click the **Help** button on the standard toolbar or press **Shift+F1** to get help on any part of the Word screen.

➤ The Help menu command is used to search for help on anything in Word. For example, Troubleshoot is a particularly helpful word to search for, in combination with another word describing your problem.

➤ Search specifically for anything your heart desires in Word by using the Find dialog box in the Help menu.

If It's Worth Saving, Save It!

One good thing about a typewriter—you type, you get words on paper, and you're finished. Not as easy with Word for Windows 95 because you have a couple of steps in between the typing and getting the words on paper. The first step is *saving* your work, and it's the focus of this chapter.

Word Doesn't Remember Unless You Save It

Start a new document in Word and type away. Now stop. Look at the screen and admire your work. Think about what happens if the power goes out or you turn off your computer at this instant. The screen goes blank, and your creation is blasted to oblivion, with no chance of ever getting it back because you didn't *save* it. What can you do to prevent such a disaster, and where do you start?

The peculiar thing about this new Word for Windows 95—a person is not required to learn *how* to save a document. It can happen automatically, if you start things off the right way.

Remember creating a document right from the Windows 95 desktop in Chapter 2? For those of you who skipped a grade, let's review, because it's important. Find the Windows 95 desktop. Click the right mouse button on an empty spot of the background to get a shortcut menu. Point to **New** and click on **New Microsoft Word Document**. A new document will appear on your desktop. Do it again, and you'll get a second, then a third, and so on. What's special about these documents? They are automatically *saved* for you and automatically *named* for you, which can save hours of time, depending on the level of your creativity to think up names for documents.

No need to worry about naming or saving these documents!

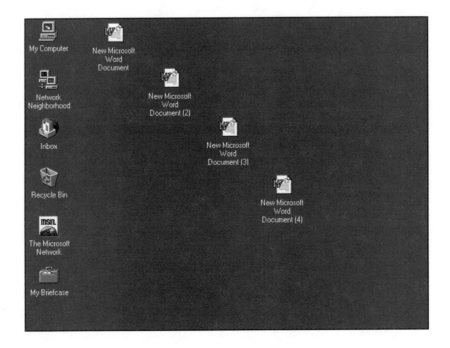

What's the catch? Does this seem too easy? Well, there is a slight penalty for this brevity. The document names are exactly what you see on the desktop. **New Microsoft Word Document #3** is certainly not what you would have picked to name your document, but that's what your computer picked. The only unique thing in these names is that tiny number at the end. Is it practical to name this way? Not unless you have a great memory.

Are you forced to live with these silly names? Of course not; you can easily change them to something more practical (by *renaming* them) with the Save As function covered later in this chapter.

Renaming Is Easier

You can also easily rename a document by clicking on it with the right mouse button. Select the **Rename** command and you can type over the old name with a new one. Then press **Enter** to save it.

Okay, so, lesson learned. New documents can be automatically named and saved as long as they are initially created from the Windows 95 desktop. But what if you are inside Word for Windows 95 and create a new document? What's the trick to save it?

How Do I Save If I Started a Document the Old-Fashioned Way?

Actually, there are two other common ways to create a new document. Experienced Word users may coerce you into trying them. The first is simply to open Word, which, as we talked about in Chapter 3, automatically puts you into a new document. The second is to create a new document from inside of Word. Once you're in Word, you simply press the **New** button on the **Standard** toolbar, and a new document screen appears. With either of these approaches, the new document is not yet named or saved. Type a word or two. You just started a new document. Now what should you do to save it?

Panic? Not required if you read this chapter and learn how to save your document (before disaster strikes)! Which of the following options will be the best for saving your work?

(A) Take a Polaroid snapshot of each screen.

(B) Scribble feverishly a copy of what you've just typed.

(C) Attend a memory-enhancement class and practice until you can memorize your entire document.

(D) Hold thermal paper up to your screen and turn the brightness way up.

(E) Press the **Save** button (the diskette icon on the standard toolbar), or press **Ctrl+S**, or click the **Save** command from the **File** menu.

The answer is E, the Save function in Word. Once you officially save your work, you can always get it back.

Check This Out...

File or Document?

Your computer classifies your document as a *file*. The first menu heading is called **File**, but you should think of it as *document*. *Saving a document* packages everything inside your document into a file, which can be stored on your computer hard disk or floppy diskette or both.

How Often Should You Save a Document?

How often should you save a file? It depends how fast you work and how much trouble it would be to re-create your progress. Here are some rules to live by, as described by famous authors from the late twentieth century:

➤ Save immediately after thinking up brilliant prose or something really funny. Save any time you think to yourself, "Wow! Did I do that?"

➤ Save before you print (in case it gets stuck and you crash).

➤ Save before you try some tricky function in Word.

➤ Save right after a tricky function if you like the results.

➤ Always save before opening a new document.

➤ Always save before closing your document.

Saving a Document the First Time

The first time you save any document is a little different than any other time you'll save it. You have to give your creation a name and a place (folder) it can call home. Save your document now by clicking the **Save** button on the standard toolbar. You will be presented with the Save As dialog box as shown in the following figure.

To make things easy, Word has already filled in a potential name for your document. Word just happened to grab the first few words of your document. Sometimes that's good enough, and you don't have to do anything more than press **Enter** (or click the **Save** button) and save your document. Or, you can type a better name in the File Name box. You can be as creative as you want in your file name, which is a big improvement over previous versions of Word.

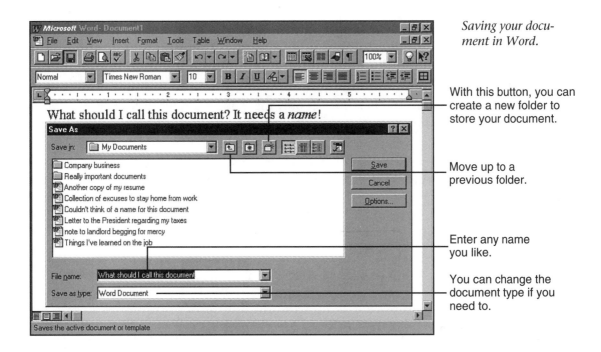

*Saving your docu-
ment in Word.*

With this button, you can
create a new folder to
store your document.

Move up to a
previous folder.

Enter any name
you like.

You can change the
document type if you
need to.

Your document will be stored in the folder shown in the Save In box. If you want to save
your document in another folder, you can search for it using the **Previous Folder** button
or by clicking on folders in the Display area.

If you don't trust your computer, or Word for Windows 95, or both, you might find it
reassuring to prove to yourself that your new document and changes have been saved.
Simply open the document once again and look at it. It's easiest to find your document
by choosing it from the selection of your last 15 documents. Click the **Start** button on
your taskbar, point to **Documents**, and click on the document you just saved. Word starts
with this document opened, and it should prove to be exactly what you hoped for.

You've Got Options in Saving

There are many document saving options you should know about. From the **Save As**
dialog box, click on **Options** or press **Alt+O**. To select an option, click on it, or press the
Alt key plus the underlined letter. Here's the scoop on what all these options are for:

Always Create Backup Copy   This option saves a copy of your original unchanged file with the extension .WBK, but you usually don't worry about extensions in Windows 95. It's useful if you need to change your mind about some changes you've made.

Allow Fast Saves   This option saves only the changes to a file instead of the entire file. With this option, saving a file often is a quick and easy process. As a precautionary measure, periodically the entire file is saved, even when this option is in effect.

Prompt for Document Properties   By selecting this option, you can make the Properties dialog box open automatically each time you perform a **Save As**, to remind you to add optional information along with your document. For example, you can add keywords that can help you quickly find this document later.

Prompt to Save Normal Templates   Refers to the Normal template file. With this option on, you'll be prompted before changes are saved to the Normal template when you exit Word. You can find out more about templates, and saving them, in Chapter 21.

Save Native Picture Formats Only   This option saves graphic files imported from a Macintosh computer in Windows format. Using this option reduces the document's file size.

Embed TrueType Fonts   With this option, the TrueType fonts you use are incorporated into the document, so they will display even when the document is opened on a system that doesn't have that particular font. Without this option, the other system is forced to find a likely substitution font, and that can affect the total look you were trying to achieve when you selected the original font in the first place.

Save Data Only for Forms   This option saves the data you keyed into a Word form in a format that's compatible with common database programs.

Automatic Save Every ____ Minutes   Use this option to put Word on "automatic." Type the number of minutes you want Word to wait between automatic saves. You can enter any number between 1 and 120, and something around 10 minutes is recommended. It depends on how much work you're willing to lose.

File Sharing Options   To protect your document against changes, use this option. You can make your document *password protected* (no one can open the document without the password of up to 15 characters) and/or *lock it for viewing only* (others can open the document and view it, but they can't change the text). You can choose **Read-Only Recommended**, which means that a person can open and edit your document, but they will see a message advising them not to make changes.

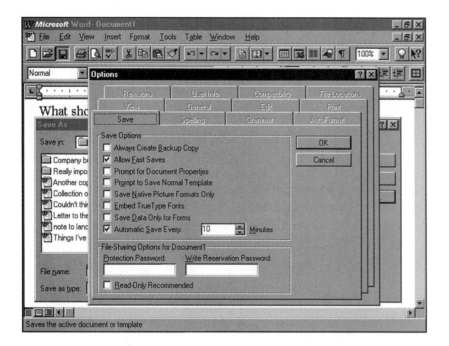

Options available to customize document saving in Word.

Saving Is Easier after That, Unless...

There are times when you *don't* want to save changes to the current document. For example, let's say you've pulled up last week's status report and want to change only the date and call it this week's report. But you also want to save last week's report, in case you need it at the hearing. If you make any changes and click the Save button, you will *lose* your previous report; it is replaced by one with the changes you've just made.

You already know how to accomplish this task. To bring up a previous document, make minor changes, and save them both, you use the **Save As** command found in the **File** menu. Remember to give this modified document a new *different* name, and both will be safe and secure.

Save 'Em All Multiple Documents Opened in Word can be saved all at the same time by clicking the **Save All** command on the **File** menu.

The Name Game Is Wide Open Now!

If you used DOS or previous versions of Windows, naming your documents used to be the hardest part because you were limited to a maximum of eight-letter file names. Finally, with Windows 95 and Word 7, you can name a file almost anything you want.

Remember the burden of having to think up an eight-character name that made sense to you (at the time)? Leave out the vowels, add maybe a number to identify the month or year, and you had something like LLBM2MEP.DOC. And how often did you need to go back and find that file, only to have forgotten what you named it?

Naming Limitations Still Exist

If you, or anyone you share files with, are using any programs that are not Windows 95 compatible, which includes older versions of Word, you may still be required to name files the old-fashioned way. To find out the DOS equivalent of a file name that is longer than eight characters, select your file by clicking the file name with the right mouse button. Select the **Properties** command from the shortcut menu. It will show you the MS-DOS equivalent file name.

Windows 95 brings relief in the form of long file names. Now, instead of LLBM2MEP, you can call the file *Letter To Landlord Begging Mercy For Two-Month Extension Since We Spent All Our Money On This New Pentium*. The file name can be up to 255 characters long including spaces, and the upper- and lowercase letters will be preserved. That means programs like Word for Windows 95 can also use these longer names.

Taking a Document Home with You

Feeling brave? Got a diskette handy? Give this trick a try and see if you're not bragging about it around the water cooler tomorrow.

Where Did That Name Come From?

When you save a document the first time, you'll notice that a name is already entered when the Save As dialog box appears. Word for Windows 95 attempts to save you some time by naming your document with the first words that appear in your document.

Use Word for Windows 95 to create and save your document. Go to the Windows 95 desktop. Use either **Find** (from the Start menu on the Windows 95 taskbar) or **My Computer** to locate an icon of your document. Click once on it with your *right* mouse button. Move to the **Send To** command and then select **My Briefcase**. Your document, documents, or entire folders for that matter, can be copied throughout the day to this thing called a briefcase. Don't ask. Now, ready to go home for the day? Stick a diskette into your diskette drive and right-click **My Briefcase**, move to **Send To** and select **3 1/2 Floppy (A)**, and then sit back and watch the fireworks. Your work will be copied to diskette.

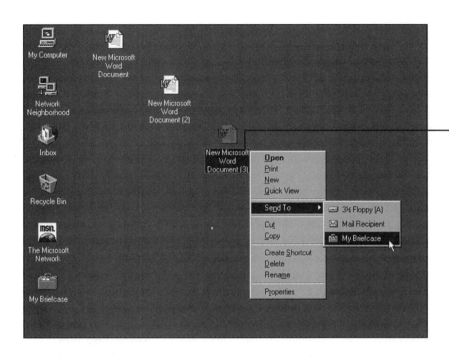

Taking your work home with you.

Click the right mouse button on any Word document on the desktop (or in Word's File Open or Save As dialog boxes) to send it to the Briefcase.

Take it home and reverse the process. This assumes you are running Windows 95 on your home computer. You can click to open and edit your work directly from the diskette, or you can save the contents of your Briefcase to a folder on your hard disk. Now you can open Word and use the File Open dialog box to open your documents directly from the Briefcase. After you finish editing your document, save it and **Send** it to the diskette repeating the steps described earlier.

The next day you're back at work with the disk in your hand. Stick your diskette into the drive and drag your briefcase from the floppy. Windows 95 is smart enough to know that the document on diskette is more current than the one stored yesterday in your computer, and you'll be asked if you want to update the old copies. This process is called *version control.*

If Your Home Computer Isn't Windows 95

You can still take documents home and not worry about maintaining the latest version. Just remember to name your document so it will be recognized on the non-Windows 95 computer. That means using the old eight-letter naming scheme, or exploring how the names in Windows 95 are created and maintaining the same name. Your document called My Letter To My Boss stored in Word for Windows 95 is actually a file named MYLETT~1.DOC, but you would have figured it out soon enough. Old DOS is gone, right?

Closing Your Document and Going Home

It's a good habit to save and close your documents before turning off your computer and heading home. This is more important than ever now, because of the way Windows 95 saves things (like documents). Your documents are hanging around in memory. When you close Word, and then close Windows 95, you guarantee that all of your documents are written to your hard drive and are now safe and sound. If you simply turn off your computer without closing Windows 95, there's a chance that a document didn't get written to disk, and is now lost forever.

The proper way to keep your documents safe and sound is to close them. If changes have been made, you will be alerted and granted time to decide on your saving options. Then you can close Word in a number of ways, like **Alt+F4**, clicking the **Close** title bar button, clicking **File** and then **Exit**, double-clicking the top left title bar button, single-clicking the top left title bar button and selecting **Close**, or simply shouting loud enough at your computer to scare Word into closing for you.

Turning Off Your Machine

Wait! There's a new commandment in Windows 95. *Thou shalt not turn off thy computer before it has been "Shutdown" properly*. So click the Start button on your taskbar. Find the **Shut Down** command and click it. Click the **Yes** button, and your computer will make sure all changes are permanently saved and properly close all files. The screen will let you know when it's okay to turn off your computer.

The Least You Need to Know

➤ Always save your documents before exiting Word, and before and after any complicated task. It's also a good idea to save your document prior to printing.

➤ File names are now wide open. Use them to your advantage.

➤ You can save a copy of your current document under a new name with the **Save As** command on the **File** menu.

➤ To set up Word for Windows 95 so it saves documents automatically, use the **Options** button within the Save As dialog box, or open the **Tools** menu, select the **Options** command, and choose the **Save** tab.

➤ To close a document window, click the **Close** button located directly below the Word Close button.

➤ Properly closing Word for Windows 95 is important to prevent accidental loss of work.

Part 2
Enhancing Your Work

Does your document look like something you ripped out of the telephone book? Is it… well… boring? Of course, neither you nor what you typed is boring, so it must be something else. Liven it up! It's called formatting! Start small; experiment with letters or small words, then work up to sentences and paragraphs, and soon you'll be competing with magazine advertisements.

Not feeling too artistic? Let Word take charge while you sit back, sip coffee, and watch automated tools bring your document to life. Now why can't other things in life be as easy?

Chapter 6

The Art of Selecting Things to Work with

In This Chapter

➤ Different ways to select text

➤ Learning how to cut, copy, and paste

➤ Moving selected text to new places

➤ Selecting things out-of-bounds

You may be thinking to yourself, "Let's skip this chapter and get to the good stuff." Well, if the term *cut-copy-and-paste* does nothing more than offer daydreams of happy times in kindergarten, you should sit up straight and pay attention! You need to know this before graduating to the fun stuff. The fun stuff depends on it.

What Is Selected Text?

Experienced Windows experts will be familiar with this subject. You always *select* text before you can format it, move it, or get excited about it.

The act of *selecting text* is also commonly known by a variety of names, most terms originating in different windows programs over the years:

➤ *Marking* the text

➤ *Highlighting* it (a term you should *avoid*, especially because Word 7 has a *real* highlighter, just like the yellow marker!)

➤ *Blocking* or *Block mark*

➤ *Choosing* the text

Windows 95 prefers the term "selecting," and that's the term used in this book.

No matter how you do it, selected text will always look the same. That's how you know it's currently selected. Selected text usually appears in reverse-video on your screen (meaning if you usually see black letters on a white background, selected text will be white letters on a black background).

Selected text typically doesn't stay selected for a long time. It's simply a middle step necessary for something major happening inside (or outside) your document.

You can select only one group of words at a time in your document. More than one would be too confusing, so it's just as well.

Selecting Text with Your Mouse

It's easiest to experience selecting for the first time by using the mouse. Open any document and move the mouse arrow to the middle of the text in your document. Now click the left mouse button, hold it down, and drag your mouse in any direction. Then let go of the mouse button. See what's there? Congratulations! You have just selected text!

This text has been "selected."

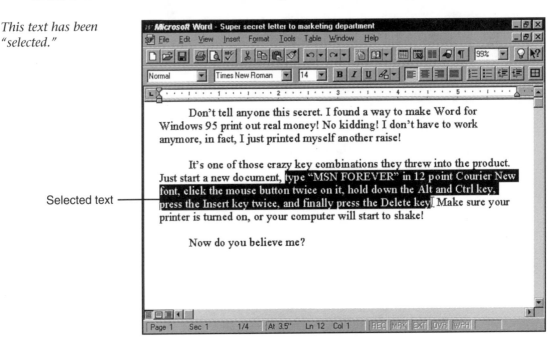

Selected text

Of course, to be useful, you have to be a good shot with your mouse. Aim well before clicking, and certainly as you finish dragging, or else you have to start the whole selection process over again. There are shortcuts, as you will soon learn, for selecting common things like words and paragraphs, but it helps to fill that toolbox in your head with all kinds of methods.

The Invisible Selection Bar

You can select an entire line with a single click if you know the trick. Take a closer look at the left border of your text screen. Can't see it, can you? That's because it's invisible, but it's still there. It's called the *selection bar*, and it always exists as a single thin strip on the left border of your entire document. By clicking in this area, you are selecting everything on this line. Try it, because it's a very common and useful way to select multiple lines or paragraphs of text. Move your mouse pointer to the far left side of an opened document, like in the figure. The cursor will change to an arrow, which can be a helpful reminder that you are now "inside" the selection bar. Click the left mouse button while you're in these areas to select text.

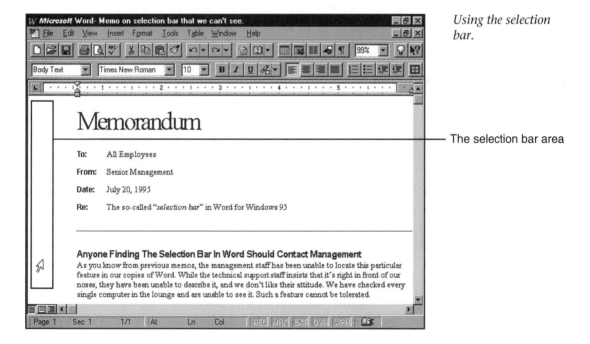

Using the selection bar.

The selection bar area

If you find this method of selecting text a drag, here are some shortcuts you can use when selecting text with the mouse:

To Select This:	Do This:
Word	Double-click on the word
Sentence	Press the **Ctrl** key and click on the sentence
Paragraph	Double-click in the selection bar next to the paragraph, or triple-click inside the paragraph
Multiple Paragraphs	Double-click in the selection bar next to the first paragraph, then drag
Line	Click in the selection bar next to the line
Multiple Lines	Click and drag in the selection bar next to the lines
Column of text	Press **Alt** and drag until the column is highlighted
Whole document	Triple-click in the selection bar, or press the **Ctrl** key while clicking in the selection bar

To extend your text selection to include more than one word, sentence, or paragraph, simply drag the pointer. For example, to select several words, double-click on one word and drag the pointer over the rest of the words you want to select.

Selecting Text with Your Keyboard

For those of you who are not into "mousing," Appendix A covers a lot of keyboard tricks that you can use as an alternative to the mouse. Many of the operations you can perform on text, but first the text has to be selected. Now you'll learn about keyboard tricks that help you select text to begin with!

It's not necessary to have a mouse to do these tricks. In fact, sometimes the mouse may be a less convenient way to select. Thank goodness for the keyboard, which provides *hands-on* selecting alternatives for professional typists.

Shifting Gets It Started

First, move the insertion point to the first letter in the text to be selected and press the **Shift** key. Then, with the Shift key depressed, use the arrow keys to reach the end of the text you want to select. Release the Shift key, and the text you selected will be highlighted in reverse video. It's selected.

Extending Your Selection

While selecting text with the keyboard, you can use any of the navigation keys I cover in Appendix A. For example, to move to the next word, you press **Ctrl+Right Arrow**. To select a word, press **Shift+Ctrl+Right Arrow**. To select text to the end of the paragraph, press **Shift+Ctrl+Down Arrow**, and so on. If you want to select the entire document, press **Ctrl+5** (use the 5 on the numeric keypad).

Unselecting Something

If you ever make a mistake and select the wrong text, simply press an arrow key or click anywhere in the document. You can also select other text instead.

Once in a while you may find yourself in a kind of selection lock, where you feel like you can't get out. Before panicking, try pressing **Ctrl+Z** once, or the **Undo** button on the standard toolbar, to clear things up.

> *Check This Out...*
>
> **To Select Any Amount of Text** Place the insertion point at the start of what you want to select, hold down the **Shift** key, then move the insertion point to the end of the selection. Release the Shift key, and you're done.

Another Way to Select Using the F8 Key

If you prefer to work one finger at a time, you can also perform the selection process with the F8 key. Start by moving the insertion point to the beginning of the desired selection and press the **F8** key once. Now use the arrow keys to go to the end—text will be selected automatically. Now you can cut or copy the text using your favorite method learned in this chapter. To remove the selection, press **F8** again.

Deleting Options for Selected Text

Once you've selected your text, you can actually do something with it. The easiest thing to do is get rid of it. Since this isn't always the most productive use of your time, maybe you should practice deleting later. We'll just tell you about it for now.

The easiest way to delete selected text is to press the **Delete** key. Bang. It's gone. You can also use the **Backspace** key. The **Ctrl+X** key combination also does the trick. Don't forget, if you really didn't mean to kill the selected text, you can always click on the **Undo** command in the **Edit** menu or press **Ctrl+Z** to undo an inappropriate deletion and give your words a second chance at life.

Another easy way to delete selected text is to simply start typing the replacement text. The first keyboard letter you press will replace selected text, saving you the time and stress of finding and pressing the Delete key.

Mouse lovers can use the mouse to do their dirty work by clicking the right mouse button anywhere inside the selected text. The pop-up menu contains the Cut command to zap the unwanted selection.

Slower methods of deleting text include using the **Edit** menu and choosing the **Cut** command, or leaving the selected text on your screen until about the year 2048 when gamma rays from outer space will have eroded the selection into nonexistence. Your choice.

Cut, Copy, and Paste

 To cut (or move) text, select it and press **Ctrl+X**, or click on the **Cut** button on the standard toolbar.

 To copy text, select it and press **Ctrl+C**, or click on the **Copy** button on the standard toolbar.

 To paste text, press **Ctrl+V** or click on the **Paste** button on the standard toolbar.

Copying and Pasting Selected Text

Sometimes you write stuff that is so good you want to use it again. You can if you first select it. Once you've selected the part you like, you can copy it by clicking the **Edit** menu and clicking the **Copy** command, or just press the copy button on the standard toolbar. You can also copy using the combination **Ctrl+C** keys. Give it a try.

Hey, big deal; nothing happened, right? Wrong! That **Copy** command just turned loose millions of little computer nerds living inside your computer. They paid attention and wrote down exactly what you've selected. Your original text is copied to the clipboard and will remain there safe and sound. Now they're waiting for you to tell them exactly where to put the text.

So go move the insertion point to the place in your document where you want to place the copy. Don't worry if there isn't enough room; any existing things will be pushed around to accommodate your copy.

Now press the **Edit** menu and click the **Paste** command (you can also use **Ctrl+V**). Almost magically your selection is copied exactly as it was previously. The trick is to remember that copying is only the first step. To be helpful, you must also use the second step called *Pasting*.

You Can Keep on Pasting and Pasting

Maybe your stuff is so good you want it sprinkled everywhere in your document. Do you have to keep going back to select a prior instance and copy it again? Heavens no. Just keep using the **Paste** command and a new copy will continue to appear, wherever your text cursor happens to be. By golly, you can even paste to completely different programs, like WordPerfect or an outgoing e-mail note in the Microsoft Network!

Cutting and Pasting Selected Text

Beginners are advised to learn copy and paste first, especially if you're computer paranoid, because you're only adding to your document. Extra stuff can always be deleted later. So if you want to move some words or a paragraph, you can now select it, copy it to the new place, and then delete the first selection. This gives you the reassurance that your selected text was moved safely to its destination before you delete the original.

But what if you feel daring and want to save time? You can *Cut* the text, which gets rid of it from the first place, and then paste it to a new location directly. This is how confident Windows experts live day-to-day. You can do it, too!

Any time you cut a selection, it's actually copied to the clipboard, which means it's still available to you. That's one of the advantages over the Delete key. If you *Delete* a selection, it's gone; but if you *Cut* a selection, you still have a chance to use it again somewhere else.

Clipboard The Windows 95 clipboard is a special storage area hidden inside your computer. Your computer uses the clipboard to store text, numbers, or graphics temporarily as it is moved or copied from one place to another. When you cut or copy something, it gets stuffed *into* the clipboard. When you paste, it comes *from* the clipboard. It's important to remember that the clipboard can hold only one thing at a time, and it's always the *last* thing you've cut or copied. You can view the current contents of your clipboard using the clipboard viewer, available in the Windows 95 accessories menu. If you don't have it installed yet, you can follow the installation steps in Appendix B.

Perusing the Clipboard for Your Cuts and Copies

Removing Those Extra Spaces When you copy or move text, Word automatically removes extra spaces that you may have selected accidentally—as long as the option Smart Cut and Paste is on. To check, open the **Tools** menu and choose **Options**. Click on the **Edit** tab and make sure that **Use Smart Cut and Paste** is selected.

If you're the least bit interested in where cut or copied text (or graphics) goes before you paste it, try viewing it with the clipboard viewer. Yes, cut or copied text or graphics are temporarily stored in something called the clipboard. The contents you place in the clipboard remain until it is placed by the next item you cut or copy. You can find the clipboard viewer by pressing the **Start** button on the Windows 95 taskbar and then open the **Programs** menu. Next, open the **Accessories** menu and choose the **Clipboard viewer**. If the clipboard viewer is not an option on your menu, you will have to install it using the installation procedure found in Appendix B of this book. When you finally get the clipboard viewer running, you will see something like the following:

You can see your cuts and copies with the clipboard viewer.

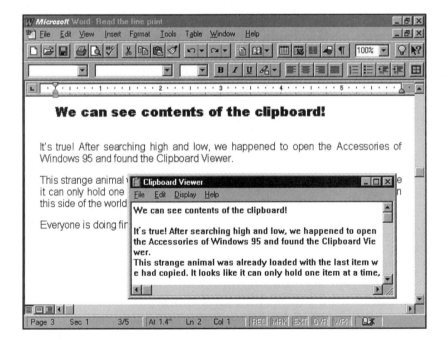

If the clipboard viewer is empty, try cutting or copying text first, and then viewing it. The clipboard viewer can be helpful if you later want to paste, and you are wondering if an item is still in the clipboard. If it is, you can continue to paste.

Moving Selected Text Around

How about that? You already know how to move text by first selecting it, then cutting it, and finally pasting it in the new spot. That's one way to move text around. Here is another.

Try using your mouse. After you've selected text, place the mouse arrow inside the selection and click and hold the left mouse button down for a few moments. The cursor will change appearance slightly (a little box appears at the bottom of the arrow) to let you know it's ready. Now drag the whole thing to a new location. When you reach the new destination, let go of the left mouse button and watch the action. Your selection is moved automatically, and you've saved some time from the alternative method of using keystrokes to cut and paste to move this selection.

Shortcut Menu

Word for Windows 95 helps you edit your text quickly with a pop-up menu that appears when you press the right mouse button on selected text. Try it and you'll see the familiar **Cut**, **Copy**, and **Paste** commands at your fingertips.

Moving Several Things at Once Using Spike

Who's Spike? Who cares, as long as he gets the job done. This subject sounds a bit strange and complicated, but you may find it helpful. You can remove several items from various locations in one or more documents and then insert them *as a group* in another location (or document) by using the Spike. You select something, spike it, then something else, spike it, and so on. All of these selections end up in what's called the *Spike*. Finally, when you find the place you want to move it all to, you ask Spike to dump it all there, in the order it was picked up. It's like having a bunch of clipboards at your service.

When you use the Spike, you remove, *not copy*, items from one or more documents. You can always insert the items into the document again after they are in the Spike. Also, when you collect text selections in the Spike, they are stored in the same order that you added them. Ready to Spike? Follow these steps:

1. Select the text you want to move to the Spike.

2. Press **Ctrl+F3**.

3. Repeat steps 1 and 2 for each item you want to collect in the Spike.

4. Click where you want to insert the contents of the Spike. Make sure the insertion point is at the beginning of a line or is surrounded by spaces.

5. To insert the contents of the Spike and clear the Spike, press **Ctrl+Shift+F3**.

View the Contents of Spike

To view the contents of the Spike, click **AutoText** on the **Edit** menu and then select **Spike** from the list of AutoText names. Word displays a portion or all of the contents of the Spike in the Preview box.

To insert the contents of the Spike without clearing the Spike (so that you can use the collected items again), place the insertion point where you want the contents of the Spike to go, type the word **spike**, and then press **F3**.

Selecting Things out There on the Edge (Outside Margins)

You may need this for future reference. It's how to change your view to see what's lurking in the margins of your page. Sometimes you have to select things outside of the normal typing area on your screen. What kinds of things? Things like:

➤ Page numbers

➤ Footnotes

➤ Headers

➤ Footers

➤ Border designs

➤ Aliens hidden in the margin

These are things you don't normally see on the screen because you're in Normal view. Headers and footers, which you will learn to add to your document in Chapter 10, are hidden in this view. The margins (covered in Chapter 9) and borders (covered in Chapter 10) on your printed page are also hidden in this view, which makes it almost impossible to select objects living in them. Views are discussed in detail in Chapter 19, but for now let's take a quick peek at our document using the Page Layout view.

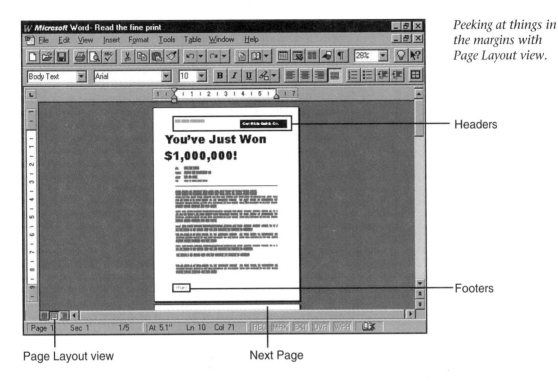

Peeking at things in the margins with Page Layout view.

Headers

Footers

Page Layout view

Next Page

Click the **View** menu and then click the **Page Layout** command, if it has not already been selected. The text area of your screen will change in appearance. Instead of a plain white background, you will now see something that looks like a sheet of paper, or more, on a darker background. You will see your document just as it will print. Travel up or down your document using the vertical scroll bar, and you'll soon see the top or bottom of the page. Notice that pages are separated from each other, appearing just as they will print.

If you've added objects such as a header or footer, you'll see them in a light gray font in the borders of the document. Of course, if you aren't using page numbers, footnotes, or headers, then you won't see any, but that's not a problem. The method for inserting things around this border area (called the margins) of your page is described in Chapter 10. Just remember that selecting things outside the border is just like selecting things inside the border. Place your mouse arrow over the object and double-click the left mouse button. This activates the feature you're trying to edit. Then you can use any of the selection techniques described in this chapter to select and manipulate the text.

The Least You Need to Know

Selecting text is a big deal. This skill deserves to be rewarded. Grab something tasty and ponder the importance of what you've learned:

➤ You can use either the keyboard or mouse to select text. The Shift+arrow key or F8 are common keyboard methods, whereas clicking and dragging the mouse does the same thing.

➤ You can cut, copy, and paste text by using the **Cut**, **Copy**, and **Paste** buttons on the standard toolbar.

➤ Selected text can also be moved around by using the mouse. Simply drag the selected text to a new location.

➤ Selecting some things can be hard work, especially if you can't see them. Change to Page Layout view to select things like page numbers, headers, and footers that hide in the margin.

➤ You can use Spike, a utility in Word, to help you cut many different text selections and then paste them all at once to a new location. Press **Ctrl+F3** to load something into Spike, and when you are finished, press **Shift+Ctrl+F3** to unload everything to one location.

Chapter 7

Making Your ABCs Look Better: It's Called Formatting

In This Chapter

➤ Choosing Bold, Italic, and Underline

➤ Selecting a different font

➤ Quick ways to change the size of text

➤ Changing multiple formats at once

➤ Copying character formatting from one place to another

So now you've got words on the page, and they basically say what you want to say. Not happy yet? You've got a feeling that things could be better somehow? You've seen it in magazines, posters, and those impersonal form letters in the mail. Just *how* do they do those *things* to get **your** Attention???

Yes, you can certainly cut out assorted fancy letters from newspapers and magazines, then paste them letter-by-letter onto your sheet of paper, but that's usually done when you want to remain anonymous. How can you get Word for Windows 95 to do the kind of stuff you'll be proud of? Sit back and enjoy; we'll break no laws (except perhaps those of good taste) on this subject of character formatting.

Who's a Character, and What's Formatting?

Character is a computer term. It means a single letter of the alphabet (or a single number or symbol). The word *antidisestablishmentarianism* is made up of 28 characters.

Character formatting is the process of changing how a character looks. For example, through character formatting you can make a word bold, italic, or underline. You can also change the size of text (its *point size*), making it bigger and smaller. You can also change its style by choosing a different *font.*

Making Your Characters Bold

To initiate bold, press the **Ctrl+B** key combination. From now on, anything you type will be in bold—that is, of course, until you want to turn it off. It's not hard to do that, either. Simply press **Ctrl+B** again!

 You can do the same thing by pressing the **Bold** button on the Formatting toolbar. Notice that the icon stays pushed-in while Bold mode is turned on. Typing anything at this point is made bold. Click the **Bold** button again, and it is turned off. The button icon returns to normal.

If you already have text on the screen that you want to make bold, you must select it first. We learned how to select things in Chapter 6, so choose your favorite method and select something. Double-click on a word if you skipped Chapter 6, as it's one of the faster ways to select a word. Once text is selected, you can press either **Ctrl+B** or the **Bold** button, and the selection will be changed to bold.

You can remove the bold formatting from existing text by first selecting it, then pressing **Ctrl+B** or the **Bold** button. Notice that the bold commands work like a toggle—first on, then off, as many times as you can stand the excitement.

Doing the Italic Thing

Likewise, to initiate italic, press the **Ctrl+I** keys. Anything typed after this will appear in italic. Press **Ctrl+I** again when you want to return to normal text.

I The Italic button is also on the Formatting toolbar, right next to our Bold friend. Click it once to start italicizing your prose; click it again to return to normal.

If you already have text on the screen that you want to accentuate by making it italic, start by selecting it. Then press either **Ctrl+I** or the **Italic** button, and the selection will be turned into italic.

If you get tired of looking at an italicized portion of your document, you can get rid of it by first selecting it, then pressing **Ctrl+I** or the **Italic** button. Just like the Bold commands, this works like a toggle—first on, then off, as many times as you change your mind.

Underlining What's Important

You've got the idea now. Press the **Ctrl+U** keys to begin underlining the text you type. Press **Ctrl+U** keys once again when you have completed the underline portion of your text to turn it off.

The Underline button accomplishes this same task and is located on the Formatting toolbar right next to Italic. Press the **Underline** button to begin typing underlined text, and press it again when finished to return to normal text.

You can remove the underlining (if no one is looking) by first selecting it, then pressing the **Ctrl+U** or the **Underline** button. Selected text will toggle between underlined and not underlined as you execute this command.

The Bold Underlined Italic Look

Yes, you can mix and match any of these formatting commands. Your text can be bold and italic, underlined and bold, or anything you feel is important. You can even rotate the letters of each word to be one of each, but you probably don't have the time.

Returning to Normal (or Regular)

You can turn off all character formatting by pressing the Ctrl+Spacebar key combination. This also works on selected text containing any combination of character formatting. Simply select the range of text and press **Ctrl+Spacebar**. If you don't like the results, you can always put the formatting back with the **Ctrl+Z** command. Ctrl+Z is known as the Great Undo-er, and will undo the last thing you've done, including character formatting. You can also press the Undo button on the Standard toolbar.

If you want to get rid of all character formatting, no matter what or where, select the entire document with **Ctrl+A** and then press **Ctrl+Shift+Z**. You'll be left with plain, unadulterated text (called *regular*) in the default font and size.

Those Little Words Shoved Higher or Lower

Superscript text flies above any normal text, like a reference to a footnote, or the degree symbol or an exponent. You can make your text superscript by using the **Ctrl+Shift+=** key combination and then typing the superscript text. You can also select existing text and press the same **Ctrl+Shift+=** keys. In fact, you don't even have to select the text, just make sure the insertion point is somewhere inside the word. The entire word will be turned into superscript.

Subscript text trudges along below normal text. You can achieve this effect by pressing the **Ctrl+=** key combination on selected text, or just before you start typing the desired

Ordinals Are Easier in Word for Windows 95 Ordinals are those numbers like 1st, 2nd, 3rd, and so on, that should be part superscript. With the AutoText feature of Word 7, you simply type 2nd and it will be turned into 2nd automatically. And that's no ordinal-ary feat!

subscript. With either superscript or subscript, you can return to normal text by first selecting the super- or sub-portion, then pressing **Ctrl+Spacebar**.

It's important to realize that both superscripts and subscripts are still the same font size as the rest of your line. That means they might not look like you expect. You can make them smaller by following the instructions in the upcoming section in this chapter.

Another important thing to remember is that some fonts can't, or won't, appear on your screen as super- or subscript, but they will print out correctly. You have to experiment for yourself.

Inserting Symbols to Suit You

Perhaps you want to include one of those unusual words you see in the comics. You know, the weird symbols representing something that shouldn't be in print, like (#!*#!*). Better yet, how about including the symbols that are easy to recognize, like a trademark, or copyright, or fractions?

All these symbols can be found by using the Symbol command in the Insert menu. You can also press **Alt+I+S** to see the Symbol dialog box displaying hundreds of symbols to choose from. You can either double-click the symbol or click it and then press Enter. The symbol will be copied into your document at the current insertion point. If the location isn't what you want, you can move it or cut-and-paste it to another location.

You can also delete the symbol, if you don't like it. Just select it and press the **Delete** key. Or, even easier, just press the **Undo** button on the Standard toolbar.

Symbols of our time.

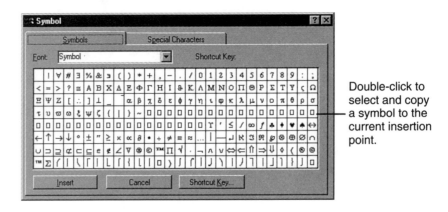

Double-click to select and copy a symbol to the current insertion point.

Fractions Are Easier in Word for Windows 95

Putting fractions into your documents will no longer slow you down with the AutoFormat feature of Word 7. When you type 1/2, for example, Word will automatically format the characters to appear as ½.

Uppercase and Lowercase Conversions

A neat trick available in Word for Windows 95 could be called the *case rotation*. It alternates letters between uppercase and lowercase in a chunk of selected text. The secret key combination is Shift+F3.

The first rotation capitalizes the first letter in all words in the selection. Press **Shift+F3** again, and all letters will be capitalized. Press it again, and they will all be lowercase again.

Case rotation is even smarter than it sounds. The first rotation after pressing Shift+F3 depends on the type of text selected. If there are punctuation marks—a period, for instance—then only the first word in a sentence is capitalized. However, if no punctuation marks exist, then the first letter in every word is capitalized.

Strange and Unusual Formatting Tips

If the other choices of character formatting still don't excite you, then here's a last attempt with some little-known key combinations.

Ctrl+Shift+A	CREATES ALL CAPITAL LETTER TEXT
Ctrl+Shift+D	Double underlines your individual words
Ctrl+Shift+H	(Creates hidden text that won't print)
Ctrl+Shift+K	CREATES ALL LETTERS THAT HAVEN'T BEEN CAPITALIZED INTO LITTLE CAPITAL LETTERS CALLED "SMALL CAPS"
Ctrl+Shift+W	Underlines only single individual words

These may not appear on your screen as they print on the page. You will have to try them and find out. Don't forget that if you try them and don't like the results, you can return them to normal by pressing **Ctrl+Shift+Z**.

Fonts and Sizes: How the Other Half Lives

Hope you aren't tired yet, because you're less than halfway through the vast character formatting jungle. Sure, the bold-italic-underline stuff helps, but the letters are still shaped the same way. That's called a *font*. You can change fonts whenever you want, and hundreds of fonts are available commercially. Word for Windows 95 gives you more than 50 to play with. And if that's not enough, you can purchase additional fonts from your computer store to install and make available to Word for Windows 95. Ask your computer salesperson for more information on purchasing and installing additional fonts.

What does a different font look like? Here's a sample:

Paragon font

Courier New font

Paradise font

Mystical font

Changing Your Font

To change to a different font, click the down arrow in the font box. A list of all fonts available will drop down for you to view. The list is alphabetical, in case you know the name of the font you desire. Browse the list with your mouse or arrow keys and press **Enter** (or click) on the font you want. The font name you picked should now be displayed in the font box. Now start typing. Everything will appear in the new font, and it should print, as well.

Squander years choosing from more than 50 built-in fonts!

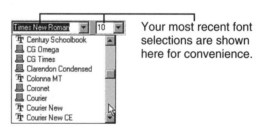

Your most recent font selections are shown here for convenience.

You can also change the font of existing text by first—you got it—selecting it. Any change of font made while text is selected will change the entire selection to that new font. If more than one font is used in the selection, they will all be converted to the single new font.

What Is a TT Font?

The TT displayed next to many of the fonts designate them as TrueType fonts, which means they print out exactly as you see them on the screen. That's a surprise to you?

Other fonts may have a little printer icon next to them. These are printer fonts, and they are built into your printer. No guarantee that you *see* the font correctly on the screen, but it will certainly *print* in that font. The other fonts are merely screen drivers, and with these there is no guarantee that you will print what you see, but usually they do.

Only in the last few years has this problem of what-you-see-is-what-you-get been solved. TrueType fonts is one way.

If Size Is Important

You can make your text appear and print larger or smaller by changing the *size* of the current font, and you have many sizes to choose from. To change the font size, click the Font Size box in the Formatting toolbar (you can also press the **Ctrl+Shift+P** key combination). Choose a larger number to make it bigger, and vice-versa.

You can also change the font size on selected text quickly with **Ctrl+]** (to make it one size bigger) and **Ctrl+[** (to make it one size smaller). The change on your screen may not be enough to notice, but it did change.

Check This Out...

Point Size The correct way to refer to font size is the term *point size*. The typical document uses a 10 or 12 point font. A point is 1/72 inch. Most fonts can be sized from 4 points to 127 points.

Sometimes a font size change looks terrible because the font wasn't designed for that particular point size. You can fix things by pressing the **Ctrl+Shift+>** (bigger) or the **Ctrl+Shift+<** (smaller) combination keys. Instead of giving you the next point size, these commands give you the next most appropriate size that the font was designed to handle.

The Whole Formatting Enchilada at Your Fingertips

There is yet another way to obtain all of the character formatting tips described in this chapter, and all of them are available in a single dialog box. It's called the Font dialog box, and you can get to it by selecting the Format menu and then clicking the Font command.

One of the best reasons to use this method is the Preview box that displays your choice of formatting *before* you apply it. Take a peek at the following figure.

Another reason to use this dialog box is to set your default font to whatever combination you like best. Set it up in the Preview box the way you like it and then click the **Default** button (or press **Alt+D**).

Click to choose font, style, and size from the lists.

The Font dialog box has it all!

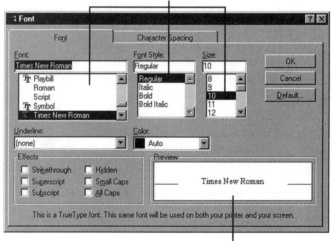

See your selection here first.

Copying the Formatting You Prefer

Suppose that you just finished choosing the most incredible combination of formatting options available and you want to apply it to existing text somewhere else. Is there a shortcut that can speed things up?

You bet. Just remember to do it immediately, or your computer might forget what it is. The magic key is **F4**. You can also copy your formatting by selecting the **Repeat** command from the Edit menu.

If you don't get around to it right away, you can still copy it later. In your document, find the area of formatting you like and click inside of it somewhere. Then click the Format Painter button on the Standard toolbar. Go to the text where you want the formatting to be applied and highlight it. That's it; the formatting will be applied automatically. When you are done, press **Esc**, or click the Format Painter again to avoid littering your document with these kind of changes.

Viewing Format Settings

Word for Windows 95 displays text as it will look when it's printed. Fanatics might worry at first that Word doesn't use formatting codes to indicate the formatting details (like WordPerfect). Fret not, I say! To check the formats of a particular character or paragraph, click the Help Pointer (the Arrow/Question Mark thingy) on the Standard toolbar. When the cursor becomes a question mark, click the text you want to check. Word will display the formatting codes for the selected text. To get rid of this screen when you are finished, press the **Esc** key.

The Least You Need to Know

You can change character formatting either before you type or after you type (by selecting the text):

➤ Use the Bold, Italic, and Underline buttons on the Formatting toolbar to quickly change text attributes.

➤ Use the buttons on the Formatting toolbar to change the font and point size quickly.

➤ You can repeat recent character formatting selections by pressing F4. You can also copy existing formatting by clicking or selecting within it, then clicking the Format Painter button on the Standard toolbar, and finally selecting the text where you want it applied.

➤ Multiple formatting decisions are more easily made using the Font dialog box (Format menu, Font command).

➤ You can view the actual formatting of a character by pointing and clicking with the Help Pointer.

Chapter 8

Formatting Bigger Things: Sentences and Paragraphs

In This Chapter

➤ Aligning paragraphs

➤ Changing a paragraph's indents

➤ Creating bullets and numbered lists

➤ Changing paragraph spacing

➤ Setting and working with tabs

So now you're familiar with selecting things like sentences and paragraphs (Chapter 6) and formatting the individual letters in your document (Chapter 7). Why not put the two together and start formatting sentences and paragraphs?

Why not also try some of the nifty automatic formatting tools that come with Word for Windows 95? Start typing a numbered or bulleted list, for example, and Word learns what you're doing so quickly that when you hit the Enter key to go to the second line, you'll find the correct number or bullet already entered and the cursor properly positioned for the next item.

Paragraph Basics: First Things First

What is a paragraph? We know you probably don't care that the definition of a *paragraph* is "one or more sentences containing a consistent theme," but you should—because using paragraphs helps the flow and clarity of what you write. Paragraphs can be as small as one sentence on a single line or thousands of sentences written across reams and volumes of paper, but most are somewhere in between.

In Word for Windows 95, a paragraph is nothing more than a collection of anything you can think of that ends in a carriage return (or a press of the Enter key). This includes normal paragraphs as well as single-line paragraphs, such as chapter titles, section headings, and captions for charts and other figures. When you press the Enter key, you are marking the end of a paragraph.

How Can I See a Paragraph?

At the end of each paragraph, Word inserts a *paragraph mark* that is normally invisible, and for good reason—they get in your way. However, paragraph marks are important because they contain all of the paragraph formatting commands contained in the paragraph. For example, you can center a paragraph between the margins, change the indentation for the first line, or change the spacing between paragraphs, among other things. Accidentally delete a paragraph symbol, however, and the formatting of your paragraph disappears!

¶ One of the more peculiar-looking buttons on your Standard toolbar is called Show/Hide Paragraph Symbols. Press it, and you'll see the special formatting codes used by Word to organize your document. These symbols will never appear on your printed document. This show/hide button is also a toggle button, and pressing it again hides the symbols again. Also, if you are allergic to buttons, you can press the **Ctrl+Shift+8** keys to do the same thing.

> **Check This Out...**
>
> **Paragraph Formatting Continues**
> When you press Enter to create a new paragraph, the formatting of that paragraph continues to the next paragraph. Once you make changes to a paragraph (such as changing its margin settings), those changes are effective forever until you change them again.

You can use the show/hide button to check on your own word processing habits. Remember the basic rule of not pressing the Enter key at the end of each line unless you want to create a new paragraph? Now you can check yourself by pressing the **Show/Hide** formatting button. You should not see any of these symbols at the end of lines unless it also happens to be the end of the paragraph. Skipped lines will also show up as a paragraph symbol at the beginning of a new line.

Where the Show/Hide
button lives

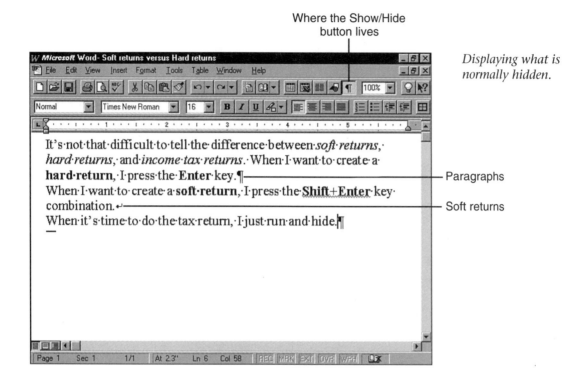

*Displaying what is
normally hidden.*

Paragraphs

Soft returns

Soft or Hard Return?

If you need to move to the next line without creating a new paragraph
(as in a list or an address at the top of a letter), press **Shift+Enter**. This
inserts a "soft return," marking the end of a line, as opposed to a "hard
return," which marks the end of a paragraph.

Center Lines and Paragraphs

To create a paragraph that's centered on the page, meaning equally distant from the
left and right margins, press **Enter** to start a new paragraph. Now press the **Center**
button on the Formatting toolbar (or press **Ctrl+E**). The insertion point will move to the
center of the page. Start typing, and you'll notice that the words spread out from the
center of the page. Press **Enter** when you're done, and you will have a completely centered paragraph. You can also center an existing paragraph by clicking it to get the

insertion point anywhere inside the paragraph and pressing the **Center** button. Selected text can also be centered the same way.

To change a centered paragraph back to a normal one, aligned with the left margin, place the insertion point anywhere inside the paragraph and press the **Align Left** button on the formatting toolbar (or press **Ctrl+L**). To transition from a centered paragraph to a left-aligned paragraph, press **Enter** to start a new paragraph, and then press the **Align Left** button (or **Ctrl+L**), and things will be back to normal.

Flushing Text Right or Left

  Flushing text sounds like a way to get rid of it, but it's not. It describes the way text aligns inside of your document. Most documents are prepared with the text *flush left*, with each line starting at the left margin. It can just as easily be flushed right for things like dates that you want to appear at the top right side of your page. Try flushing some text.

Flushing is not a way to get rid of text. It's the accepted term used to line up text to the right or left, and left is the most common.

Place the insertion point where you want to type. Press the **Align Right** button on the Formatting toolbar, or press **Ctrl+R**, and things will line up to the right. Press **Ctrl+L** when you are finished to return to normal.

Changing Line and Paragraph Spacing

Someday your boss may ask you to read between the lines, and your vision may not be so good. You can try to increase the distance between lines in your Word for Windows 95 document.

Normally, all lines are single-spaced. However, you can quickly change the line spacing of any paragraph by placing the insertion point anywhere in the paragraph and pressing the desired key combination listed here:

➤ Press **Ctrl+1** (the number one) for single-spaced lines.

➤ Press **Ctrl+2** for double-spaced lines.

➤ Press **Ctrl+5** for one-and-a-half spaced lines.

Besides adjusting the spacing between lines, you can also adjust the spacing between paragraphs. Open the **Format** menu and choose the **Paragraph** command. In the Spacing section of the Paragraph dialog box, enter the number of lines to place before or after (usually not both) this paragraph. If you set up a paragraph so there is a blank line following it, you won't have to press the Enter key twice between paragraphs.

Before leaving the Paragraph dialog box, notice the Line Spacing drop-down box, which is another method you can use to change line spacing.

Indenting a Paragraph

Regular paragraphs are indented by using the Tab key to indent the first line. That's fine, but sometimes you just have to call attention to an entire paragraph by indenting the whole thing, not just the first line.

To indent an entire paragraph, place the insertion point anywhere in the paragraph and press **Ctrl+M** or press the **Increase Indent** button on the Formatting toolbar. To return an indented paragraph to the original margin, press **Ctrl+Shift+M** or click the **Decrease Indent** button on the Formatting toolbar.

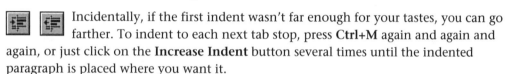 Incidentally, if the first indent wasn't far enough for your tastes, you can go farther. To indent to each next tab stop, press **Ctrl+M** again and again and again, or just click on the **Increase Indent** button several times until the indented paragraph is placed where you want it.

If you want to indent both right and left sides, use the method called *double-indenting*. Move the insertion point to the beginning of a new paragraph and open the **Format** menu and choose **Paragraph**. In the Paragraph dialog box, choose the **Indents and Spacing** tab to bring it to the front. Now click the **Left** box and enter something like .5 (half inch), or simply play with the up/down arrows and pick a number. Click the **Right** box and enter .5 again. You should keep each side the same, but no one will arrest you if you don't. Click **OK** or press **Enter** and start typing. Your text will be double-indented. I'll tell you more about the Paragraph dialog box later in this chapter.

Making a Hanging Indent

For some reason, certain people like to do exactly the opposite of what you expect. That's what the hanging indent looks like. Instead of the first line starting comfortably inside the paragraph, the hanging indent sticks out from the rest of the paragraph. It looks backwards—but it can be put to good use, as you'll read in the next section.

To create a hanging indent, click anywhere in an existing paragraph (or start a new one) and press **Ctrl+T**. Press **Ctrl+T** again to indent even more. To undo any or all of this, press **Ctrl+Shift+T**.

Hanging Around Numbered and Bulleted Lists

A special kind of hanging indent is a *numbered* or *bulleted list*. This kind of list is special because a number or symbol (that sometimes looks like a bullet) is placed to the left of all the other lines in the paragraph.

 You've seen bulleted lists used throughout these chapters to:

➤ Create snazzy lists like this one.

➤ Highlight what's coming up.

➤ Summarize the important points that were covered.

Faster Bullets and Quicker Numbers
Now with Word 7, creating numbered or bulleted lists can happen as quickly as you can type! Numbered lists are automatically created when you type a number followed by a blank space and then some text. Bulleted lists are automatically created when you use a symbol like *, o, or > followed by a blank space and text. In either case, when you press Enter, you will see the next bullet or number automatically created.

Numbered lists are especially helpful when you want to explain the specific steps for doing something, such as step 1, step 2, and so on. Ready to number or bullet? Here's what to do.

Click on the appropriate button on the **Formatting** toolbar, and then start typing. What you type becomes a bullet on a list. Press **Enter** to start a new bullet. You can stop the bullets from appearing by clicking the same button of the Standard toolbar once again. You can also stop a running list by pressing **Ctrl+Shift+N**, which starts a new paragraph with the Normal style.

You can interrupt a numbered list by clicking the right mouse button and selecting **Skip Numbering** from the menu. To resume numbering later in your document, click the **Numbering** button on the Formatting toolbar.

Doesn't Look Like a Bullet?

If you want to create different bullets or numbering, use the Bullets and Numbering command on the Format menu. You can change the type and size of bullets, the numbering system (letters, Roman numerals, or decimal numbers), and the amount of space between the number or bullet and the rest of the paragraph. If you're using the keyboard, you can press **Ctrl+Tab** to move between the Bullets and Numbering sections; then use the forward arrow to select a style and press **Enter**.

Using Tabs

What are *tab stops*? They're a way of moving, or indenting, your way consistently in a paragraph. Press the **Tab** key, and you move in one tab stop. Normal tab stops are set every half inch.

If you want to change the distance between tab stops, or change the type of tab you want to use, do something weird first. Place the insertion point *to the left of where you will be adding the desired tab stop* (this prevents existing text, and you, from getting confused when the change occurs). Now take a look at the ruler near the top of your page. If you don't see your ruler, or aren't sure, open the View Menu and choose the Ruler command so a checkmark appears next to it. At the far left of the ruler is a box with a strange symbol inside. These symbols are Tab symbols, and change as you click this box. Any tab symbol appearing in this box will be applied to the ruler when you click anywhere else on the ruler. Click the left mouse button on the Ruler, and a little corner will appear, indicating a tab stop location. You can change the tab stop location by dragging it with your mouse to the left or right.

You can get rid of tab stops by clicking and dragging them off the ruler completely.

Tab Markers

Word for Windows 95 uses four different types of tabs which can be viewed on the Ruler.

- ➤ **Left Tab**   The most common tab is the left tab, which operates just like a typewriter.

- ➤ **Right Tab**   The right tab causes text to line up right-justified at that tab stop. This can help create interesting titles, which are, of course, single-line paragraphs.

- ➤ **Center Tab**   This is great for one-word columns of text. The center tab lines all the words up in the center, left-justified.

➤ **Decimal Tab**   This tab is used to align numbers by their decimal point. The number is right-justified before you press the period key and then left-justified on the decimal.

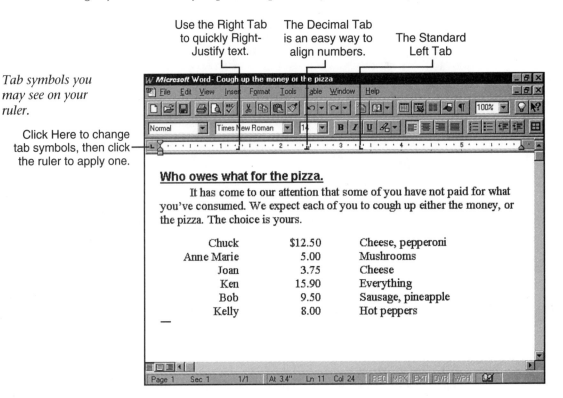

Use the Right Tab to quickly Right-Justify text.

The Decimal Tab is an easy way to align numbers.

The Standard Left Tab

Tab symbols you may see on your ruler.

Click Here to change tab symbols, then click the ruler to apply one.

Who owes what for the pizza.

It has come to our attention that some of you have not paid for what you've consumed. We expect each of you to cough up either the money, or the pizza. The choice is yours.

Chuck	$12.50	Cheese, pepperoni
Anne Marie	5.00	Mushrooms
Joan	3.75	Cheese
Ken	15.90	Everything
Bob	9.50	Sausage, pineapple
Kelly	8.00	Hot peppers

Using Leader Tabs

Sometimes tabs can be used to provide interesting effects in your document. For instance, have you ever wondered how they get that line of dots that extends out to the page number in a table of contents? Me neither. But it just so happens that you can use something called a *leader tab* to get the job done.

No dots (the default)   X

Little dots X

Dashes ————————————————————X

Underlining _____X

To create these leader tabs, start by positioning the insertion point on the line where you want to start them. Set a tab stop as described previously, then choose the **Tabs** command from the **Format** menu. You will see the Tabs dialog box.

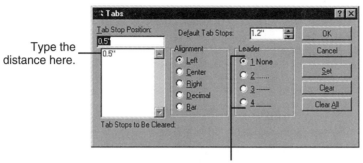

Type the distance here.

Word running your tab for you.

Pick your leader type.

Now select the style of leader you prefer by clicking the option button (you can also press **Alt+1** through **Alt+4**) and then press the **OK** button (or press **Enter**).

Now start typing. Type the text to appear before the tab stop. Press the **Tab** key. Bingo! The leader will appear, and all you are left with is to decide what to type at the other end. Press the **Enter** key to end each line containing a leader tab.

The Paragraph Dialog Box

Yes, the paragraph is so important that it has its own dialog box inside of Word for Windows 95. All of the features and procedures described in this chapter (and a whole bunch more!) can also be performed from this dialog box. You can find it by selecting the **Format** menu and then choosing the **Paragraph** command. You can also click the right mouse button to see the formatting shortcut menu, and choose the **Paragraph** command. You'll see these dialog boxes:

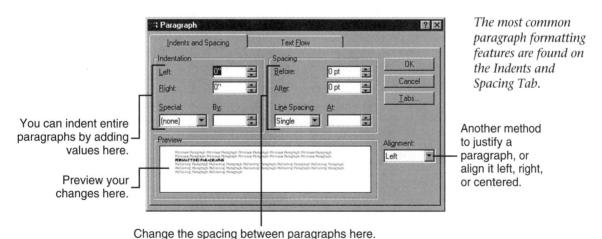

You can indent entire paragraphs by adding values here.

Preview your changes here.

Change the spacing between paragraphs here.

The most common paragraph formatting features are found on the Indents and Spacing Tab.

Another method to justify a paragraph, or align it left, right, or centered.

You've already learned how to make all these changes in this chapter. This dialog box simply provides one place where you can do all this at once. The remaining paragraph formatting functions can be found by clicking the **Text Flow** Tab to bring it to the front. Here, you will find less-known features, like preventing single lines from appearing on an entire page with the Widow/Orphan Control option.

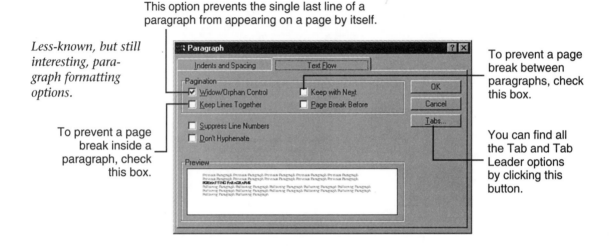

This option prevents the single last line of a paragraph from appearing on a page by itself.

Less-known, but still interesting, paragraph formatting options.

To prevent a page break inside a paragraph, check this box.

To prevent a page break between paragraphs, check this box.

You can find all the Tab and Tab Leader options by clicking this button.

Copy the Formatting of a Paragraph

In Chapter 7, you learned that you can quickly copy character formatting by using the **Format Painter** button. You can use this same button to copy the formatting of one paragraph to another, which can save you lots of formatting time. Start by selecting the entire paragraph that is formatted to perfection. Now click the **Format Painter** button located on the **Standard** toolbar. Finally, locate the paragraph you want to have the same formatting and click anywhere inside of it. The paragraph formatting is applied instantly. You can repeat these steps as often as you like throughout your document, or even apply the formatting to paragraphs in other documents.

The Least You Need to Know

Now you can have your paragraph and format it, too. This chapter reviewed helpful tips and reminders such as:

➤ A paragraph is created when you press **Enter**.

➤ You can use the buttons on the Formatting toolbar to change formatting, indenting, and paragraph alignment.

➤ Press **Ctrl+Shift+N** to return a selected paragraph to the Normal paragraph style. To remove manual formatting, press **Ctrl+Q**.

➤ Change the spacing before, after, and within paragraphs with the Paragraph command on the Format menu.

➤ To copy a paragraph's formatting, you could try osmosis. If that doesn't work, press the **Format Painter** button on the selected text of the preferred paragraph formatting. Then simply click anywhere inside the paragraph you want to fix. The paragraph formatting is changed instantly to match the preferred paragraph's.

Chapter 9

Formatting Even Bigger Things: Pages and Documents

You are now beyond formatting letters and words, sentences and paragraphs. You've reached the formatting of entire pages and documents! That's impressive power—power to make a major visual impact with your document. I can tell you're trembling with excitement. Control yourself. To harness all that power, you might want to review some of the tips in this chapter.

Since this is an entire chapter on formatting pages, I want to make sure you're comfortable viewing a whole page. With any document appearing on the screen, open the **View** menu and take a peek at the top four viewing choices. All you care about for now is the Normal and Page Layout views. Try selecting each of them to see the difference on your screen. Page Layout view actually looks like a sheet of paper, while Normal view is nothing to write home about; at least not yet. Get comfortable switching between these views, because you'll need to do it in this chapter to see the various page formatting commands, and the effects of those commands. You can also switch views by clicking on one of the three buttons at the left side of the horizontal scroll bar. You can learn more about views in Chapter 19, but for now let's return to the subject of page formatting.

Starting a New Page

After a few minutes (or days) of typing, you may find that it's time to start a new page. You're probably now familiar with the *soft page breaks*, a single line of dashes that appears when text you're typing fills one page and spills onto another. You always get a new page in Normal view when the page is filled up and text flows to the next page. But what if you intentionally want to start a new page, and it's somewhere in the middle of your document, like a new chapter heading or title? You need to use the *hard page break*.

The Hard Page Break

The most important difference between a soft and hard page break is that you have control over where this hard page break happens. Instead of pressing the Enter key 49 times to get to the start of the next page (which guarantees nothing), you simply place your insertion point at the exact spot you want and press **Ctrl+Enter**.

When you press **Ctrl+Enter**, a tight row of dots, which also includes the words **Page Break** in the middle, gets inserted in your document. It looks different from the soft page break, and it's hard to miss.

You can delete a hard page break by pressing the **Backspace** or **Delete** keys at the top of the page.

Creating Section Breaks

A *section* is a part of a document that has different formatting settings from the main document. These settings might include margins, paper size, headers, footers, columns, and page numbering. A section can be of any length: several pages, several paragraphs, or even a single line (such as a major heading). There are a lot of good reasons why you might want to include sections in your document. Here are a few ideas:

➤ To create multiple chapters in a long report. Each chapter would have its own chapter title (called a header), and you could easily have Word generate a table of contents or an index for the whole document.

➤ For legal documents that require line numbering in some sections but not in others.

➤ To create a company newsletter with various formats. You could create a section just for the front-page heading so that it reaches from margin to margin on a single line.

Underneath, you could change to a three newspaper-column format for the text of the newsletter.

➤ For business reports printed in portrait orientation (for example, 8 1/2-by-11 inches) with a chart that's printed in landscape orientation (11-by-8 1/2 inches).

➤ In a small manual, where each section has its own page numbers. The table of contents section could use Roman numerals (I, ii, and so on) for page numbers. Each section after the Table of Contents could start with page 1. Since the title page wouldn't need a page number, you could suppress page numbering on just that page.

What Are Those Double Lines I See? In Normal view, sections are marked by a double line. Section marks are like paragraph marks; they contain the formatting for that section. So if you delete them, that section will revert to the formatting of the section before it. It's best to learn to ignore these lines; they won't print, and deleting them causes you to lose your formatting for your section.

➤ To include text in two different languages (for example, a human resources memorandum). The document could be divided into paired sections—one section for English and another for Spanish.

Before you create your first section break in a document, do yourself a favor. Set the most common document options first. For example, if you want most pages to have two newspaper columns, go ahead and set them up *before* you start dividing your document into sections. Otherwise, you'd be left to duplicate the common options within each section, and you have better things to do with your time.

When you're ready to start dividing up your document, place the insertion point at the desired continental divide, open the **Insert** menu, and choose the **Break** command.

Under Section Breaks, choose from these available options:

Next Page   The section starts at the top of the next page.

Continuous   The section starts right after the previous section, even if it's in the middle of the page.

Odd Page   The section starts on the next odd-numbered page. That's typically the next right-hand page.

Even Page   Yes, the section starts on the next even-numbered page, which is typically the next left-hand page.

When you have made your selection, press the **OK** button to close the Section dialog box, and you're done!

Choosing a break in your document.

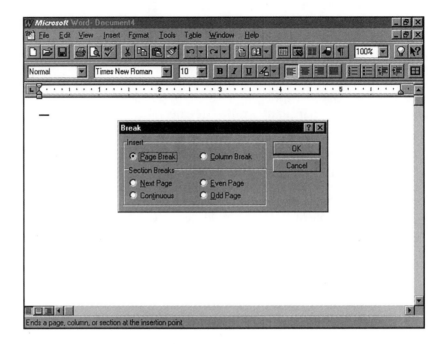

So Now That I Have a Section, What Do I Do with It?

These are some of the changes you can make that affect a section of a document, instead of the document as a whole:

Margins If you decide to create different sections in your document, you can change the margins within each section separately. You'll learn to do this later in this chapter.

Paper Size and Page Orientation You can choose from lots of paper sizes (such as 8 1/2-by-11 inches and 11-by-14 inches), and even change the paper size by section (but that could cause printing delays if a paper tray is empty, or not supported, by your printer). Certain sections may look better with a different orientation (landscape versus portrait). I'll tell you more about page orientation later in this chapter.

Headers and Footers A *header* is stuff that's printed at the top of the page, and a *footer* is stuff (like page numbers, filename, and so on) printed at the bottom. You'll learn how to create these in the next chapter, but you get the idea that these are ideal candidates for section use in a document.

Page Numbers   These are usually included as part of a header or footer. You can change the page numbering system from the default of 1, 2, 3 to something else, such as I, ii, iii or A, B, C. You can change the page numbering system within a document by creating sections and using different headers and footers for each section.

Newspaper-Style Columns   You can create columns in your document that appear like those you find in a newspaper or a magazine. If you ever want to vary the number of columns inside of the same document, you are required to set up a new section. You will learn how to set up columns of text in Chapter 18.

Deleting a Section Break

Select the section break you want to delete, and then press the **Delete** key. Be careful! When you delete a section break, you also delete the section formatting for the text above it. That text becomes part of the following section, so it picks up the formatting of that section. If you really didn't want to do this, press **Ctrl+Z** or the **Undo** button on the Standard toolbar.

Copying the Formatting Between Sections

When a document has more than one section, you can copy section formatting by copying the section break. When you paste the section break into a new location, the text above the section break automatically picks up the formatting of the new section break.

Formatting in the Last Section

The section formatting for the last section in a document is contained in the final paragraph mark of the document. You can replace any existing paragraph mark with the last paragraph mark by using the **Copy** and **Paste** commands on the **Edit** menu.

Centering Your Page on the Paper

If your document doesn't fill up a single page, you will have some empty space near the bottom. If that bothers you, why not center what text you have, with equal spacing from the top and bottom edges of the page. Even inside a large document, you may want the effect of having some important text centered from top-to-bottom in the middle of a page by itself. Word for Windows 95 provides an easy way to do this.

Check This Out...

Confused?
If you thought this section described how to center a line between the left and right margins, you missed by one chapter (line centering is covered in Chapter 7).

Easy stuff first: here's an example of a single page document, with just a few sentences or paragraphs wanting to be centered, between top and bottom, on the printed page. Open the **File** menu and choose the **Page Setup** command. When you see the Page Setup dialog box, click the tab that says **Layout** to bring it to the front. Near the bottom of this box you will see the label Vertical Alignment. That's it! Click it to pull down the choices, and in this case, choose **Center**. Press the **OK** button, and Word will center your text on the page.

Click here to choose the type of section you want to create.

Formatting your document with the Page Setup dialog box.

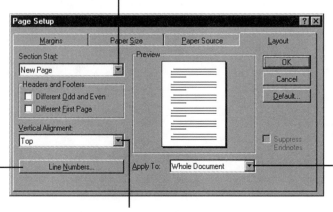

You can also number all the lines in a document by clicking and choosing options here.

Be sure to apply your changes to the whole document, or you won't see any changes yet.

Click here to align the text on your page either top, center, or justified.

Centering a Page Inside a Large Document

Centering one page inside a large document is a little bit different than centering a single-paged document. You see, the page settings are things that affect all pages in a document. So if you jump to the middle and try to center one page using the Page Setup command, you are really changing the alignment of an entire document. Here's the correct way:

Find the page containing the text you want to center. Place the insertion point at the top of that page. You have to mark both the beginning and the end of the page you want centered with a section break, so open the **Insert** menu and choose the **Break** command. Select the **Next Page** option for the section break. The double line of dots will be inserted, marking a new page and a new section.

Now open the **File** menu and select the **Page Setup** command and follow the same steps as before (choose **Center** from the Vertical Alignment drop-down box on the Layout tab). Press the **OK** button and observe the results. Don't forget that new pages in this section will have centered text unless you set up a new section break to isolate the page you just created.

If you have existing text you want to have centered, and it happens to appear in the middle of your document, you can take a shortcut. Simply select the text you want to have centered, open the Page Setup dialog box from the **File** menu, and choose **Center** on the Vertical alignment. Word 7 will automatically insert section breaks before and after the selected text, to isolate the centered formatting.

Margin Review

Word for Windows 95 automatically sets your margins at one inch from the top and bottom, and 1.25 inches from the right and left sides. If you aren't happy with these default settings, you can change them.

Adjusting Your Margins Using the Ruler

The quickest way to change your margins is to use the **Ruler** located below the **Formatting** toolbar (if the Ruler is not displayed, select the **View Ruler** command to display it). Change to Page Layout view by clicking the **Page Layout** button on the horizontal scroll bar. Next, move the mouse pointer to the Ruler. Position the pointer over the Indent markers, and the cursor will change to a double-headed arrow. Drag the markers to the desired location and release the mouse button.

Adjusting margins with the ruler.

Click and drag the margin boundary.

Ruler

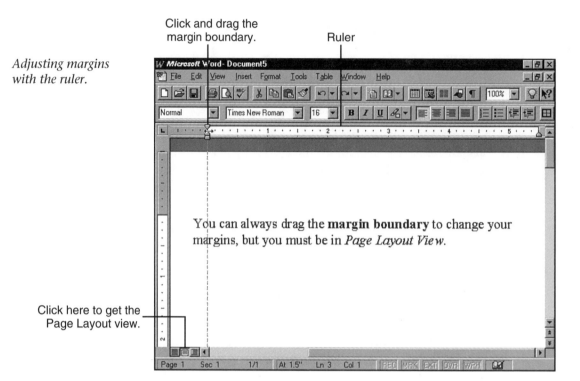

You can always drag the **margin boundary** to change your margins, but you must be in *Page Layout View*.

Click here to get the Page Layout view.

Adjusting Margins Using the Page Setup

Open the **File** menu and choose the **Page Setup** command. In the Page Setup dialog box, click on the **Margins** tab if it isn't in front. The actual margin settings are listed near the top left of this box, and you can change them easily by typing over the value (you can leave off the inch symbol) or by clicking the increase/decrease arrow buttons for any item.

Check This Out...

Laser Printers Can't Print Here
Remember not to set your margins less than 0.5 inch on the left or right side if you plan to print using a laser printer. Laser printers are designed to ignore text within a half-inch of the paper edge.

Don't forget to look in the Preview box. The sample document demonstrates the effect of your changes immediately. This is a live picture of a sample document that changes as you choose different margin values.

Now look at the Apply To drop-down list near the bottom of the Page Setup dialog box. Big decision time. If you happen to be in the middle of your document and you are changing your margins, you must decide if you want them changed starting at this point, or changed throughout your entire document. Choose either **Whole Document** or **This Point Forward**.

Margins on a Smaller Scale

If any text happens to be selected when you open the Page Setup dialog box, the available options change and allow the margins to be applied only to the text that is selected.

Click the **OK** button, and your new margins will be applied to your document. Automatic formatting will occur to adjust any existing text, columns, or pictures.

Type number (to indicate inches) directly here…

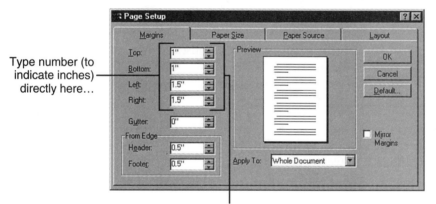

Changing your margins in the Page Setup box.

Or click to increase or decrease margins.

Setting the Page Size

Although you probably plan to print on standard 8 1/2-by-11 inch paper, Word for Windows 95 will allow you to change the paper size to anything you want. Start by placing the insertion point at the beginning of the document or the top of the page.

Open the **File** menu and choose the **Page Setup** command. Click on the **Paper Size** tab to bring it to the front. When you click on the **Paper Size** drop-down list, you will see the paper sizes offered by Word. Make your selection and prepare to click the **OK** button.

Wait! There's the Apply To box again. You must decide if you are changing paper for your entire document or if you really want a mixed-bag of different paper sizes making up this single document (probably not). Since that's unlikely, don't wait; just click the **OK** button to change the size for the entire document.

Deciding Between Landscape and Portrait Mode

The world of art struggled over this concept for ages. It's the struggle of humans over frame type for the picture. What shape are pictures? Have you ever seen a square picture? They aren't too common. Why not, and who did this to us? Rectangle, yes, even diamond and circle, but very few squares. Now you get to struggle over the same issue in formatting your document. If documents were square, there would be no need for this decision. Most pages, by convention, are printed in a rectangular format called *portrait* mode, like this book page.

If you think of pictures hanging on a wall, you will get the idea. Portraits (pictures of people) are usually taller than they are wide. Scenery or landscape shots are usually wider than they are tall. Documents are easier to hold and read in portrait mode. Spreadsheets are easier to follow in *landscape* mode. Presentations are usually created in landscape for the same reason. Landscape is also called sideways printing.

To change your document to landscape mode, open the **File** menu and press the **Page Setup** command. Click the **Paper Size** tab to bring it to the front. Choose either **Portrait** or **Landscape** and watch the Sample document rotate in the Orientation area to demonstrate the effects of your selection. Press the **OK** button, and the change will be applied to your document.

Constructing a Master Document

You can make a document as large as you want, but you will notice that Word for Windows 95 starts to get sluggish with lots and lots of pages. It makes sense to break up larger documents into smaller pieces like chapters and work on them individually. But what if you want to tie them all together at the end to print the whole thing at once, or to use features like building a table of contents or index? You can use the Master Document feature.

Start with the tough job. Create all those smaller documents, and save them. Remember what they're named. Then create a new document (try the **New** button on the Standard toolbar). Now open the **View** menu and choose the **Master Document** command. You will see the Outline toolbar with the Master Document toolbar included on the right side.

 Create Subdocument   Use this if you want to create a document that doesn't exist yet. It's just like a new document, but it's already included in the master.

 Remove Subdocument   This does not delete the document but removes it from being considered part of the master document.

 Insert Subdocument   Easiest button to use; it means go get an existing document and consider it part of this master.

 Merge Subdocument   This silly button should read Merge Subdocuments because it can take multiple subdocuments listed in the Master document and create a single, big document. Pressing this button is like saying, "I've changed my mind and don't want subdocuments; make them a single document."

 Split Subdocument   Use this to split up one of the documents into two documents. You'll need to supply a name for the new addition.

 Lock Document   If you are on a network and don't want people changing any part of your master document while you print it, press this button and lock everyone out. You can lock individual subdocuments or the whole thing based upon where you place the insertion point.

Page Numbers

With Word, you can insert a page number, include text with page numbers, and start page numbering on a page other than the first page of a document. You can also change the page number format in different sections of a document so that a preface or an appendix is numbered differently from the main document.

Changing the Page Number Format

To change the page number format for the entire document, click **Select All** on the **Edit** menu. If you want to change the page number format for only a section of a document, click anywhere in the section you want to format. For example, you can number the section that contains the table of contents with Roman numerals and number the body of the document with Arabic numerals.

On the **Insert** menu, click **Page Numbers**. In the Page Numbers dialog box, click the **Format** button. Now you've reached your destination for the request. In the Number Format box, click the format you want.

AutoFormatting

If you are feeling daring and no bungee cords are at hand, give AutoFormatting a try. No, not on a real document, but just a scratch document (scratch means you can live without it). Type up a few sentences in a new document to test out this feature. It's supposed to help you by taking care of everything—lock, stock, and barrel. Unfortunately, it rarely works. But don't take my word for it; screw up a document yourself. Here's how:

1. Type some words and sentences on a page.

2. Open the **Format** menu and choose the **AutoFormat** command.

3. Click the **Options** button to have a gander at what interesting things might happen.

4. Click the **OK** button to run it.

5. Don't like what you see? Click **Reject Changes**, and everything will return to normal so you can do this process manually.

Am I being unfair to this feature? Probably, because if you happen to create a scratch document the way Microsoft intended, AutoFormat will do a good job. But if you pay that much attention to the way you enter text, you might as well spend the time learning how to control the formatting yourself. Give it a try. It might help improve the readability of files you get off the Internet, especially the longer text files and e-mail.

The Least You Need to Know

➤ You can change margins, paper size, page numbers, and the number of newspaper columns for individual portions of your document by creating sections.

➤ Create a section break with the **Break** command on the **Insert** menu.

➤ If you need to start a new page but not a new section, use a page break. Force a hard page break anywhere in a document by pressing **Ctrl+Enter**.

➤ You can change the margins for several sections at once by using the **Page Setup** command on the **File** menu.

➤ AutoFormatting (on the Format menu) can be used by anyone refusing to read this chapter.

Chapter 10

Headers, Footers, Arms, and Legs

In This Chapter

➤ Making your page look more interesting

➤ Creating Headers and Footers

➤ Editing Headers and Footers

➤ Working with Footnotes

You may not be satisfied with the constraints of a normal page of text in Word for Windows 95. If you are interested in journeying beyond the normal confines of a typical document, this chapter gives you the know-how to create elements that appear in the margins, such as headers, footers, and footnotes.

Natural Extensions to Your Pages

If you open a textbook or a novel and look closely at the pages, you will notice there is a lot more information than just the words on the page. You will find *page numbers* at the top or bottom of each page, either in the corner or centered. Usually you find information at the top of each page. By convention, the top of the left page of an open book contains information such as the *book title* or *section name*, whereas the top of the right page includes the name of the current *chapter* or the *title* of the article. Often you find *footnotes* at the bottom of pages, as well. These bits of helpful information are referred to as *headers* if they are located at the top of the page, and *footers* if at the bottom.

If you attempted to add these professional touches to your own documents by staying within the margins, you would quickly notice a substantial loss of writing real estate. Luckily, you can add all of these features to your documents in space that otherwise wouldn't be used—the margins.

Adding a Header or Footer

You can make your document more interesting by creating your own headers and footers, and placing whatever information helps to clarify your document to your reader.

To make your document even more interesting, you can use a unique header or footer on the *first page only* of the document or each section, or omit a header or footer on the first page of the document or section. And for anyone creating a document large enough to be printed on both sides of the page, and then bound like a book, you can use different headers and footers on odd and even pages or for each section in a document.

Headers and Footers

A *header* is information that can be printed in the top margin of a page, either on every page, every odd page, every even page, or just the first page. Typical information included in a header includes book titles, chapter headings, and sometimes page numbers. A *footer* contains information such as page numbers and footnotes and is printed at the bottom of the page, in the bottom margin.

Putting Useful Things in Headers and Footers

Large documents really benefit from constructive use of headers and footers. An open document lying on your desktop can be instantly identified with the title or subject of discussion, and the page number provides a relative location within the document.

But don't waste toner; always put *useful* things in your header or footer! Include good information like the date, document name, page number, title, and other information that helps identify your document or where you happen to be within the document. And understand that certain conventions apply to where you place information. For instance, if your document will be bound, you will have right- and left-hand pages. Book titles usually appear on the left-hand page header, while chapter or section titles are on the right-hand page header. Although Word doesn't provide a way to automatically insert book titles and section headings into headers, they aren't that hard to create. What does Word provide? Certainly some of the information is very helpful, like the date or time, the author, or the name of the document. These examples are simple enough to learn, so let's get started.

To create a header or footer, open the **View** menu and choose the **Header and Footer** command. You'll see the Header and Footer toolbar. If needed, click inside the header area to establish the insertion point, and begin typing the desired text. Press the **Tab** key one time to center this text, and twice to right-align it. You can add character formatting, such as bold or italic, by clicking on the appropriate buttons on the Formatting toolbar. If you'd rather be in the footer box, click the **Switch Between Header and Footer** button.

Just in case you tried, you cannot edit text and graphics in the main document while the header or footer areas are visible.

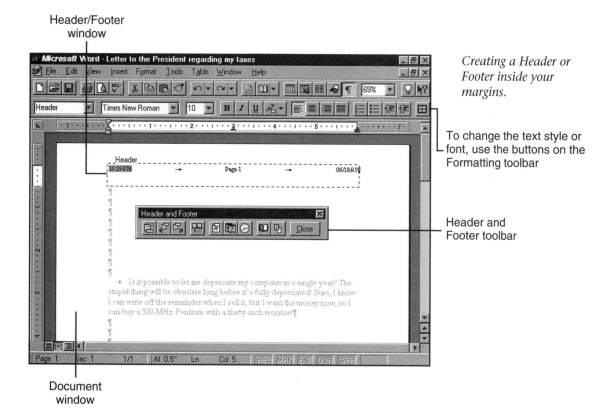

Header/Footer window

Creating a Header or Footer inside your margins.

To change the text style or font, use the buttons on the Formatting toolbar

Header and Footer toolbar

Document window

In the Header and Footer toolbar, there are several buttons for creating the header and footer information you want. Here's a rundown on what they do:

Button	Name	Description
	Switch Between Header/Footer	This moves you quickly between two.
	Show Previous	Take a look at the previous page header/footer.
	Show Next	If you're in the middle of a document, take a peek at the header/footer on the next page.
	Same as Previous	Copy the previous one to this location.
	Page Number	Inserts a page number.
	Date	Inserts today's date into your header/footer.
	Time	Inserts the current time.
	Page Setup	Brings up the Page Setup dialog
	Show/Hide Document	Helps you concentrate on the header/footer by hiding your document temporarily (until you press it again).
Close	**Close**	Returns you to your document, saving the header/footer changes.

There's an Easier Way to Do Page Numbers

You don't have to create headers and footers just to add the page number to every page in your document. Open the **Insert** menu and select the **Page Number** command. For more details, check out Chapter 9.

You can type whatever you want to have appear, such as a title or heading, or you can choose from a whole list of prepared header/footer items provided by Word. The list provided by Word includes *intelligent fields*, which are placeholders for information that can change, like the date or time, or things unique to the document, like the title or author. The instant these intelligent fields are placed in your document, they change to become the name or value of what they represent. You can easily add the three most common—Page Numbers, Date, and Time—because they are included right on the Headers and Footers toolbar. Just place the insertion point at the location in the header or footer where you want them, and press one of these three buttons. You can mix or match any combination of them in the same header or footer.

You Can Add More Intelligence

Intelligent fields, that is. Word provides almost 100 detailed fields you can choose from, like the date the document was printed, and they are stored in categories to help you find the one you want.

To add an intelligent field to your header or footer, be sure you are in Header/ Footer view. Place the insertion point where you want the field to appear. Open the **Insert** menu and choose the **Field** command. Browse through the different categories provided in the Fields dialog box. To select the type of field you want to insert, click a category in the Categories box. If you aren't satisfied with these choices, click **All** to see all available field types in Word for Windows 95. Next, in the Field Names box, click the field type you want to insert. Press the **OK** button to insert that field into your header or footer. When you've finished, click the **Close** button to resume the normal view and save the header/footer changes.

A popular item to add to a footer is the actual filename and location of the original document. Find the field named FileName, and then click Options. Click the Field Specific Switches tab, click \p in the Switches box, and finally press the Add To Field button.

Using Different Headers/Footers on the First Page

You can use a unique header or footer that appears only on the first page of the document, like a special title. You can also get rid of a header or footer on the first page only of the document or section, for instance, if you want to use letterhead that would be overwritten with a header. Word also provides the capability to put a header or footer only on odd or even pages, and you can also limit your headers and footers to appearing in only a particular section of your document.

By clicking on the **Page Setup** button on the Header and Footer toolbar, you can select special options such as Different First Page (for a header that's different on the title page, for example) and Different Odd and Even Pages (for headers that are different for the left- and right-hand pages). If you want, you can also change the placement of the header or footer in relation to the edge of the page.

Customizing Headers/Footers in the Page Setup dialog box.

Check this box to alternate headers or footers by page.

Check this box to remove headers/ footers from first page.

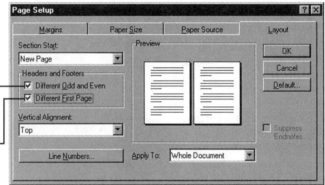

Watermarks

A *watermark* is usually a large, slightly visible graphic printed as a background decoration in the center of your printed sheet of paper. A watermark is considered a graphical object in Word, and you can insert these objects in headers and footers, just like in regular text (inserting graphics is reviewed in Chapter 11). You can create a watermark (it can be text or a graphic) that is printed on every page by inserting a drawing object in the header.

To insert an object, be sure you are in Headers and Footers view. Open the **Insert** menu and choose **Picture**. Locate the picture in your folders and click to select and preview it. Press the **OK** button to insert the picture into your header and footer. If you need to adjust the size, shape, or location of a graphic, refer to the details contained in Chapter 11.

Viewing Headers and Footers

So where are they, you ask? You certainly created them, and you may swear to this fact, but they disappeared from view when you pressed the **Close** button. Don't panic, unless you have doctor's orders, then it's okay. The headers and footers are really there, trust me. Of course you could print your document to see them, but in the interest of saving paper, you can also view the headers and footers if your document is in the Page Layout view.

Open the **View** menu and choose the **Page Layout** command. Your normal editing view will be replaced with a more accurate rendering of what your pages really look like. The headers and footers in the margins are printed in a slightly lighter color on your screen so you don't confuse what they are.

To learn more about the Page Layout view, take a peek at Chapter 19.

Editing Headers and Footers

To edit a header or footer that you've already created, go to the page containing the header or footer you want to edit. Open the **View** menu and select the **Header and Footer** command. You will see the Header and Footer toolbar. You may have to press the **Switch Between Header and Footer** button if the other one is displayed first.

Now make any changes you want by typing over what's there (or use your normal editing technique), and press the **Close** button when you are finished.

You can also take a shortcut to the Header and Footer toolbar if you happen to be in Page Layout view. You'll notice the header or footer you've created is exposed in the margins. Double-click in this area and it will activate the header/footer toolbar for quick editing of your header or footer.

Creating Footnotes

If you really want to impress your boss, try placing *footnotes* in your status reports, referencing conversations you've secretly recorded. It's easy to make simple documents look impressively professional by following these tips on creating footnotes.

You remember footnotes from high school or college. The little numbers are strategically placed to interrupt your reading by sending subliminal messages to your brain urging you to look down to the bottom of the page to see what was so important that it warranted this number. Maybe you were tricked and didn't see anything at the bottom of the page, because they weren't footnotes, they were *endnotes*, which appear at the end of a document.

Your First Footnote Is the Hardest

If you have trouble making decisions in life, stick with the defaults, and you won't go wrong. This philosophy also applies to footnotes because the hardest part about creating them, besides writing them, is deciding where they should appear on your page. Some people like them at the bottom of the page (the default), some prefer just below the current paragraph, still others at the bottom of a table or the end of a document (but technically, that's called an *endnote*); the rest of us don't bother with footnotes.

Endnotes are special footnotes that can be placed at the end of the section or the end of the document.

When you're ready to create a footnote, start by placing the insertion point where you want the footnote to be referenced. It can be a word or a sentence (or paragraph). For a word, place the insertion point at the end of an individual word, and Word will automatically place the footnote mark in the conventional location—slightly raised and to the right of the word. If you want to footnote an entire sentence, place the insertion point at the end of the last word of the sentence.

Open the **Insert** menu and select the **Footnote** command. You will see the Footnote and Endnote dialog box.

Deciding where a footnote should be seen.

Click here to have your footnotes automatically numbered.

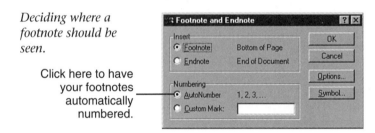

Make sure you leave **AutoNumber** selected so your footnotes are correctly numbered and organized.

You may also want to try the **Options** button, which helps adjust the placement of notes, set note numbering and formatting options, and convert notes to footnotes or endnotes (or vice versa). And if you would prefer to use a different symbol as a custom note reference mark, click the **Symbol** button.

When you press **OK**, you will be transported to the footnote area at the bottom of the page. You normally don't see this part of your page because your view is set to, well, Normal. If you insert a footnote while in Normal view, the window splits and the cursor is transported to a footnote editor. Working in Page Layout view will move the cursor to the bottom of the page, where the footnotes are located.

Now start typing your footnote. You can place almost anything in a footnote, including text, pictures, and charts (and even sounds and video for multimedia buffs). Footnotes can be long, also, and can exceed a page in length. Don't fret, for Word for Windows 95 will take care of the formatting.

When you are finished typing, click the **Close** button (if you happen to be in Page Layout view, you don't have to do anything—you're done). Now admire your work. Little numbers appear properly, and the page is adjusted to fit the footnote.

The good news is that once you've set your footnote options, you don't have to come back to this dialog box each time you add another footnote or endnote.

Spewing Forth Footnotes after That

After the first footnote has been placed, the rest are easy to create—even if you have to place one earlier in your document. Place the insertion point at the next point of text you want to reference, and select the **Footnote** command from the **Insert** menu. You are now in the footnote editing area. Type away and press the **Close** button when finished. No more menus to worry about, and the numbering is taken care of for you.

Graphics in Footnotes?

Check This Out...

If you're serious about sticking things like pictures, charts, or graphs in your headers, footers, or footnotes, you need to see a doctor soon. In the meantime, you can review Chapter 11, which shows you how to add pictures just about anywhere, including in footnotes.

Editing Footnotes

If you need to change the wording of a footnote or two, they can easily be edited. All you have to do is double-click the little footnote number, and the handy footnote editing window will appear, with the cursor already at the start of the footnote text. Or, if your aim is not so good on those little numbers, you can switch to Page Layout view and see the footnotes directly. Open the **View** menu and choose the **Page Layout** view, and if you move to the bottom of the page, you will see your footnotes. Either way, once you are inside the footnote area you are ready to edit your footnote directly.

Once the cursor is inside the footer area, you can update the footnote text by using any of the editing or formatting tools you are comfortable with. When you have finished editing the footnote, click on the **Close** button. You will be returned to the Normal view of your document. Or, if you are in Page Layout view, simply click in the main body of your document to return to it.

Deleting Footnotes

Now here's a demonstration of Word for Windows 95 doing something really helpful for you. Let's say you've got 27 footnotes in your research document on the livers of aquatic emus, and you just realize the first one is incorrect and has to be deleted. Word not only blasts it away and reformats the entire document, but more importantly *renumbers* and *re-references* the remaining footnotes automatically. Now *that's* what you bought a computer for.

To delete a footnote, you must go to the footnote number in your document, not the header and footer area. You don't have to be in Page Layout mode when you delete a footnote. Select the footnote's number (it's called a *reference mark*) in your document (it will appear highlighted) and press the **Delete** key.

To delete all automatically numbered footnotes or endnotes, open the **Edit** menu and choose the **Replace** command. Click **Special** and then click **Endnote Mark** or **Footnote Mark**. Make sure the Replace With box is empty, and then click **Replace All**. You cannot delete all custom footnote reference marks at one time.

Cutting, Copying, and Pasting Footnotes

Power users will be amazed that you can even cut and paste a footnote from one area to another if you need to. Select the footnote and press **Ctrl+X** or press the **Cut** button. Find the proper location for the footnote and press **Ctrl+V** (or the **Paste** button). If you pass another footnote during the move, everything will be renumbered automatically and referenced correctly for you.

Copying is just as easy for those popular *IBID*'s and *See Footnote #1*'s. Select the footnote and press **Ctrl+C** (or the **Copy** button) and go find the next location. Press **Ctrl+V** (or the **Paste** button), and you've got a newly numbered visitor here to stay.

The Least You Need to Know

Footnotes, headers, and footers are natural extensions to our documents, and there's no reason to avoid them—especially now that you've learned that:

➤ Headers and footers are helpful bits of text or graphics that can be created in the margins of your document; they can include titles, dates, filenames, page numbers, and so on.

➤ Creating headers or footers in the margins of your document is easy once you open **Insert** menu and choose the **Headers and Footers** command.

➤ Editing an existing header or footer is easy if you are in Page Layout view—simply double-click on it, and the editing box will be activated.

➤ Footnotes are easily created by clicking where you want them, then choosing the **Footnote** command from the **Insert** menu.

➤ To move or copy a footnote, use the **Cut**, **Copy**, and **Paste** buttons (or **Ctrl+X**, **Ctrl+C**, and **Ctrl+V** combination keys).

Chapter 11

Placing Pictures in Your Work

In This Chapter

➤ Placing a picture (also called a graphic) in your document

➤ When to use a frame with your picture

➤ Adjusting pictures in your documents

➤ Drawing a box around your picture

➤ Placing captions on your graphics

A picture may be worth a thousand words, as long as it's legal and no one gets hurt. Think of how much typing you'll save! Even if your picture isn't worth a thousand words, illustrating your document with pictures can make your pages more appealing and help convey meaning much faster to your readers—assuming you pick the right picture and put it in the right place. You pick the picture and the location. The time is now, and here's how you do it.

Adding Pictures to a Document

We need to come to terms with our terms. Everyone knows what a picture is, and a picture by any other name looks as sweet. Shakespeare would have told Microsoft that the word *graphic* is an adjective, but in the modern computer world, it is also the term used for anything resembling a picture.

You have a lot of freedom working with graphics. The freedom starts by finding or creating any possible graphic you can think of, and you have lots of sources and tools to help you. Next you get to choose how and where you place the graphic in your document. Finally, you have the ability to adjust and manipulate the graphic in unlimited ways.

Where Can You Find a Good Graphic?

If you aren't an artist, you will have to hunt for graphics to use. Lucky for us that we live in the digital age, where computer graphics abound, so the hunt for existing graphics is relatively easy—especially compared with creating a graphic from scratch. Most computer programs, like Word for Windows 95, come packaged with lots of graphics ready for your use. You are free to use the graphics that came with Word without worrying about who owns them. The pictures that come with Word are called *clipart*. Clipart describes the format of simple graphics that are stored electronically. You can browse through all the Word clipart and choose one to insert into your document from the Insert Picture dialog box. You'll learn how to do this a little later in this chapter.

If you are an artist, you can create your own graphics using simple programs like Paint (you have it already; it came with Windows 95) or more sophisticated drawing programs available for purchase. You create and view the graphic on a computer screen, and print it on a computer printer. The software program allows you to save the graphic as a computer file that can be stored on a diskette. Once you've stored the graphic as a file, it can be imported into your document in Word for Windows 95. You can also draw your graphic on a piece of paper, using a pen or pencil, and then scan it using a scanner. A scanner converts a picture on paper into an electronic file (graphic) on a computer disk or diskette.

Check This Out...

Graphic
A *graphic* refers to a picture used in a document. Computer graphics are pictures stored electronically as files, on hard drives, diskettes, or CD-ROMs. Graphics come from lots of sources, including software packages, friends, electronic bulletin boards, and the Internet.

You can purchase graphic images at a store, by looking for software packages containing graphics categorized by subject. You can find ready-to-use computer graphics in topics ranging from Aquatic Animals to Zealous People Climbing To The Top, and the price ranges from cheap to you-want-how-much?

If you don't want to pay for graphics, you can find a wide assortment of public domain graphics on computer bulletin boards and many locations on the Internet. Look for directories, categories, folders, or other storage locations with names like pictures, graphics, bitmaps, PIX, GIF, PCX, and TIF. Be forewarned that lots of graphics contain mature themes, with content that may shock and offend you. Sometimes you can't tell the nature of the graphic by the name or location until you download and view it. Still, you can find lots of quality graphics free for the asking if you are patient enough to look for them.

All of these graphics have file formats associated with them, and the most common have extensions like PCX, BMP, GIF, TIF, and WMF. Who cares? You should, if you want to use the graphic in your document. Make sure the graphic is in one of these common forms that you can work with, or you won't even be able to get started. If you see a nice graphic created on someone else's computer and you have permission to copy it, you must ask for it in a file format you can use. You ask for a graphic by asking for the format you want, something like: "Could you please save it in PCX or bitmap format for me?"

Who Owns a Graphic?

Speaking of artists, it must be pointed out that most graphics (drawings as well as pictures taken by camera) are considered art, created and owned by an artist, and should be treated as such. Many graphic images (especially popular images) are copyrighted material in many countries. That means you can't simply copy them or scan them and then use them as your own in your own document; you are required to obtain permission from the author or owner of the graphic, and even reference the source in your document.

Also, you can't just take a picture of someone and use it without permission. It's a privacy issue, and a legal one as well. To avoid such problems, look for graphics that are considered *in the public domain*, which essentially means they are free to copy and distribute as you like. The graphics that come with Word for Windows are free for you to use in any way you like.

Graphic Formats Word 7 Can Use

You can insert many popular graphic file formats into your document. Word 7 provides these graphic converters, called filters, to allow your graphic to become a part of your Word document. Some graphics, like bitmap images, don't even need a filter. If you didn't install the filter you need when you installed Word on your computer, you can run Setup and add the filter (see Appendix B for more details on running Setup).

➤ AutoCAD Format 2-D (.DXF)

➤ Computer Graphics Metafile (.CGM)

➤ CorelDRAW! 3.0 (.CDR) file

➤ Encapsulated PostScript (.EPS) file

➤ HP Graphics Language (HPGL) file

➤ Kodak Photo CD (.PCD) file

➤ Micrografx Designer/Draw (.DRW) file

➤ PC Paintbrush (.PCX) file

➤ Tagged Image File Format (.TIF) file

➤ Targa (.TGA) file

➤ WordPerfect Graphics (.WPG) file

➤ The Macintosh PICT (.PCT) filter

➤ The CompuServe GIF (.GIF) filter

Adding a Graphic to Your Document

The next big questions to tackle are where to put the graphic and how to insert it. Word for Windows 95 provides three basic ways to place a graphic in your document.

➤ The first is to simply copy and paste the graphic without any preparation. The graphic will appear wherever you've placed the insertion point. But you'll find that although it's the easiest, it may not always be the best way. Graphics just pasted at the insertion point do not allow text to flow around them, and you can't move the graphic once you've pasted it into your document, except to delete it.

➤ The second choice is highly recommended, and worth the effort: simply insert your graphic into a *frame* placed on your document. You'll learn how in a moment.

➤ The third is the miscellaneous category; you can place graphics directly into special parts of your document, like a table, header, footer, or footnote. Basically, Word will let you stick a graphic just about anywhere your heart desires. Whether or not you or the reader of your document will be able to see it is based on the size, quality, and location of the graphic you choose.

No Preparation, Just Sticking a Graphic in Quickly

Here's the easy way first: pasting an existing graphic into your document. We will use clipart from Word for Windows 95 so you can follow along. Start by opening or creating a document and finding a location to place your graphic. Click the insertion point at that location.

Now let's find a graphic. Open the **Insert** menu and choose the **Picture** command. The Insert Picture dialog box will automatically open and display the contents of the Clipart folder in alphabetical order. The Preview box will display each picture as you select it from the Name list. You can scroll up and down the list of pictures and preview them yourself. When you've found a picture you want to put in your document, select it and click **OK**.

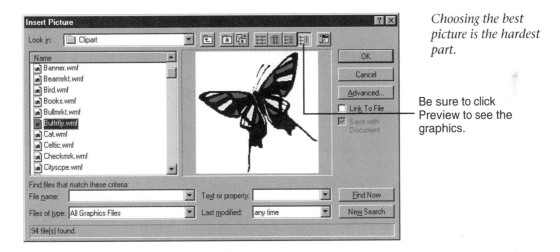

Choosing the best picture is the hardest part.

Be sure to click Preview to see the graphics.

You can also navigate through the different folders on your computer or network to find the location of the graphics you want to use. Once you've found the graphic you want, press the **OK** button. The graphic will be placed in your document.

Frame Your Picture for a More Professional Result

Did you notice the empty space around your picture in the last example? Not exactly what you expected? We can do better. The problem with simple pasting is that a graphic takes up all the space to the left and right of it. Nothing flows gracefully around it.

You can make text flow gracefully around your graphic by placing it in a frame. A frame is just an invisible box that contains your picture. Once your graphic is inside a frame, you can move the frame around, and text will flow around a frame.

Let's get rid of that last picture by deleting it. Just click on it to select it. A selected graphic contains handles, those little black boxes on the corners and the sides, which you will learn about next. Press the **Delete** key. It's gone without a trace. Now let's put another one in, but place it in a frame. You can place your insertion point where you want the graphic to appear, but it's not as necessary because you will be able to move the graphic around easily once it's inside a frame.

To create a frame, you must be in Page Layout view. Get there by opening the **View** menu and choosing the **Page Layout** command (or you can click the **Page Layout View** button on the Status bar). Now open the **Insert** menu and choose the **Frame** command (if you aren't in Page Layout view, Word will remind you at this point and help you get there). Now you have a different mouse pointer on the screen, indicating you are about to create a frame (be still my heart). Move the pointer to the top left area of where you want the frame, and click and drag the left mouse button to the bottom right. You will see a frame created before your eyes. Let go of the mouse button, and your frame is finished.

Framing a picture leads to professional results.

Graphic placed in a frame

View frames in Page Layout view

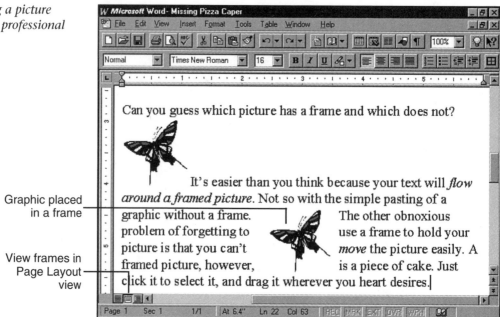

Once the frame is built, you can stick a graphic inside it. Be sure the frame is selected by clicking on it (it will have handles around it). Open the **Insert** menu and choose **Picture**, just like in the last example. Find the desired picture and press the **OK** button. The graphic is now placed securely inside your frame.

Including Pictures Inside a Table

Why use a table at all for importing graphics? The main reason is the capability to place descriptive text to the left or right of your graphic. You can also get around the problem of moving a graphic that's not placed in a frame. By placing a graphic in a table *cell*, you can move the table border, and the graphic will move with it.

It's easy to place a graphic inside a table, now that you've got the two basic techniques down. A *table* is made up of cells, and any graphic inserted into a table is always placed into a single cell. Give it a try. Find or create a table (Chapter 12 covers how to create and edit tables), and place the insertion point inside the cell chosen to hold your graphic. Now open the **Insert** menu, choose **Picture**, and select the desired picture. The graphic will be inserted into the table cell.

The cell size, and therefore the table size, will automatically expand if the default size of the imported graphic is too large. You can still modify either the size of the cell (see Chapter 12) or the size of the graphic (see below), or both.

Editing Graphic Images Inside Your Document

Now that the original graphic has become a part of your document, is there anything more we can do with graphics, once they're inside of our document? Only squishing, stretching, elongating, enlarging, shrinking, and moving it all around. If that's not enough, you can also delete them.

Moving Graphics Around

If you want to move a graphic around inside your document, you better hope you inserted it correctly. Here's why: If you did not create a frame for your graphic, you won't be able to move it, even if you are Superman. Nestled safely inside a frame, however, a graphic can be moved anywhere inside your document. You actually grab the frame and move it; the graphic just goes along for the ride. Without a frame, that graphic is stuck to your document tighter than your high school shorts.

To move a graphic, you must start by selecting it. When you click on it once, the frame will be selected. Using the left mouse button, you can now drag the frame around your document. Don't worry about the underlying text on the page—it will be moved automatically and flow around the new graphic location.

Word won't let you split a graphic between two pages, so anything extending beyond the bottom margin will be pushed to the next page. The same goes for the sides—Word won't allow a graphic to spill over the edge of your paper. You should consider that helpful.

Making a Graphic Bigger or Smaller

You can change the size of any graphic whether or not it resides on a frame. Simply select the graphic by clicking it once. A selected graphic will reveal its object *handles*, which are the eight little black boxes on the sides and corners of the box surrounding your graphic. Once you've located these handles, you can grab on to them and size the graphic. Click and drag a corner handle inside and out and watch as it resizes automatically. The top and bottom handles make a graphic taller or shorter, while the side handles make it skinnier or fatter. Corners do both at the same time.

Putting a Border Around Your Picture

Some graphics look better with a border. If the graphic did not come with a border, you can create one. Borders can be placed around any graphic, whether or not it has been placed inside a frame. First select your graphic by clicking once on it, so Word will get the idea of what you want a border around. You can certainly open the **Format** menu and choose the **Borders and Shading** command, but why not try the shortcut mouse commands for a change? Click once on your graphic to select it. With the mouse arrow on top of the graphic, click the right mouse button. A pop-up menu will appear that's called the *Shortcut menu*, because it's one-stop shopping for all of your formatting and editing needs. Choose the **Borders and Shading** command with either mouse button, and you'll arrive at the Borders and Shading dialog box in a snap.

A shortcut to adding a border to your pictures.

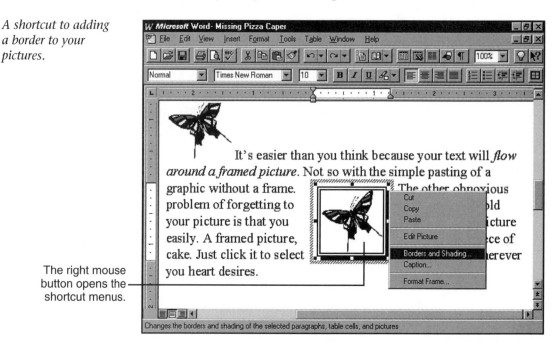

The right mouse button opens the shortcut menus.

Once inside, make sure the Borders tab is in front by clicking on it. Near the top left of the dialog box under Presets, you'll notice three small icons of a sample page labeled None, Box, and Shadow. Click on **Box** and you start the process that creates a border around your graphic. You can double-click on the different line sizes to change the appearance of the border. You can also click the Shadow button to add a three-dimensional appearance to your frame, in addition to a border.

To remove a border or shadow from any graphic in your document, select the graphic and open the **Format** menu. Choose the **Borders and Shading** command and click on the **None** button in the Presets area. You can also use the shortcut menu (clicking on the graphic with the right mouse button) to quickly find the **Borders and Shading** command.

If you aren't totally bored with the subject of borders, you can learn more about them in Chapter 18.

Adding Captions to Things

You may need to do some explaining on certain pictures imported into your document. You can do this by adding descriptive titles to objects like a graphic, table, figure, equation, or others. These descriptive titles are called *captions*, and Word provides an easy way to apply them. You can automatically add a caption to an object when you insert it. Or you can manually add a caption to an item in a document that already exists.

Placing a Caption on an Existing Object

If you have a graphic, table, or other object you want to add a caption to, first select the object. Once an object is selected, you can open the **Insert** menu and choose the **Caption** command. The Caption dialog box allows you to select from existing caption names (like Figure or Table), but you can also create your own by typing in the New Caption box.

You can also select the position of the caption by clicking and choosing from the list of options presented in the Position pull-down box. You can choose from above or below your object.

Adding Captions Automatically

If you plan to add several graphics to a document, and want a caption for each, make it easy on yourself by turning on AutoCaptions. If you set this up while placing your first graphic, you'll save tedious steps for the rest—the captions will be placed automatically. You can automatically add a caption to a table, figure, equation, slide, video, spreadsheet, sound recording, and just about anything else you can think of.

Open the **Insert** menu and select the **Caption** command. In the Caption dialog box, click the **AutoCaption** box. Select the options you want to be captioned automatically when you insert them in a document. Captions will now be inserted automatically when you add the type of item selected in the AutoCaption dialog box. Better yet, they will be consecutively numbered to your specifications if you prefer, so you won't have to remember the last number you used.

Use captions to clarify which graphic you discuss in your text.

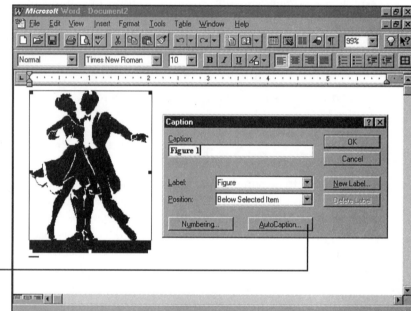

Click here to add a caption automatically when you insert an item in a document.

Linking and Embedding

It's time to congratulate yourself. You've learned more than you may realize. Sure, you know how to insert a graphic into your document, but did you realize you have been *embedding* them? Embedding is a fancy way to say that you've included all the required tools to edit that inserted object. But don't take my word for it, see for yourself. Double-click on any of your inserted pictures included in Word 7 and watch what happens. The application used to create and edit these pictures, Microsoft Paint, opens up inside of Word, allowing you to directly edit your graphic. This is the advantage of embedding objects; you embed everything necessary to edit that object later.

Now it's time to learn even more. Suppose that graphic you are inserting belongs to someone else, and he is continuing to update it, perhaps storing the latest version on a network. If you simply embed the graphic, you will only have the latest version as of the date you embedded it. To get a later version, you would have to delete the currently embedded object and replace it with the more updated version existing elsewhere. But there's a better way to do this, which you will learn now, and it's called *linking*.

Linking simply means you make a connection between a graphic (or any object) in your document and the original source of the object. That way, if the original object is ever updated or changed, even if the owner forgets to tell you, your document can have the latest update appear automatically.

To create a link to the selected picture rather than embedding it, select the **Link To File** check box in the Insert Picture dialog box. The picture will appear just as it did before. The only difference is that each time you open this document, Word will automatically update the picture with the linked source, and you will see the latest updated version of the picture.

Finally, this whole discussion applies to much more than simply pictures and graphics. Object Linking and Embedding, also known as OLE, applies to spreadsheets, presentations, drawing and painting programs, and even other documents, or portions of documents, included inside of your document, or inside of any other OLE-compliant application. Your Word document could be included as an object linked or embedded in a Paint picture, or Excel worksheet, for example.

So What's Embedding?

The alternative to simply pasting a graphic or linking it to an existing graphic is called embedding. The difference between linking and embedding is where the actual object is stored. When you import a graphic and link it to its original application, the graphic is not stored as part of the document. Instead, a link (or connection, if you prefer) is maintained between your document and the program that created the graphic. Because the graphic is not actually part of your document, when you open that other program and make changes to the graphic, those changes are not reflected within your document until you update it. The link helps your document find the changed graphic and update the linked version of it.

With embedding, on the other hand, a graphic is stored as part of the Word 7 document. Just as in linking, however, there is a special connection between the document and the program that created the graphic, but this time the connection takes a different form. When you want to make changes to an embedded graphic, you don't go to the program that created it, but to your document. Double-click on the graphic, and you'll see the original program used to create the graphic right inside your Word document, where you can work within its program window to make your changes. Finish making your changes, exit the graphics program, and you're returned to your document where the graphic already reflects your changes. Unlike a linked object, an embedded object is updated immediately as changes are made. That's because you're not making changes to an object that's stored somewhere else, but to the one that's stored within your document.

OLE Application
Windows applications that support object linking and embedding (OLE) can exchange information between objects. Use *linking* to automatically update the information in an object when the source information changes. Use *embedding* to insert an object from one application into another. Both applications must support object linking and embedding.

To embed an existing graphic into your document, start with the graphics program. Open and select the graphic, then open the **Edit** menu. Choose the **Copy** command. Now switch to Word for Windows 95 and place the insertion point where you want the graphic to appear. Open the **Edit** menu and choose the **Paste Special** command. In the Paste Special dialog box, make sure that the Data Type has correctly identified your graphic (usually it's a Picture or Bitmap, but often it's actually the name of the other program used to create the graphic). If everything is in order, click on the **Paste** button and press **OK**. Your graphic should appear, and is now officially embedded into your document. Remember that all you have to do to make changes to your graphic is double-click the graphic, and the graphics package will open automatically.

The Least You Need to Know

Anyone can place quality graphics into a document because Word for Windows 95 already comes packaged with a selection of clipart. Here are the highlights to remember:

➤ You can quickly place a picture (a graphic) into your document by opening the **Insert** menu and choosing the **Picture** command. Find the picture you want, press **OK**, and the picture will be included in your document.

➤ A better way to include a graphic is to create a frame for it to live in, because then it can be easily moved around your page.

➤ Graphics can be shaped by selecting them to reveal their handles, and then clicking and dragging any of the handles in the direction needed for the desired shape.

➤ Captions can be placed above or below your graphic. Captions can also be made to increment automatically if you plan to place more than a single picture in your document.

➤ You can choose to either embed or link a graphic into your document. If the source of your graphic is subject to change, and to keep the storage size of your document small, you should link the object. To carry everything you need to edit the graphic with your document, you should embed the graphic.

Chapter 12

Your Table Is Being Prepared

In This Chapter

➤ Creating a table to organize your information

➤ Making your table look nicer with borders and shading

➤ Moving around inside a table

➤ Putting a caption on a table

➤ Getting rid of tables you hate

The word *table* possibly comes from the Latin word *Tab-Bleh*, which loosely translates to "Using only the Tab key to create a table makes it look like Bleh!" You don't want your tables to look like Bleh, and neither do I, so this chapter was written especially for the subject.

Microsoft Word for Windows 95 provides a Table feature that builds good tables with a minimum of effort. Using the Table feature is a good way to line up information neatly.

And just because it's a table doesn't mean it has to be a box with gridlines separating your words or figures, either. Tables can be subtle, even invisible, and still have the power to control the placement of your information.

Setting the Table

What Is a Table? A *table* is a collection of rows and columns, just like a simple spreadsheet. Each row and column inside a table is made up of units called *cells*. A single cell is where a row and a column intersect. A cell is where you type a table entry.

Sooner or later you will have information which you will want to appear organized in your document. You should consider putting the information in a table. What exactly is a *table*? If you say a box with rows and columns, that's right, and in Word, the box is not even needed.

Tables present information in rows and columns. They're great for organizing information in your faxes, letters, memos, and reports. You can use tables to show lists of data, personnel rosters, financial information, scripts, and procedural steps. A reader usually finds it easier to locate and understand detailed information when it is presented in a table. You will discover that you can place just about anything in a table, including pictures, and then format the content of the table using all of the features you learned in the past few chapters.

A common resume is one of the best examples of a document that's easier to create and edit using a table rather than tabs or margins. You might not think it at first, until you generalize that tables are nothing more than text lined up neatly in columns. A resume has dates or companies lined up on the left, and experiences described to the right. A perfect match for a table. Tables are also an easy way to align paragraphs side-by-side. What about table lines, you ask? Well, tables don't always require lines or borders, which aren't always needed or wanted. Let's *table* any further discussion until we review the basics.

Creating a Table Years Ago—Using the Tab Key

There is nothing wrong with the Tab key. By golly, it's one of the few keys on the keyboard for which you know exactly what happens when you press it. A nice indent. Or many indents, if you press it many times, that always line up evenly within a paragraph. Yes, they should make a movie about the good old reliable Tab key someday.

Well, okay, that's stretching it. But I bet you have used the Tab key in the past to create simple (or complicated) tables. There's nothing wrong with that at all. In fact, a very small table with two columns and short words can still be created easily using nothing but the Tab key. But, if your table requirements include any of the following, you may find that tabs just don't make the grade when it comes to controlling the appearance of your tables:

➤ The need to hold more than a column or two of information

➤ The desire to line up paragraphs side-by-side

➤ The desire to use the length of tables that will extend beyond a single page

➤ The desire to apply special formats to individual rows or columns

➤ The desire to add gridlines and borders to show off your table

Any or all of these requirements point you to using the Table feature of Word, which can be as easy or cumbersome as you want to make it.

The Cool Way to Create a Table

By far the easiest way to create a perfect table in Word 7 is using the Table feature and the mouse. You can also use the keyboard; it's covered later, but you have to think more when using the keyboard. The mouse way is a no-brainer. The basic concept is that you fill in a table after you create it. So let's create one.

You must first open or create a document, and it should be the one where the future table will exist. Now decide where you want the table to exist in your document, and place the insertion point there. Did I mention it's always a good habit to save a document before going on vacation or trying a stunt like this? Now click the **Table** button on the Standard toolbar. The table grid will drop down, presenting the most popular table sizes. Picture in your mind the size of the table you want, then use your mouse to select it. Drag the mouse down and to the right to highlight the size of table you desire. As you drag the mouse pointer, the grid expands to create rows and columns like a miniature table. The resulting table size will be displayed at the bottom of this grid. When you release the mouse button, your table will be created precisely the way you sized it. An empty table is instantly created in your document, waiting to be filled with your wisdom. How's that for simplicity?

The easy way to create a table using the Table button.

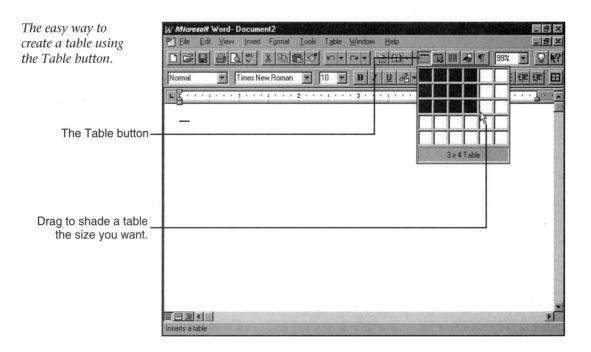

The Table button—

Drag to shade a table the size you want.

Still Another Method of Preparing Your Table

If your mouse died, you could still create a table using the keyboard. Word actually offers more options this way, but there are steps to follow. Once again, make sure you have the document you want opened and saved. Place the insertion point where you want the table to be created. Now open the **Table** menu and select the **Insert Table** command. The Insert Table dialog box will appear.

Word's table manners improve with this dialog box.

Type in any number of rows or columns to get you started.

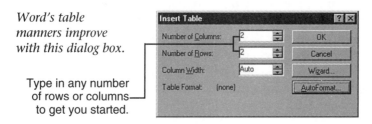

Enter the number of columns in the first box. Press the **Tab** key to move to the second box (or click it with the mouse button). Enter the number of rows in the second box. You don't have to be exact at this point because you can easily change the shape after the table is created. Leave Column Width set to Auto to let Word manage them (if you type

134

more, the column will automatically get bigger). Of course, you can set your column width now if you know the size you need. Now click the **OK** button to create your table.

There you go—a table built to your specifications. But it's empty, and empty tables serve little purpose in a document (unless you are creating graph paper), so now it's time to fill it in.

Gridlines Prevent Gridlock

If you have trouble coloring between the lines, you will be thankful for table *gridlines*. Word displays dotted gridlines in a table so that you can see which cell you are working in. When a cell is selected, the area inside the bordering gridlines is highlighted. You can switch between displaying and hiding table gridlines by opening the **Table** menu and clicking the **Gridlines** command, which will toggle between on and off.

Filling in Your Table with Useful Stuff

Once a table has been created, it's a straightforward process to fill it in. If your insertion point isn't already in the first table cell, you can get it there by clicking anywhere inside the cell. Once inside, just start typing. The cell will automatically adjust to accommodate what you type. You can type in words, numbers, or even place pictures in a cell.

Pressing the **Enter** key inside a cell puts a new paragraph in the same cell. Think of each cell as its own little document, which means the rules of editing and formatting apply.

Big Cell/Little Cell There's no limit to the number of characters you can add to a cell. You could include pages of text in a single cell, for example. Practically speaking, however, you will want to keep the quantity of information to a reasonable size for a given cell, or else your reader is likely to miss the purpose of your table.

The Magic of Table AutoFormat

Once you enter information into your table you may be so excited that you print your document to see it for real. Surprise! Not what you expected, I bet. No gridlines, no box around it; in fact, except for lining up your information, it doesn't look like a table at all!

We can fix that—easily, in fact—using another miracle of Word for Windows 95 called Table AutoFormat. Just click inside your table anywhere, it doesn't matter where. Now open the **Table** menu and choose the **Table AutoFormat** command. This is the dialog box you will see, and it's full of ideas on making your table the best it can be.

Fancy tables await you in Table AutoFormat.

Scroll this list to see preformatted tables.

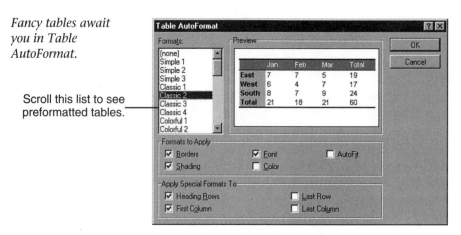

Scroll up or down this listing of preformatted sample tables using your **Up** or **Down** arrow keys. Watch the Preview box to see if any choices come close to what you want. Don't worry if your table is a different size; the formatting will apply to the size of your table. If the table you're planning will be much smaller than the samples, however, you may not get a heading or column format as in the Preview screen. If you can't decide between a few of them, try them all! One at a time, of course, and you can always click the **Undo** button on the Standard toolbar to get rid of an end table that doesn't match the rest of the furniture in your document.

If, at a later date, you decide you prefer another style of table, go get it! The information you have already stored in your table will be preserved and placed in the new table format. Select your existing table, open the **Table** menu, and run the **Table AutoFormat** command. Choose a new table format from the list and press the **OK** button.

Formatting the Contents of Cells

Once your table is formatted, you may still wish to format the individual contents of cells, or even whole rows or columns. No problem, just remember the basics of selecting (Chapter 7) and formatting (Chapters 8 and 9).

Anything you can type in a cell is fair game for the formatting tools of Word. You can apply any of the character formatting options to any cell, group of cells, entire row, entire column, or the entire table. First select the cell or cells containing the text or numbers you want to format. The table below can assist you in the selection process. Once it's selected, you can apply any of the tools on the Formatting toolbar. Maybe the Bold, Italic, and Underline are growing old on you. Try changing the font or font size, or arrange the contents with the Center or Right Justify button, or even create a numbered list inside a single cell.

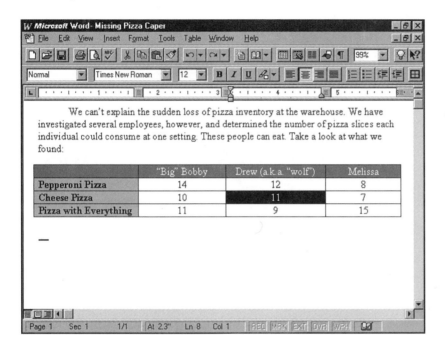

A selected cell inside a table.

Helpful Hints for Selecting Items in Your Table

To...	Do This...
Select a cell	Click the left edge of the cell.
Select a row	Click to the left of the row.
Select a column	Click the column's top gridline or border.
Select multiple cells, rows, or columns	Drag across the cell, row, or column; or select a single cell, row, or column, and then hold down the Shift key while you click another cell, row, or column.
Select text in the next cell	Press the Tab key.

continues

137

Helpful Hints for Selecting Items in Your Table   Continued

To...	Do This...
Select text in the previous cell	Press Shift+Tab.
Select the entire table	Click the table, and then press Alt+5 on the numeric keypad. Num Lock must be off.
When in doubt	You can also select rows, columns, or the entire table by clicking in the table and then using the Select commands on the Table menu, or by using keyboard shortcuts.

Check This Out...

Can't See Text in a Cell?

Sometimes you can't see some or all of the text in a cell. What should you do? You may need to adjust the indents within the cell. On the **Format** menu, click **Paragraph**, and then specify new measurements under Indentation.

Another check is to see whether you've set an exact row height that's smaller than the text you are trying to display. On the **Table** menu, click **Cell Height And Width**, and then click the **Row** tab. In the Height Of Row box, click **Auto**.

Some tables look better with a heading on the top row. But with multiple columns in a typical table, you always have those column dividers preventing a nicely centered title. You can get rid of column dividers on any given row using the **Merge Cells** command. To create a heading for your table, select the entire first row. Open the **Table** menu and choose the **Merge Cells** command. The multiple cells will be merged into one across the width of a table. Now you can enter and format your title in this new cell.

Moving and Squirming Around Inside Your Table

One entry in a table is boring. It's time to move to the next cell. After filling in the first cell, you can move to the next cell by pressing the **Tab** key. If the insertion point is in the last cell of a table, pressing Tab adds a new row. To move backwards to a previous key, press the combination **Shift+Tab** keys. You can also use the Arrow keys to move around between cells inside your table, but you will find the Tab key is faster.

Navigating Your Table

To...	Press...
Move to the next cell	Tab
Move to the previous cell	Shift+Tab
Move to the previous or next row	Up or Down Arrow Keys
Move to the first cell in the row	Alt+Home or Alt+7 on the numeric keypad
Move to the last cell in the row	Alt+End or Alt+1 on the numeric keypad
Move to the first cell in the column	Alt+Page Up or Alt+9 on the numeric keypad
Move to the last cell in the column	Alt+Page Down or Alt+3 on the numeric keypad
Start a new paragraph	Enter
Add a new row at the bottom of the table	Tab at the end of the last row
Add text before a table at the beginning of a document	Enter at the beginning of the first cell

Editing an Existing Table

You can move or copy a cell's contents to a new location in your table. If you need to move a cell's contents, select the contents by clicking in the middle of the cell. Then drag the cell to its new location. You copy the contents of one cell to another with a similar technique. To copy a cell, hold down the **Ctrl** key as you drag.

If you don't like the contents of any cell in your table, you can get rid of it easily. You can delete a cell's contents by first selecting the contents, then pressing the **Delete** key. Notice that the table cell is still intact; it's just empty. The only way to completely remove a cell from a table is to completely remove the row or column to which it belongs.

You can get rid of an entire row or column of your table. Place the cursor inside the offending row or column and then open the **Table** menu and choose **Select Row** or **Select Column**. Now open the **Table** menu again and notice the new command that appears—either Delete Row of Delete Column, depending on what you've selected. By choosing this command the row or column will be completely eliminated from your table.

You may want to do more than simply change the format of the contents of a table cell or cells. You can also change the inside and outside dimensions of any part of your table.

To change the width of any column in your table, drag the column's right edge to its new location. The left edge can be moved, as well. If you want to let Word adjust the widths of columns automatically, you can double-click on either edge of a column.

More Headroom in a Table You can also change row height by using the vertical ruler in Page Layout View. On the **View** menu, click **Page Layout**. On the vertical ruler, drag a row mark to the location that adjusts the size to your taste.

Unless you specify otherwise, the height of each row in a table depends on two things: the contents of the cells in that row and the paragraph spacing you add before or after text. You can vary the height of each row, but all cells in the same row will have the same height. You can add more space between the rows of a table if you want. First, select the rows you want to change. On the **Table** menu, click **Cell Height And Width**, and then click the **Row** tab. To make the row height fit the contents, click **Auto** in the Height Of Rows box. If you don't select Auto and the cell contents exceed the listed height, Word cuts off the bottom of the contents. Not good.

To add more rows or columns to your table, select the area where you want the new row or column placed, then choose either the **Insert Columns** or **Insert Rows** command from the **Table** menu. The new table addition will be added, and the table size will be adjusted to accommodate the new size. You can easily make a table bigger by moving the insertion point to the last cell (the bottom right) and pressing the **Tab** key. A new row of cells will be added.

Sorting Table Information Automatically

Do you get the shakes when you need to prepare a table in alphabetical or numerical order? Shake no more, my friend, and say hello to the powerful sorting features of Word for Windows 95 that removes the pain of sorting—any sorting, in any kind of table, including sorts by date.

For important reasons known by logicians and the people who create the phone book, it's always a good idea to select your entire table when performing a sort, not just a single column. Selecting only a single column in other word processors, including previous versions of Word, can cause misalignment of other related information in your table. By selecting the entire table, all related information contained in a row gets sorted at the same time, so it all stays together nicely.

Select your table and open the **Table** menu. Choose the **Sort...** command, which opens the Sort dialog box. You can choose to sort any column by clicking and selecting the column heading in the **Sort By** text box. The default is the first column, which is usually what you want anyway. Press the **OK** button, and a-sorting it will go. If the results look good the first time, save your work and quit while you're ahead. If not, press the **Undo** button (or **Ctrl+Z**) and try again.

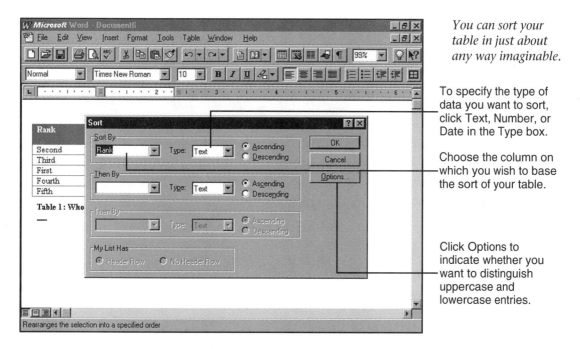

You can sort your table in just about any way imaginable.

To specify the type of data you want to sort, click Text, Number, or Date in the Type box.

Choose the column on which you wish to base the sort of your table.

Click Options to indicate whether you want to distinguish uppercase and lowercase entries.

Techno Talk

Numbering the Lines in Your Table

Here's an easy method to number the cells in your table. First, select the range of cells you want to number. To number the beginning of each row, select only the first column in the table. Then click the **Numbering** button on the Formatting toolbar, and the Table Numbering dialog box will appear. You can choose between numbering your cells across rows or numbering down columns. Press **OK** and your cells will be automatically numbered. You may have to adjust the size of the column or row to accommodate the new numbering additions.

Adding Borders to Your Table

Most tables you see in books and magazines are surrounded by crisply detailed lines called borders. Adding a border to your table can help call attention to it on a page. Borders are so common, in fact, that Word for Windows 95 includes an entire toolbar dedicated to creating these borders. And borders aren't limited to tables. Once you learn the method of placing a border on a table, you'll find that it also works on words, paragraphs, and entire pages. Don't forget that the dotted lines you may see in your table are gridlines that don't print. If you want to print the lines of a table, you must apply the **Borders and Shading** command.

If you already used the **Table AutoFormat** command, it's possible that you already have a border because several of the format choices create a border and shading in the most common and visually appealing combinations. But you don't have to be limited by it. You can create your own custom borders using the **Borders and Shading** command on any table, no matter how it was created.

Creating Custom Table Borders and Shading Manually

If you're a perfectionist, you may not like any of the table format choices in Table AutoFormat. Whether your table already has a border you don't like, or no border at all, you can create your own custom border (or shading) for it. Start by selecting the entire table (to add borders and shading to only specific cells, select only those cells, including the end of cell mark). Open the **Format** menu and choose the **Borders and Shading** command. Click the **Border** tab to make sure it's in front. The easiest way to border your table is to click the **Grid** box, and optionally change to a heavier line width by clicking a fatter line on the right side of the dialog box. When you press the **OK** button, the custom border will be applied to your table.

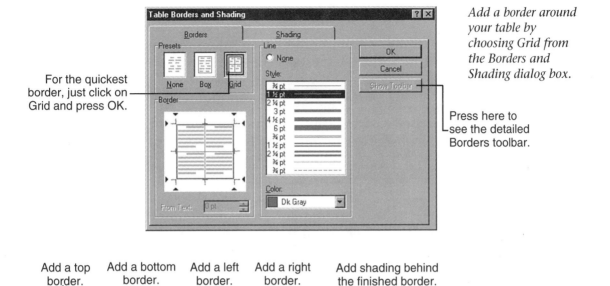

For the quickest border, just click on Grid and press OK.

Add a border around your table by choosing Grid from the Borders and Shading dialog box.

Press here to see the detailed Borders toolbar.

Add a top border. Add a bottom border. Add a left border. Add a right border. Add shading behind the finished border.

Customize your own border with the Border toolbar.

Choose a line style for your border. Create inside borders. No borders. Add only outside borders.

Removing Borders and Shading from Your Table

Regardless of how the border was applied to your table, there's an easy way to get rid of it. First, select the table by clicking anywhere inside of it. Open the **Table** menu and choose the **Table AutoFormat** command (even if you created the border using the Border toolbar). In the Formats box, click **None**. Press **OK** to close the dialog box, and you will discover the borders have disappeared from your table.

Dealing with Tables That Spread over Multiple Pages

There's nothing worse than table headings appearing at the bottom of a page, with rows and columns of unlabeled data appearing at the top of the next page. Word provides protection from this sort of thing by either preventing smaller tables from being broken up in the first place, or by providing table headings on every page for large tables.

Preventing a Table from Breaking Across Pages

If your table fits comfortably on a single page, and you want to keep it that way, you can tell Word to take care of it. Then, if text editing ever pushes or pulls your table toward a natural page break, Word will push your table in its entirety to the next page.

To protect your table from ever splitting, first select it by clicking on it. Open the **Table** menu and click the **Cell Height And Width** command. Now click the **Row** tab to bring it to the front. Clear the **Allow Row To Break Across Pages** check box by clicking on it. Press the **OK** button and your table will be forever protected (until you decide to fill that check box again).

If Your Table Extends Beyond a Single Page

To break a table across pages, click the row you want to appear on the next page. Press **Ctrl+Enter**, and the table will be conveniently split between pages, including formatting and borders that may have been applied.

Putting a Table Heading on Each Page

To repeat a table heading on subsequent pages, use the Headings command. First, select the rows of text, including the first row, that you want to use as a table heading. Then open the **Table** menu and click the **Headings** command. Word automatically repeats table headings only for tables that are split with automatic page breaks. Word will not repeat a heading if you insert a manual page break within a table. These repeated table headings are visible only in Page Layout view.

Messing Up a Table with Margins

If you change your margins with an existing table, you will notice the table isn't affected at all. It's stuck right where you put it. That's because existing tables are not affected by changes to the page margins. If you want to maintain the same relationship between table width and page margins after changing the margins, you will have to adjust the table width manually.

To change the width of columns in a table, first select the columns whose width you want to adjust. Next, on the **Table** menu, click **Cell Height And Width**, and then click on the **Column** tab. You can specify an exact measurement by entering a number in the Width Of Column box, but there's an easier way: to make the column width automatically fit the contents, click **AutoFit**.

Don't forget that you can also change the width of a column by dragging the column boundaries in the table itself or by dragging the column markers on the horizontal ruler. To display column-width measurements, point to the horizontal ruler, and then hold down **Alt** while you click the mouse button. You will see the table markers appear in the Ruler.

Completely Blasting Away a Table Permanently

There is still no "delete the whole table" key in Word for Windows 95, which is bad news if you create lots of bad tables. You can still get rid of them however, but it takes an extra step.

To completely eliminate a table, select the entire offending table first. Then open the **Table** menu and choose the **Delete Rows** command. It's gone forever, unless you want to bring it back with the magic **Ctrl+Z** keys. But why would you?

The Least You Need to Know

➤ You can organize small amounts of information in columns by using tabs. But tables are better to use than tabs if you have large amounts of data to organize.

➤ If you need to move a cell's contents, select the contents by clicking in the middle of the cell. Then drag the cell to its new location. To copy a cell, hold down the **Ctrl** key as you drag.

➤ To add more rows or columns, select the area where you want the new row or column placed, then choose either the **Insert Columns** or **Insert Rows** command from the Table menu.

➤ To add a heading to a table, merge cells across the width of a table by using the **Merge Cells** command on the Table menu.

➤ You can add more space between the rows of a table by using the **Cell Height** and **Width** command on the Table menu.

Part 3
Final Touches: Pampering, Proofing, and Printing

Formatting didn't help? Document still boring? Have you considered that maybe what you're writing about is actually boring? No? Okay, then let's make sure the language is doing justice to your thoughts. Contained in these pages are tips for inspecting, dissecting, and healing your documents so they're good enough to print.

Chapter 13

Importing a Fine Piece of Text

In This Chapter

➤ Loading and saving a DOS text file

➤ Opening a WordPerfect file in Word for Windows 95

➤ Copying existing work from a DOS application

➤ Saving documents in other formats

Being human, we have to communicate with others. We can communicate using speech, our hands, even shaking our legs. If you understand the language, it's so easy you don't even think about it. If you don't, you stare in wonder and try to keep from laughing.

Computer files are like that. Pick up a diskette with a document stored on it. Can you read the document? Even if you break it open and hold it up to a strong light? No, because that document is stored in a form unbeknownst to humans. We need a computer to translate those bits and bytes of magnetic ink into words and special formatting, and then splash the resulting document on our color screens.

But computers also have trouble understanding files that aren't stored in their repertoire of languages. So before you share a document with a friend who's using a different word processor or a very different type of computer, you might want to review these helpful tips on file formats. Or, if you've been given a file on diskette that you can tell your computer is laughing at, fear not, for you can help your computer in the conversion.

Opening a Non-Word Document in Word for Windows 95

All word processors create documents and store them as files on hard disks or diskettes in something called a *file format*. Each word processor has its own format design, trying to be better than the competitors. The default file format for Word is different from the file format in WordPerfect, as you might expect. This sounds like it could lead to utter chaos in the world of computers, especially if you have to share documents between word processors. But amazingly, it works! The companies decided to make life easier for us by including *import filters* for most of their competitors' file formats. An import filter converts a document from one format to another. For example, the WordPerfect 6.1 import filter in Word for Windows 95 converts WordPerfect files into Word documents.

The good news for you is that Word does all the work! When you try to open a non-Word document, those import filters kick in automatically to examine and convert the file if necessary. Some formats are converted without telling you at all. And when you're finished, Word puts the document back into the format it came from, unless you request otherwise. So the next time someone hands you a diskette with a document on it, you can feel reasonably confident that Word will be able to open and edit it.

What If You Can't Find It?

A trusted companion gives you a diskette, explaining that the document it contains tells you how to make money while you sleep. You rush to your desk and pop the diskette into your computer and start Word for Windows 95, hoping to double your salary by morning. You open Word, then click the **Open** button on the Standard toolbar. You insert the diskette into your computer and click the Look In box. Locate the icon of a diskette labeled "3 1/2 Floppy" and click to select it. All the files stored on the diskette will be displayed.

Don't be discouraged if you don't see anything at first. It doesn't mean the diskette is empty. This can happen often if you share documents with a friend who uses another word processor. Word is simply expecting Word documents, so if the file on the diskette is in another format, Word won't immediately recognize it. You'll have to manually invoke one of those *conversion filters*, or all of them. You will find them at the bottom of the File Open dialog box in the Files of Type box.

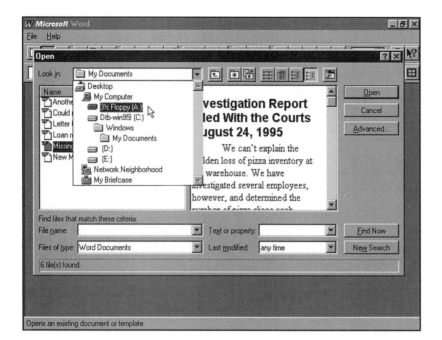

Looking for files on diskette.

Open the **Files of Type** drop-down box by clicking on it once. The drop-down box will list the available word processor products, so find yours and click to select it. If you aren't sure or want to see all of the files on the diskette anyway, select the entry called All Files. This option allows you to view all the files on your diskette (and also your hard drive), not just the Word for Windows 95 documents.

If the diskette contains folders, you can navigate through them by double-clicking them, or search through them following tips provided in Chapter 23. Watch the preview box in File Open, because Word will actually convert and preview any non-Word documents it finds. This can also help you locate and identify documents even if you aren't familiar with the filename. If these documents are large, the conversion could take several seconds, even for the simple preview. You can press the **Escape** key to quickly (and safely) ignore a preview at any time.

When you find the file you want, press the **OK** button and Word for Windows 95 will kick into conversion action. Word will do the best it can to maintain the contents and formatting of the original file, but if it can't, you will at least receive a message describing the problem. Most of the time, these problems relate to page formatting, so you have to decide if it's worth the effort to continue.

To see files on a diskette, choose either the product type or just All Files.

Files on diskettes are found on "3 1/2 Floppy."

Scroll through list to view non-Word files.

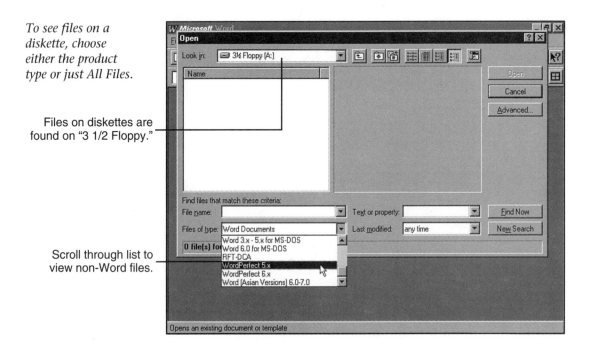

Sometimes an external style file may be required, and you can either ask for the style from the person who gave you the document, or try to continue by pressing the Ignore button (it may not look great, but at least the words should show up).

Now that the document is open, you can enrich it with your talents and all of the features of Word for Windows 95. You don't have to know a lick about the original word processor product. For now, it's considered a Word document. And sooner or later, you will want to save it. Let's try.

Saving and Closing Non-Word Documents When You Are Finished

At any time during the editing of a non-Word document you can save your document (press the **Save** button on the Standard toolbar), but you will see the Save As dialog box. Word knows you've been working with a different type of file format, and when you want to save it, Word wants to know *how* you want to save it—in Word format, or the other word processor format? The dialog box will present both choices as a button. Simply select the one you want. Remember that if you added any fancy formatting to this document while in Word, those items may not translate back to the other word processor format. Follow these tips to decide how to save your document:

➤ If you will be using Word to edit this document from now on, save it as a Word document.

➤ If you want to apply Word formatting to this document, you're better off saving it as a Word document.

➤ If the document has to be used again with the other word processor, avoid using any special formatting inside Word, and save the document in the other word processor format.

➤ If you haven't a clue, press **Cancel**. Your document will wait while you go find someone to help you.

You can also save your non-Word document in another non-word file format using the **Save As** command on the **File** menu. Click the pull-down arrow on the **Save As Type** box and choose the file format you desire.

If you open a non-Word document, edit it, and attempt to close it before you have saved it, you will see the same dialog box. Once again, you have to decide in which *format* you want the document. You have two choices: it's either Word or the word processor format in which the file was originally created. Decide based on who is going to use the document next. If it's you and you always have Word for Windows 95 available, then save it as Word, of course. If you are returning the file to your friend using WordPerfect or Word Pro, you'll be doing them a favor by choosing that format. Otherwise, they might not have a file converter for Word 7 documents and won't be able to open your document.

Decide on the format you want, then press the **Save** button on the Standard toolbar (or press **Ctrl+S**), and you'll see a dialog box similar to the one shown here:

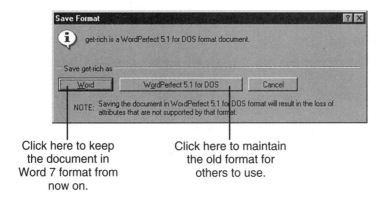

Word keeps track of the original format, so you don't have to.

Click here to keep the document in Word 7 format from now on.

Click here to maintain the old format for others to use.

Press either the Word or the other word processor's button, and the file will be saved. When it's time to close the file, Word will ask if you want to save your changes. Just remember that Word considers any open document a Word document (except for some plain text files), so you may be asked to save changes even when you didn't make any. That's Word asking one last time if you want to keep it as a Word document. If it's a WordPerfect document, for example, and you haven't made any further changes, you can press the **Cancel** button to prevent Word from replacing it in Word format.

Inserting a Whole File into a Word Document

What's the difference between opening and inserting a file? Glad you asked, because you can save yourself editing time if you choose correctly. The last few pages described how to open a file, regardless of the word processor that created it. When finished, that file is saved. One file is opened; the same file is closed. Inserting is taking the contents (some or all) of one file and placing it inside a Word document.

Check This Out...

Take the Easiest Road to Inserting Text The Insert command is best used to copy the entire contents of a file into your Word document. If you only want part of the file, you can still insert the whole thing and then delete the portions you don't want. And don't forget Windows' Copy and Paste commands. You can bypass the Insert command entirely by opening and copying the portion of text in one file, then opening your Word document and pasting the contents into it.

With your Word document open, decide where you want the inserted text and place the insertion point there. Open the **Insert** menu and click the **File** command. Although you can insert other types of program files, such as spreadsheets or presentation graphics, the focus here is on text files, such as those created with other word processing programs. Locate the file you want, highlight it, and press the **OK** button. The file will be *imported*, which means the words and formatting will be automatically converted to Word for Windows 95 format and become a permanent part of your document. You may need to do some cleanup using Word's formatting tools, but the result is much improved over previous versions of Word. Remember to save your work when finished.

If you're shocked and disgusted by the inserted file, you can quickly remove it by pressing the **Undo** button (or **Ctrl+Z** keys). Maybe you inserted the wrong file. Try again, because the **Insert File** command really works.

Lots of Formats to Choose From

In the earlier example, you used the Files of Type drop-down box in the File Open dialog box to see the selection of available word processing formats. If you installed all of the *converters* available in Word for Windows 95, you'll be able to choose from many versions of WordPerfect and Word, and even Word for the Macintosh; over twenty converters are available.

If you can't find the converter you need, it may have been deleted or moved, or not installed in the first place. Run the Microsoft Word Setup program again, and install the converters you need.

Formatting Issues

Nothing is perfect in life, and you may find that the file converter you used creates a document that looks different from the original. If the original contained a font you don't have in Word, Word will replace it with something else. A margin setting may be lost, causing heading locations and page counts to change. You may find that character formatting is changed. Page formatting like footnotes, headers and footers, and page numbers are often not converted due to the complexity. In these cases, headers and footers may show up as regular text, and page numbers may disappear completely.

Have You Been Converted? A converter is used to take the text and formatting of a document created in one program and make it appear as similar as possible in another program. Microsoft Word for Windows 95 comes with converters for over twenty different programs, making it easy to convert documents created in those programs into Word 7 documents.

If all the words are there, you should consider the conversion at least a partial success. Retyping words usually takes much longer than adjusting the formatting, so at least you saved *some* time.

Handling Graphics

If graphics are a part of the file you are inserting, you can kiss them goodbye. Although text is usually successful, graphics rarely make it through a file conversion. If yours didn't, don't give up hope; just look for a different way. Since graphics are usually individual components stored inside a file, you can try to find where the original graphic came from. Maybe it's clipart stored on a diskette or CD-ROM, and you can copy it directly from the original source. Or you can copy and paste it from the original computer into another Windows program that might have better success, like Paintbrush, or another graphics program. Then you can store the graphic in a format you can insert using the **Picture** command on the **Insert** menu. Finally, if all hope seems lost, you can always print the graphic from the original computer and scan it in as a new graphic, using the scanner method described later in this chapter.

Inserting Only Portions of Text from Other Sources

Sometimes the information you want to insert is part of something bigger. Maybe it's a quote or a short paragraph from a large document, or a table or brief article. Maybe it's the reference section or an appendix from a useful instructional document—important information that you don't want to retype and risk accuracy or a deadline.

The source of the text information you need may be portions of documents created in other Windows or non-Windows programs, DOS applications like the DOS versions of WordPerfect or the DOS editor, or even words on paper that you don't want to retype. Here are some tips for making those words productive.

You Can't Beat Cut and Paste

Since you are running Word 7 using Windows 95, you can do many things at once. You may have discovered that other programs, including other word processors, can run at the same time on your computer. Imagine having a document opened in Word, another opened in WordPerfect, Word Pro, WordPad, Notepad, even a text file opened in the DOS Editor, all at the same time. With good eyes and lots of memory, you can even tile your screen with all your open windows at once. What can you do with such a mess? You can perform miracles.

Okay, maybe *miracles* is stretching it a bit, but to be able to move text so easily from one running program to another feels like a miracle if your only alternative is to import the entire document and edit out the parts you don't want. Just as you can copy and paste between two opened Word documents, you can copy text from another program into your Word document (and sometimes vice-versa).

First get your programs running and the documents or files opened in each. You don't have to tile and view all windows at the same time. The Windows 95 TaskBar makes it easy to switch between running applications. You can select and copy text in one full-screen program, choose another program from the TaskBar, and paste the text into that full-screen program. In fact, Windows 95 remembers what you select and copy from any program, even after you close that program, so it's not absolutely necessary to have both programs running at the same time—it's just easier to explain and prevent mistakes.

If the other program happens to be a Windows program, you'll be happy to know your cut and paste keys usually work the same. Select the text in the other program and press **Ctrl+C** to **Copy** the text (or you can use the menu commands from that other program).

The same rules apply to non-Windows programs. Only copy text from them—*never* cut text—to prevent losing it in case of an accident. But you've got bigger fish to fry using a non-Windows DOS-based program, like WordPerfect 5.1 or the DOS editor.

Once you switch back to Word 7, you simply place the insertion point where you want the text pasted and paste it, using the familiar **Ctrl+V** keys or click the **Paste** button on the standard toolbar with the left mouse button. You can also open the **Edit** menu and choose the **Paste** command. The text is pasted into your document.

> **Ctrl+X Works**
> Yes, the **Ctrl+X** key also provides the Cutting function, but don't use it; it's not worth the risk. It's like throwing a bag of food to a friend on the other side of a raging river. If your pal catches it, that's great; if not, your dinner's gone down the river.

If the pasted text looks good, congratulate yourself and then save your Word document for safe keeping. If the pasted text looks different than you expected, you may have to do some adjusting.

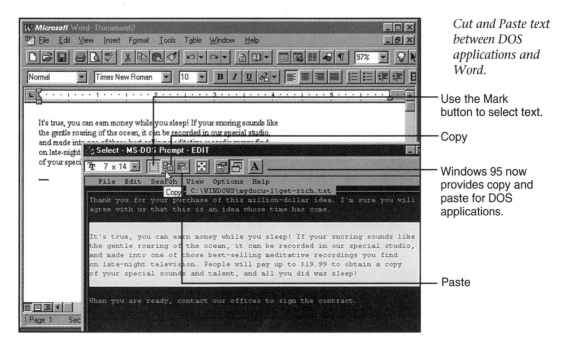

Cut and Paste text between DOS applications and Word.

Use the Mark button to select text.

Copy

Windows 95 now provides copy and paste for DOS applications.

Paste

Grabbing Text from the Internet

The Internet is a great place to find just about anything you can imagine. You can download text files from bulletin boards and news groups and retrieve e-mail from friends. Find a friend who has experience downloading files from the Internet if you want to explore this subject further, or buy one of the thirty gazillion books available on the subject, such as the *Complete Idiot's Guide to Downloading*.

Acquiring Text from the Microsoft Network (MSN)

Using the Microsoft Network is one of many ways to access the Internet, and the Microsoft Network also has an enormous treasure of information of its own that can be helpful.

You can capture chats you have with other people, copy contents of e-mail and paste them into your document, and search bulletin boards and subject categories for things that are interesting or helpful in your work. Since you are probably running MSN on the same computer as Word, you can easily copy and paste text directly from MSN into your document using the familiar **Ctrl+C** (**Copy**) and **Ctrl+V** (**Paste**) commands.

Obtaining Text from Older Files You May Have

If the file you want is on a diskette or an older computer, chances are good that you will be able to recover at least some of the text contained in it, unless it was stored in a completely obsolete word processing package format and no other copies can be found. Before you give up on some text that you hope to save, review these quick tips:

➤ You can convert files stored on 5.25" diskettes to 3.5" using a computer that has both types of drives; copy from one drive to the other.

➤ If you have only a 5.25" drive on a computer, you can still connect it to a modem and upload the file to a bulletin board. Then download the file to a computer with a 3.5" diskette drive. Better yet, try using the Dial-up feature of Windows 95 to move a file between two computers. You can find detailed explanations of how to do this in *The Complete Idiot's Guide to Windows 95*.

➤ If the file you need exists on an older computer, use the application stored on that computer to open it. If it opens, save it in a format you'll be able to import, like DOS text (a.k.a. ASCII file).

➤ When a file exists on a minicomputer or mainframe at work, contact the support staff and request the file. They can usually provide the file you need on a diskette in ASCII format.

➤ Does the file you need reside really far away? Have a person send it to you via e-mail, or as an attachment to e-mail, which you can then download and insert, or copy and paste.

Scanning in Your Own Text from Any Source

The sky's the limit. Well, actually the copyright laws are the limit. Here's how to take any piece of paper containing almost any kind of text and get those words into Word for Windows 95. This can be a real life-saver if your computer crashes and the only remaining copy of your 500-page thesis is a draft you printed last week. Use this technique when the alternative—retyping all those pages—would be interminable hell.

The solution is called *scanning*. A *scanner* is a machine that comes in many shapes and sizes, with costs to match. It's usually attached to a computer. A scanner takes a paper document and turns it into a computer file. Think of it as a printer in reverse. You don't have to buy a scanner; you probably already have access to one, or at least have a friend who does. Many offices have scanners, and many computer stores offer scanning services for a small fee.

Here's the routine: you walk up to a scanner with your report and blank diskette in hand, feed the scanner your document, and place the diskette into the attached computer. You press a button or two on the computer (ask for help if you need to), and the scanner stores the file onto your diskette.

Sound too easy? You knew there was a catch—and there is—because the scanner just takes a picture of your paper document, which might contain rips, folded corners, pictures, smudges, grape jelly, and what-have-you. That's why most scanners also come with a software program called *OCR* (*Optical Character Recognition*). The OCR looks at the scanned picture of your page, determines if there's any text on it, and reads only the text, or at least tries. So the single file saved to your diskette is only the text found on all the pages (no pictures or jelly). Lots of smudges and folds will reduce the accuracy of the file, and it's always important to check the quality of your file before using it.

When the scanning and OCR is complete, your file is usually stored in ASCII format, and sometimes you have many more choices. That shouldn't scare you, now that you're equipped to handle such file formats. You know that Word for Windows 95 will have no problem converting ASCII to Word format. Some OCR packages will even try to capture the character formatting and save the document in a Word (or other) format, saving you even more time. Don't push your luck, and remember the real value in scanning is saving the time of retyping. Do the rest yourself.

All that's left is to take the diskette back to your computer and import the file into Word. Once again, remember to check this new document for errors before using it. Word will help you catch lots of errors using the Spelling and Grammar Checker. See Chapter 16 for more information on proofing a document.

Saving Documents for Use in Other Word Processors

You've got the document that other people want, and you've created it in Word for Windows 95. But you've discovered that not everyone on the planet has converted to Word yet, and even two or three of those are a version or two behind. If you give a copy of your Word 7 document to a person who does not have Word 7, they will not be happy. Earlier versions of Word (like Version 2, and who knows what happened to 3, 4, and 5) cannot read Word 7 format, and the error message will be "unrecognizable file format." (Word 7 documents are compatible with Word 6. Users of Word 6 will have no problems reading Word 7 documents.) Other word processors like WordPerfect and WordPro will also have trouble, unless you obtain and install special file converters from the manufacturer.

But that doesn't mean you can't share your documents. In its infinite wisdom, Word for Windows 95 includes document converters, which takes your document and creates a copy in a different format, usually with a different name, that can be opened by others using those programs.

Saving in Other Word Processing Formats

It's important to note that you always create and edit your document in Word 7 format, regardless of how you ultimately want it saved. The trick to saving your document in another format is in using the **Save As** command on the **File** menu (the **Save** button on the standard toolbar won't let you change file formats).

Even Word for Windows Version 2 is considered an outside format. A friend using Word 2 will not be able to open your Word 7 document. You must convert your Word 7 documents to Word 2 format, or another format that Word 2 can recognize, such as a DOS Text file.

Saving Your Document as a Text File

If you want a reason to save your Word document as a text file, I've got one. There are over a billion DOS-based computers on our planet, and who knows how many on other planets, and they can all understand a DOS text file! That means you could take the file anywhere, even in the foreseeable future, and feel confident that your words will be recognized. A text file is considered the lowest common denominator of file formats.

Saving a DOS Text File

If your document is a DOS text file, you simply have to save it back to disk (or diskette). You can use either **Ctrl+S** keys, open the **File** menu and choose the **Save** command, or press the **Save** button. Word for Windows 95 will remember that you opened this file as a DOS text file and will keep it the same. If you made any formatting changes, such as using bold face type, you will be asked if you want the document saved in Word format.

DOS Text Files Are Easier to Identify
Locating and identifying DOS text files has been made easier because they are automatically converted and displayed in the Preview box before the file is even opened.

If you started a new document in Word, it is automatically created in Word format. To save a Word document as a DOS text file, you have to follow a few more steps.

Open the **File** menu and select the **Save As** command. You cannot use the **Save** command for this. The **F12** key also works. The Save As dialog box will appear. You must change the format, which appears in the Save File as Type box. Click the down-arrow button next to the Save File as Type box to see the drop-down list of choices. Find the one called **Text Only** and click it to select it and press the **Enter** key. Now click the **File Name** box and think up a name for this file. Since this will be an ordinary text file, you should follow DOS naming conventions, which are really restrictions. The restriction is that the name must fit in eight letters, with no spaces or fancy symbols. Now press the **OK** button, and your file will be saved to disk.

If the file already exists, or you typed a name that is already taken by another file, you will be asked if you want to replace the existing file. Think about it for a second or two, and press either **Replace** or **Cancel**. Press **Y** (or the **Yes** button) to replace the existing file.

What Gets Lost When You Save as a Text File?

A lot of weight gets lost when you save a file as plain text. The file size drops to a mere fraction of its size in Word. That's because some things don't convert to this format called ASCII. Which, you ask? How about all of the character formatting you've learned (like fonts, font sizes, bold, italic, and underline), all of the paragraph formatting (like bullets and numbering, centering, spacing, and margins), and certainly all of the page formatting (page numbers, pictures, borders, and margins).

Hey, that's everything! Yes, basically, all the neat features of Word for Windows 95 that you choose to use are applied on top of a basic ASCII file. So if you want the plain ASCII file, you have to rip away all of the Word things. All word processors are like this, including WordPerfect, Word Pro, Write, and countless others. They all create the same words;

they just have their own way to make them interesting. Strip away those formatting features, and you have nothing more than a plain ASCII file.

Saving As Both Text and Word for Windows 95

You can save a document both as a Text file *and* a Word for Windows 95 file. First, save the file normally as a Word file, then save the file as a text file by choosing **Text Only** in the Save As Type box in the Save As dialog box, which automatically adds the extension .TXT. You will then have a text file, which anyone can read, and also a Word 7 file, which can have all the formatting your heart desires.

The Least You Need to Know

Converting files and importing text is the way your computer acts like a language translator. You may become fluent performing these acts if you remember the highlights of this chapter:

➤ Opening documents created in programs other than Word 7 is a breeze. Word does all the work. Press the **Open** button on the Standard toolbar (or choose the **Open** command from the File menu or press **Ctrl+O**) and be sure to change the file type to All Files (*.*) to allow you to see the names of non-Word files.

➤ If you only need a few sentences or paragraphs from another document, it's often easiest to select, copy (**Ctrl+C**), and paste (**Ctrl+V**) the text between the two programs. This even works for non-Windows programs running in Windows 95.

➤ Saving a document for a friend who doesn't have Word 7 is easy using the **Save As** command. The **Save As** command allows you to save documents in other file formats, like WordPerfect or DOS text.

➤ Remember that the words ASCII and DOS Text File, or just plain Text File, mean just about the same thing, and it's the special format that is supported by every word processing package. Save a file as DOS text when you're sharing a document with an unknown word processing partner.

Chapter 14

Search, Find, and Replace

In This Chapter

➤ Finding words in a document

➤ Using Find and Replace to quickly update a document

➤ Fancy ideas using Find and Replace

➤ Changing the past, present, and future forms of a word

➤ Getting rid of things with Find and Delete

Suppose that you've just finished creating a big marketing document minutes before meeting with your new client, only to find out that your client just changed its name from Bud's Cheese Shop to Cheese Products International. You can use the Word for Windows 95 Find and Replace feature to replace all occurrences of the incorrect name right before your meeting with the Head Cheese. It only takes a matter of seconds. You can also search for a word without replacing it, which can be helpful to locate a particular part of a document. Or you even can search for things to automatically eliminate, like the accidental extra spaces between words or sentences, or tabs that may be hanging around. Since it's almost always easier to attempt to repair a document instead of completely recreating it, this chapter has been prepared to help you with all the shortcuts related to the feature of Find and Replace.

Finding Something Inside Your Opened Document

No matter what it might be, if you typed it inside your document, you can find it. You might be looking for a word, a phrase, a name, a number, or a special symbol for any number of reasons. Finding these items can help you return to a particular part of a large document, find out if they exist at all in your document, or find other words that are usually close by.

To find a word or a phrase in your document, open the **Edit** menu and select the **Find** command, or press **Ctrl+F**. You will see the Find dialog box. Type the word or phrase you're looking for in the Find What text box. Here are some handy options you can choose from.

If it's there, you can find it.

➤ If you want to locate only the word you typed, and not words that include it as a part (for example, you want to find "search" but not "searching"), use the **Find Whole Words Only** check box.

➤ If you want to match upper- or lowercase letters (for example, "Word" but not "word"), then use the **Match Case** check box.

➤ If you want to search backward through the document, open the **Search** list and select the **Up** option.

➤ If you want to search for a word with particular formatting, click on **Format** or press **Alt+O**, select **Font**, **Paragraph**, **Language**, or **Style**, and make the selections you want.

➤ To search for a special mark, such as a page break or a tab, click on **Special** or press **Alt+E**, then select an item from the list.

Shorten Up That Search

Word for Windows 95 finds any matching text in your document. It can find things so well, however, that it can drive you crazy. Search normally for the word *me* and you're likely to be bombarded with words like *home*, *tame*, *meander*, and *remedial*. To make Word for Windows 95 more precise—to locate only the whole word *me*, for example—select the **Find Whole Word Only** check box in the Find dialog box. When that box is checked, the Find command locates only whole words and not letters stored in other words.

When you have selected all the options you want, click on **Find Next**. Word for Windows 95 begins the search from the current location in the document, but you can continue the search at the beginning by clicking on the **Yes** button when the message appears.

Word will look for the first occurrence of the selected word. If you want it to continue looking, click the **Find Next** button. To return to your document, click on **Cancel**. To continue your search at a later time (searching for the same text or formatting) or in another document, press the **Shift+F4** key combination.

Finding Special Characters

But what if you want to find something strange, like the next Tab marker located in a document? The Tab is one of many keys that you can't simply type in the Find What text box. The Enter key, which creates the next paragraph, is another. To find these special characters, click the **Special** button. You will see a pop-up list of various characters that Word for Windows 95 can search for but you aren't able to type. Click on the character you want, and it will appear in the Find What box, ready for the search. You will also see a symbol next to it called a *caret* (^) that has to be there, but you can ignore it.

Finding and Replacing Things in Your Document

Believe it or not, the reason most people usually want to find something in a document is to get rid of it, or change it to something else. Word for Windows 95 has a special feature to help you with this, and it's called Find and Replace.

Find and Replace has become incredibly powerful. Sure, it will search your entire document for a particular word (or words) and replace it with whatever you want, and maintain whatever format is found. But it's also very flexible and allows creative searching. Imagine being able to search for any occurrence of a particular font (no matter what the words) and replace it with another font. Or find anything in bold or italic and change it

165

to normal text. You can even search to find things to get rid of, and delete them in an instant.

Searching and Replacing Plain Old Text

The text you replace doesn't have to be plain or old, and what you replace it with can be anything you can think of (well, almost anything). You can even search for combinations of letters inside words, like acronyms used in your business that change, and replace them easily.

The process of finding and replacing text looks very similar to just finding text, except you start the process differently. Open the **Edit** menu and choose the **Replace** command, or take a shortcut and press **Ctrl+H**. In the Replace dialog box, type the text you want to find in the Find What box and press **Tab** to move to the next box (incidentally, if you already opened the Find dialog box, you can click on the Replace button to turn it into the Replace dialog box). In the Replace With box, type the replacement text. Now press the **Find Next** button to search for the next occurrence of what is entered in the Find What box. The dialog box stays with you as the search travels through your document, stopping at each occurrence. Press the **Replace** button to replace the text, or skip it and move to the next occurrence by pressing **Find Next** again.

Replacing what you find automatically.

If you are the bold and decisive type, go ahead and try the **Replace All** button. No holds are barred with this button; it blasts through your document replacing every occurrence before you can scream "OH NO!" Don't panic. Just remember the Undo button (or **Ctrl+Z**), which works well at restoring the previous state of your document, and possibly your health.

Replacing Text That Has Been Formatted

You can get particular with the words you search for by selecting the format of the words. For example, you may want to tone down a document by replacing every bold **NO** with normal text. Or you can take normal words and replace them with formatted versions of the same thing, and the formatting is limited only by your imagination. You can also search for words in different fonts and sizes, and replace them with yet another font or size.

Here's a simple example to get started. Replace every bold **No** in your document with a plain No in normal text. Open the **Edit** menu and choose the **Find** command. Type the text you want to find in the **Find What** text box, and apply any of the formatting to it using any of the character formatting commands on the Formatting toolbar (just press the **Bold** button and type the word **No**). Then press the **Replace** button and type the replacement text in the **Replace With** box, and indicate the format of the replacement in the same manner (type **No** without any formatting). You can use any combination of the formatting options for your search or replace. Now press the **Find Next** button to begin your search. The dialog box will remain on the screen as it displays the found words in your document (you usually see enough of the surrounding text to confirm that you really want to replace it; if not, just move the dialog box around the screen by dragging the Title bar of its window). To replace the text, press the **Replace** button. To move to the next occurrence, press the **Find Next** button. Continue this process until you return to the beginning of your document.

If you don't have any specific words to search for, but still want to replace any words using a type of formatting with another type (like changing any words in 10-point Courier font to 12-point Times New Roman), use the Find Font dialog box. To begin such a search, open the **Edit** menu and choose the **Find** command to display the Find dialog box. Click on the **Format** button near the bottom of the dialog box to reveal the many formatting options available for searching. To search for anything related to fonts, choose the **Font** command from the pop-up menu. This will bring up the Find Font dialog box, which allows

> *Check This Out...*
>
> **Always Type Something in the Replace With Box** If you happen to leave the Replace With box empty, whatever you type in the Find What box will be systematically deleted. This process is sometimes referred to as "Find and Delete" and is described later in this chapter.

you to specify the type of formatting for your search. Just as before, enter what you want to find, and what you want to replace it with. Press the **OK** button to return to the Find dialog box. Then begin your replacing by pressing the **Find Next** button, and pressing the **Replace** button as needed each time the discovered font appears.

Finding fonts, attributes, and other symbols.

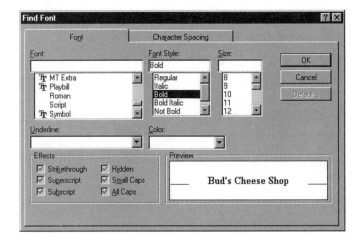

Replacing Formatting Only

Sometimes you don't care about the words, only the formatting. You can search for and replace all occurrences of a specific formatting, regardless of the text. Here's another way to change the formatting of *any and all* words in your document from, say, Bold text to Normal text.

Open the **Edit** menu and choose the **Replace** command (or press **Ctrl+H**). Delete any text in the Find What box and the Replace With box that might be lingering from a previous search or replace. To specify the formats you want to find and replace, you can click the appropriate button on the Formatting toolbar. Press the Bold button, for instance, and the word Bold will appear just below the text box as the description of what will be searched for. Do the same after pressing the Replace button, and here's the trick—if you want Bold changed to Not Bold, just press the Bold button twice. The description will read Not Bold. Then press the Find Next button and you'll be on your way. Each and every entry of bold text will appear in order on your screen, and you have the option of changing them to normal text by pressing Replace, or leaving them alone by pressing the Find Next button.

Word will even let you totally destroy a document by, say, replacing all normal text with nothing. Just leave the Replace With box completely empty. I can't think of a practical reason to do this, but it serves as a good warning to you. Make sure you know what is in your Replace With box before starting one of these experiments.

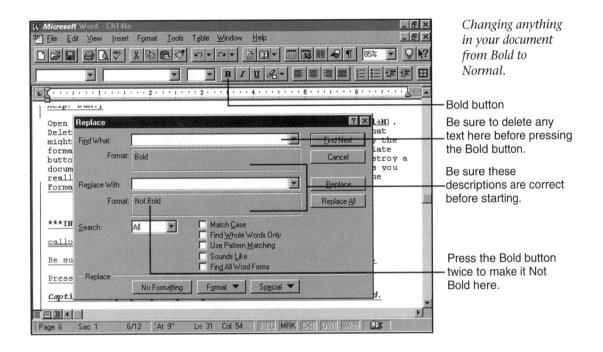

Changing anything in your document from Bold to Normal.

Bold button

Be sure to delete any text here before pressing the Bold button.

Be sure these descriptions are correct before starting.

Press the Bold button twice to make it Not Bold here.

Finding and Replacing Graphics, Fields, and Annotations

If you use lots of graphics in your document, you may be happy to know you can find and replace any of them. Who knows, it could be helpful in really large documents. And if you create templates or create annotation comments, you may find it helpful to search on either fields or the inserted annotations.

Open the **Edit** menu and choose the **Find** or **Replace** commands. In the dialog box that appears, click the **Special** button. Now click **Graphic**, **Field**, or **Annotation Mark**. If you are replacing something, type what you want to use as a replacement in the Replace With box. This can also be text, graphics, fields, or annotations. Now start your search by pressing the **Find Next**, **Replace**, or **Replace All** buttons.

Stop That Search! You can press the **Esc** (Escape) key on your keyboard to cancel any search in progress, especially if it's taking too long or if you've changed your mind.

Special Characters You Can Find and Replace

Word has preloaded almost all of the special codes you are likely to need to search on. If you happen to know the special code, you can just type it in the Find What box. Otherwise, press the **Special** button and choose the plain English description of the symbol

169

you want to find. The special code for the symbol you have chosen will appear in the Find What box, and it won't look like anything you're expecting. You can just ignore these special codes; Word uses them to find what you're looking for.

The symbol code will appear here.

No need to memorize special codes anymore.

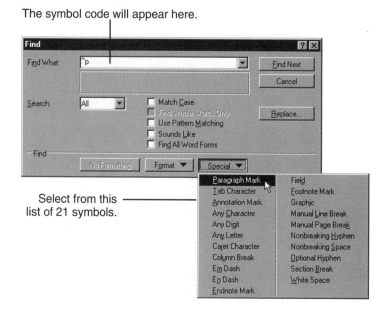

Select from this list of 21 symbols.

White Space?

That last option on the Special button may have you wondering what's included in this thing called *white space*. After all, isn't the background considered white space? Not all of it. White space includes any number and combination of normal and non-breaking spaces, tab characters, and paragraph marks. Most people search for white space during paragraph and section formatting.

So what else is useful to search for and replace? Spaces are a popular item. They end up a lot more than they should at the end of sentences—like twice as much. A single space between sentences is now considered correct, not the two most people prefer to type. Although they may not be causing you harm, you can still get rid of them easily using Find and Replace. Simply open the **Edit** menu and choose the **Replace** command, and type two spaces into the **Find What** box, and only a single space in the **Replace With** box.

Pretty simple, huh? Since you probably don't want two spaces in a row appearing anywhere in your document, you can press the Replace All button to save yourself some time. Every occurrence will be replaced immediately. If you are still a bit chicken, press the Find Next button to see them one at a time. Then press the Replace button to change them to a single space.

Need another example to get you excited? After importing a text file, you may find five spaces used instead of the appropriate single Tab key. It's a real pain if you are trying to align the document. Taking it from the top, open the **Edit** menu and choose the **Replace** command (or press **Ctrl+H**). In the **Find What** box, enter five spaces. In the **Replace With** box, select **Tab character (^t)** from the **Special** menu. Now press the **Replace All** button, and all those spaces will be turned into tabs, which are much easier to align.

Getting Fancy with Find

Using advanced criteria, you can specify some pretty complex search patterns. First, from within the Search or Replace dialog boxes, select **Use Pattern Matching** or press Alt+M. Then click on **Special** and select one from the list, or enter your search pattern in the Find What text box. Here's a sample list of patterns and what they can do:

Pattern	What It Searches For	Examples
?	Any single character	s?t finds "sat" and "set."
*	Any string of characters	s*d finds "sad" and "started."
[list]	Any character in the list	w[io]n finds "win" and "won."
[range]	Any character within range	[r-t]ight finds "right," "sight," and "tight."
[!c]	Not character c	m[!a]st finds "mist" and "most," but not "mast."
[!x-z]	Any single character except x, y or z	t[!a-m]ck finds "tock" and "tuck," but not "tack" or "tick."
c{n}	n occurrences of c	fe{2}d finds "feed" but not "fed."
c{n,}	n or less occurrences of c	fe{1,}d finds "fed" but not "feed."
c{n,m}	range n-m of occurrences of c	10{1,3} finds "10," "100," and "1000."

continues

continued

Pattern	What It Searches For	Examples
c@	Any occurrences of c	lo@t finds "lot" and "loot."
<(char)	char found at beginning of word	<(inter)finds "interesting" and "intercept," but not "splintered."
>(char)	char found at end of word	(in)> finds "in" and "within," but not "interested."

Finding and Replacing All Forms of a Word

What a pain it used to be worrying about all the different forms of a word during a word replace. Famous authors and politicians complained that they couldn't, for example, change all the words *go* with the word *leave*, because they might also have additional steps to find occurrences of *going* or *gone*. These people pushed their weight around Microsoft and got them to include some pretty fancy innards in this version. Accurate replacement of words usually means painstakingly determining the different word forms, or tenses, and finding and replacing them. It works, and it's fun. You can also change the entire gist of a letter by replacing words with ones of opposite meaning (called an antonym).

To invoke this new wonder, open the **Edit** menu and choose either **Find** or **Replace**; it works for both functions as well. In the dialog box, click to check the **Find All Word Forms**. Now all your searches will include the past, present, and future with the press of a single button.

Buy, Buying, Bought

Word for Windows 95 now features linguistic technology to understand the meaning of words and their different forms. For example, if you want to replace the word *buy* with the word *sell* throughout your document, Word applies some smarts and changes not only *buy* to *sell*, but also *buying* to *selling*, and *bought* to *sold*. Now you can send form letters to your stock broker.

I Don't Know, but It Sounds Like...

Did you experience the parental spelling paradox as a child? When asked how a word was spelled, your answer was to "go look it up." It usually results in going out to play, because how can you look up a word in a dictionary when you don't know how to spell it in the first place?

This paradox no longer frustrates the youth, or the elderly for that matter, with the Sounds Like feature in Find and Replace. You don't have to know the exact spelling of a word to find or replace it, you just have to come close enough for Word to guess it. The better your attempt at spelling, the more accurate your search will be. But you don't even have to be close and Word will still go at it. Have

Don't Get Too Crazy with Word Forms This intelligence of replacing word forms is powerful, but it can't change the underlying structure of your sentence. It won't replace all forms of a verb with a noun, for example, or vice-versa, but why would anyone try that anyway?

some fun. In either the Find or Replace dialog boxes, check the **Sounds Like** check box. Enter your best attempt at spelling the word in the Find What box, and press **Find Next** to start the hunt for the real word. Don't be so bold as to press the **Replace All** button during one of these, unless you are quick with the **Undo** button (or **Ctrl+Z**).

Getting Rid of Words and Symbols with Find and Delete

You may not see this feature advertised in Word for Windows 95 because it can lead to really confusing sentences in the wrong hands. But you might already have figured it out.

If you don't type anything in the Replace With box, the **Replace** command systematically deletes all of the Find What's. It's great to use on imported text files where each line ends with a paragraph symbol. This process can quickly blow them all away—although you might prefer replacing them with a single space. You might also try using it to remove all words of a particular size or font, by searching for character formats instead of words.

Open the **Edit** menu and select the **Replace** command (or use the shortcut **Ctrl+H** keys). In the Find What box, type the text you want to find. Any previously searched text appears at the prompt. Edit it or type in new text or the special symbols you want to search for. Don't type anything in the Replace With box. Leave it empty because replacing something with nothing leaves nothing, and nothing is considered a deletion. Finally, press either the **Find Next** button (to go slowly and carefully) or the **Replace All** button (being decisive and ruthless), and the text will be replaced with nothing, a neat trick for deleting things.

If you don't like the results, you can always press **Ctrl+Z** or the **Undo** button on the Standard toolbar. Words and symbols replaced with nothing will suddenly reappear to your relief.

The Least You Need to Know

Finding the important points of this chapter is much easier than replacing them:

➤ To search for words in a document, use the **Find** command on the **Edit** menu or press **Ctrl+F**.

➤ To replace words in a document, use the **Replace** command on the **Edit** menu or press **Ctrl+H**.

➤ Just about anything you can think of can be found and replaced, including formatting, fonts and font sizes, bold, italic, or underlined text, and even special characters you normally see in a document.

➤ The past, present, and future meaning of words can be replaced quickly with the Find All Word Forms feature found on both the Find and Replace dialog boxes.

➤ Leaving the Replace With box (in the Replace dialog box) blank (empty) is a way to perform quick search and delete operations on your document.

Doing Two Things at Once: Multiple Documents

Sometimes one document just isn't enough. Sure, it's open on your screen and you're comfortable with all the controls, but you're sure there's more to life. You need more than this document. You probably need additional information stored in another document, and you want them both open at the same time.

If that's how you feel, this chapter will show you how to get not one, not two, but up to a gazillion documents open on your screen at once (if you have enough memory). You'll also learn how to copy or move information (or yourself) between them. And to keep things interesting, you'll also learn how to create your own form letters for fun or for profit.

Opening Many Documents at Once

Why would anyone want to have more than one document open at the same time? An informal poll of the entire human population was taken last week, and here are the preliminary results:

➤ It's the easiest way to cut, copy, and paste between them.

➤ It's quick when you need multiple reference documents available fast.

➤ It's easy to move graphics and text back and forth.

➤ It makes your boss think you're doing more work.

➤ It's the best way to slow down really fast computers.

Whatever your reason, having *multiple* documents open on your screen is as simple as opening one document, then opening another, and so on. Although you probably see only a single document at the moment, the rest are right behind it, waiting for you to bring them forward. You can see the list of all open documents by opening the **Window** menu (if you have more than nine opened documents, you will see the last entry as More Windows... which, if selected, takes you to a dialog box containing the complete list of all opened documents). Choose between any of the opened documents by clicking with the mouse, or use the keyboard and type the number of the document.

Use the Window menu to track open documents.

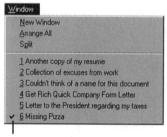

The checkmark indicates the currently viewed document.

Opening Many Documents at the Same Time

If you need to have many documents opened at the same time, you can try this to save yourself some time: open the **File** menu and choose the **Open** command to see the File Open dialog box. Locate the folder storing the documents you need. This time, instead of double-clicking on a single document (which opens only that document), hold down the **Ctrl** key and click once on several documents to highlight them. All selected documents will be opened at the same time when you press **Enter** or the **Open** button. You can even select documents stored in different folders. You can also click **Advanced** and search for documents, and select several of them from the results listing. Finally, when you press the **Open** button, all selected documents will be opened, in the order you selected.

Select in multiple folders

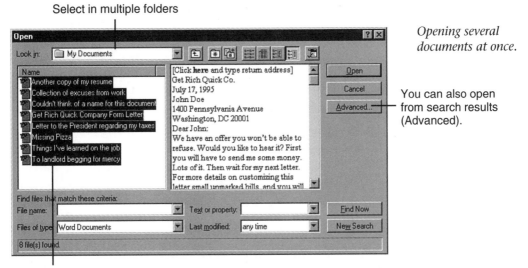

Opening several documents at once.

You can also open from search results (Advanced).

Multiple selections to open

You Opened Them, but Where Are They?

You're fairly certain you just opened 16 documents, but only one is staring you in the face. Where are the rest? In Word for Windows 95, each document is stored in its own window. Normally that window uses the entire screen, so a single document is all you see at the moment. You can see this list of windows by opening the **Window** menu.

Word for Windows 95 will display a numbered list of all opened documents for you to choose from. They are in alphabetical order, which was more helpful back in the old days of eight-letter document names.

You can also switch between open documents by pressing **Ctrl+Shift+F6**, which takes you to the next window on the list. It's easier to press Ctrl+F6 to go to the previous window on the list, however, since most people just switch windows until they find the one they want. The Ctrl+F6 key combination is most helpful if you have two documents open and want to switch between them.

Limited Only by Your Memory
Word for Windows now lets you open as many documents as you want, as long as your computer has enough memory to support all of them.

So What Can You Do with Two Open Documents?

Probably the best thing you can do with multiple opened documents is easily cut, copy, and paste anything between them, and it can be anything stored in any of the documents. Just follow the rules from Chapter 6 to select the portion of text, figures, or objects from any document. Then press **Ctrl+C** (or the **Copy** button) to copy the selection to the clipboard. Now find the spot in any document you want to copy to, place the insertion point there, and press **Ctrl+V** (or the **Paste** button), and the selection will be pasted instantly. The **Cut** command (**Ctrl+X** or the **Cut** button) works fine also across multiple documents. In fact, even **Spike** works across multiple documents. For a refresher on **Spike**, see Chapter 6.

Word for Windows 95 handles each window independently, in case you were wondering why only one document printed when you pressed the **Print** button. Each command affects only the current document, which is the one you're looking at. Spell checking, formatting commands, and printing are examples of tasks that are performed only on the current document.

Viewing Multiple Documents at Once

Instead of seeing a single document on the screen at a time, you may decide you want to see more than one, or all documents. Just open the **Window** menu and choose the **Arrange All** command. All opened documents will be placed on your screen, each in their own smaller window. This works best for two or three documents because each window has to share space on your screen, and too many open windows make it difficult to work on any single document.

Check This Out...

Cut, Copy, and Paste
Incidentally, multiple documents do not have to be open at the same time to cut, copy, and paste between them. You can select and copy from one document, close it, open another document, and paste it just fine. Fewer steps are required when both documents are opened.

Although you can *see* more than one document on the screen at a time, you are still limited to working on one. Only one insertion point is active at a time. The active document has the highlighted title bar with the Title bar buttons. You can click the title bar of any of them to make it the current document. In fact, you can click anywhere in another window for its document to become active. You can also toggle through them by pressing the **Ctrl+F6** keys.

Clicking on the Maximize Title bar button on the active document will cause that document to be maximized, moving its Title bar buttons to the Menu bar of Word 7. The remaining documents are still there, just covered up at the moment. You can get to them again by choosing from the Window list, pressing **Ctrl+F6**, or by minimizing the current window (press the **Minimize** Title bar button) or restoring it to a smaller window (press the **Restore** button, which toggles between Restore and Maximize) to expose the other active documents.

See Multiple, Use One It's easier to find the active window when you have many windows open. Word 7 places the Title bar buttons (Minimize, Maximize, Restore, and Close) on *only* the active window. This makes it much less confusing on a busy screen.

You can resize them and move them around just as you can any window. Another quick way to see all open documents at once is to open the **Window** menu and choose the **Arrange All** command. You will see all of your active documents sharing the available space. Once again, to return to focusing on a single document, you can maximize that window by pressing the **Maximize** button in that window's title bar.

Viewing Multiple Parts of the Same Document

If you like working on two things at once, even if the two things are in a single document, then you'll love this screen manipulation. You can view different parts of a large document at the same time, in different windows on your screen.

Start by opening the document you want to work with. Open the **Window** menu and choose the **New Window** command. This creates another window on your screen where you will find another copy of the same document. These aren't two different copies—just two different views of the same document. Make a change in one, and it's instantly updated in the other view also. Your documents are also labeled in the Title bar with something extra—a colon and a number after the filename—which helps you identify the views. For example, you may have Quarterly Summary Report:1 in one window and Quarterly Summary Report:2 in the title bar of the second window.

What's this dual-view good for? Cutting and pasting in very long documents. Clicking on the different views or using **Ctrl+F6** pops back and forth between them.

When you are finished editing either part of this document, save it and close it by opening the **File** menu and choosing the **Close** command. You'll only have to do this once because closing one will close both.

Splitting Your Viewing Screen

You can save some space on your viewing screen and still have two views of the same document by using a slightly different feature of Word 7 called *screen splitting*.

To view two parts of a document simultaneously, open the **Window** menu and choose the **Split** command. A horizontal bar will appear about halfway down your screen. Now just click your mouse button and you will have a split screen. The bottom window will contain an exact duplicate of your document. Try clicking in this new window and scroll around. The other window will remain still, allowing you to see different parts of the same document at the same time.

Seeing double using the old Split-Screen trick.

Place the cursor here to drag up or down for a new window size.

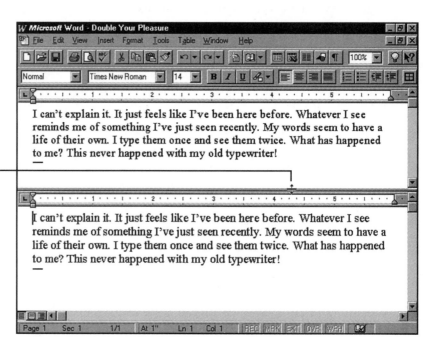

Split screen view is often used to copy or move text between parts of a long document. Display the text or graphics you want to move or copy in one pane and the destination for the text or graphics in the other pane, and then drag the text or graphics across the split bar. Instant success and feedback. What a concept.

When you are tired of this view, you can quickly get rid of it by double-clicking the split bar in the vertical scroll bar, or by simply opening up the **Window** menu and choosing the **Remove Split** command. Or if you have lots of time to waste, you can try to click and drag that little arrow shape on the vertical scroll bar all the way back up to the top.

Saving Multiple Documents at Once

You can save all open documents at once by opening the **File** menu and selecting the **Save All** command. Any document containing any new changes since it was last saved will now be saved. You'll be able to watch each document flash in the status bar at the bottom of your screen. (If your status bar is hidden, you can bring it back to see this action, but it's not necessary. Open the **Tools** menu, select the **Options** command, click the **View** tab to bring it to the front, and click to check the **Status Bar** box.)

Of course, if you are going to be away from your computer for more than a few minutes, it's best to also close all of your documents.

Closing All Documents at the Same Time

Press and hold down the **Shift** key (either one) and use the mouse to open the **File** menu. It changed! There's now a **Close All** command, and by selecting it, all of your documents will be closed. Of course, if any documents have changes not yet saved, Word will stop before closing them and ask if you want to save the changes.

These dynamically changing menus may have you wondering what else might change if you hold down a key and open a menu. If you have time to waste, it really would be wasted because there aren't any more.

Mail Merge

You may not know what *mail merge* is, but you have experienced the results of a mail merge. Anytime you receive junk mail with your name pasted next to the possible winner of $1,000,000, you have experienced a mail merge.

If it's done well, a mail merge is ideal for communicating more personally to a large number of people, like your friends during the holidays, the customers of your business, or the tax base of your country.

What Is a Merge?

Mail merge is the process of taking a single form letter, mixing it with another containing a bunch of names (or other information), and then *merging* both to create several documents. Each of the documents is customized by using the list of names and information that you provide.

First some definitions. The document that contains the names and other information is called the *data source*. The file that contains the form letter is called the *main document*.

Now the process. You start by creating the *main document*, complete with formatting. But leave blank the places you would normally enter a name or address, or anything else that might change from document to document. In these blank spaces, you add something called a *field*. Each field is replaced with a real name or address during a merge.

Next you find or create a *data source*. The *data source* is a document that contains a collection of the names and addresses (or anything else) that you want. Unlike a regular document, however, this one is created in a different format called a *database*. For example, this could be a database of all your customer names and addresses. Got it? One database file, many names and addresses. Each combination of name, address, and other information in this data source is called a *record*.

When you say go, Word for Windows 95 creates a bunch of customized documents (as many as you have *records* for in your data source), one form letter for each customer in your database. Then it's very easy to print all of these custom documents as a final step, without the need for saving all of them—or you can save them all. In fact, you can e-mail them all if the names came from your address book provided with Windows 95. You can get to it through the **Insert Address** button on the Standard toolbar.

Using the Mail Merge Command

This won't be so bad, I promise. If you follow the steps to the end, I'm certain your sentiments will be something like "Wow!", "How about that!", or "Who cares, I'm hungry."

The easiest way to explain mail merge is to use an example. You just had a birthday and got lots of presents. You know you'll keep getting presents if you send a personal thank-you note to everyone. You decide to send the same note to everyone since they all live in different parts of the country. Only the names and addresses will change.

What's first? Building the basic thank-you note. Start by opening the **Tools** menu and choose the **Mail Merge** command. You see the Mail Merge Helper dialog box. The large numbers 1, 2, and 3 make you guess you'll be finished in a snap. Guess again! This example goes on for pages! See the **Create** button? Push it. Now select **Form Letter** from the list. You can press **New Main Document** next, to begin the creation of your form letter.

After pressing the New Main Document button, two new buttons will appear—an Edit button and a Get Data button.

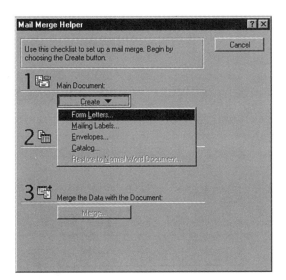

The Mail Merge Helper dialog box leads you through the process.

Creating Your Data Source

Press the **Get Data** button to reveal the pull-down listing of potential sources of data. Choose **Create Data Source** for now. We're going to build a list of our generous friends from scratch.

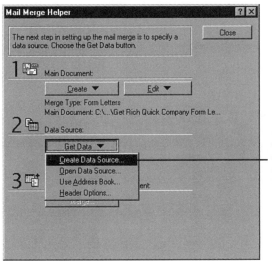

Creating the data source (the names and addresses for your form letter).

Build your list of names by choosing Create Data Source.

183

In the Create Data Source dialog that appears, just press the **OK** button. It's a shortcut for quickly creating the file that will contain your names and addresses. You are now asked to save what you've just created. What have you created? Nothing yet, but call it **People Who Gave Me Presents This Year** to give you an idea. Press the **Save** button in the Save As dialog box to continue.

Next you will find a dialog box asking what you want to do next. It says that the data source you just created contains no data records. No kidding. So let's add some. Choose the **Edit Data Source** button to begin adding names to our mailing list.

Press OK when you finish adding
all your names and addresses.

Adding to a list of names for your merge.

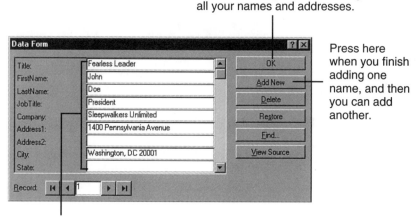

Press here
when you finish
adding one
name, and then
you can add
another.

These are called Fields.

What's this, you ask? It's called creating your *data source*, and it's easier than it looks. Think of the best present you got. Now think of who gave it to you. (Stumped? Don't worry; everyone is getting the same letter anyway. Guilty? You should be, since you should have done this sooner!) Type their first name right next to the First Name box. That's it! Unless you want to add more information about this person (by pressing the **Tab** key to move to each field), you are ready to move on to the next person. Do this by pressing the **Add New** button and don't panic. Although it looks empty again, you can relax because the first entry was saved. Fill in the second person's name. Press **Add New** for the third person, and so on.

When you've finished adding everyone's name, press the **OK** button, and your database will be saved, and you will be returned to the document screen.

Creating Your Form Letter

Now be creative as you compose a generic thank-you note. When it's time to add something personal, like a first name after Dear, click that **Insert Merge Field** button on your Mail Merge toolbar. Choose **First Name** from the list of fields. This ties directly back to those names you entered earlier.

Don't worry about the formatting, those silly <<things>> will be replaced later. Keep on creating the thank-you note.

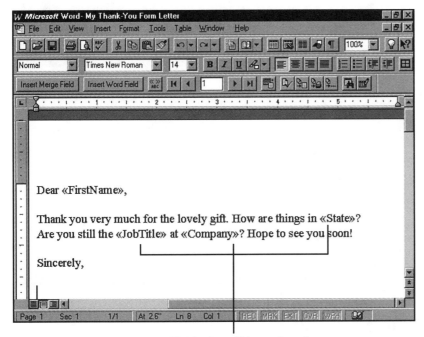

A generic thank-you note ready to be merged.

Fields that will be replaced

Merging at Last

You're so close to the end of this example, you should be able to taste it. Open the **Tools** menu and select **Mail Merge** again. Press the **Merge** button to see the Merge dialog box. The most common defaults are already selected in this dialog box, like the option to merge to a new document. You can also choose to merge directly to your printer, or even e-mail, by pressing the **Merge To** pull-down arrow and choosing another destination.

Now press the **Merge** button in the Merge dialog box to finally start the merging process. You may be surprised how quickly your computer can accomplish this merging, and you will want to inspect the results to make sure the proper merging took place. If the merge was less than spectacular, you can delete the merged results (by closing them without saving) and trying again. All of the tedious merging steps have been saved, so you are taken to the very last step to try again.

The finished product.

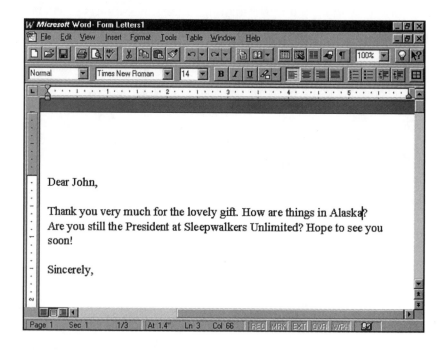

The Least You Need to Know

Humans have no problem doing 50 things at once. Now our documents can keep up with us. This chapter reviewed ideas on using multiple documents and provided these words of wisdom:

➤ You can open as many documents as your heart desires. You can track multiple opened documents by opening the **Window** menu.

➤ You can view two (or more) opened documents at once by opening the **Window** menu and choosing the **Arrange All** command.

➤ You can work on two sections of the same document by splitting the window into panes.

➤ A mail merge takes a single master document and mixes it with another (like an address list) to create many new documents (also known as "form letters").

Chapter 16

Spelling, Thesaurus, Grammar, and Grandpa

In This Chapter

➤ Spell Checking your document

➤ AutoText and AutoCorrect miracles

➤ Using a Thesaurus

➤ Getting to know the Grammar Checker

Once in awhile, you run into a gadget that makes you feel like you've arrived in the future. Maybe it's your first jet ride, that laser at the supermarket checkout, or your first pair of inline skates. The new Spell Checker in Word does it for me. The improved Thesaurus and Grammar checker that come with Word for Windows 95 help you find better words and use them correctly.

You won't waste anymore of your precious time running the Spell Checker at the end of a document. It runs continuously while you type, looking up each word and underlining it with a red wavy line if it's not found in the dictionary. It even stores the suggested spelling along with that wavy line, hoping that you will ask to change it.

Those Wavy Red Lines

Unless you're an expert speller, you may notice that several words you typed are underlined with a wavy red line. These words are misspelled or don't exist in Word's dictionary. Word for Windows 95 has installed a little computer troll under your keyboard, watching each word as you type it. The instant you misspell a word, the troll does the wavy underline thing (you actually have to move the insertion point off the word, indicating that you are finished with it, before the Spell Checker analyzes it). The red wavy line doesn't print, and no formatting tool can get rid of it, but you can make it go away by correcting the spelling mistake.

How do you find the correct spelling? Try placing the mouse pointer over the word that has a wavy red line under it and click the right mouse button. Word displays a list of suggested spellings. Click the correct spelling from the list displayed.

Spell Checking faster than you can misspell.

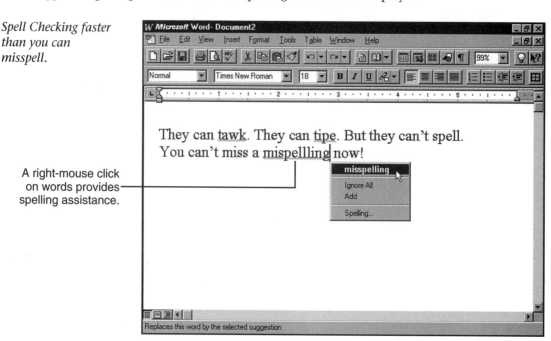

A right-mouse click on words provides spelling assistance.

Is Your Spell Checker Turned On?

If you don't have any red wavy lines, you're either a great speller or else your Spell Checker is turned off. To turn on the Spell Checker to check automatically while you type, open the **Tools** menu and select the **Options** command. Click the **Spelling** tab to bring it to the front. To have Word check spelling automatically as you type, select the **Automatic Spell Checking** check box. Press **OK** to return to your document.

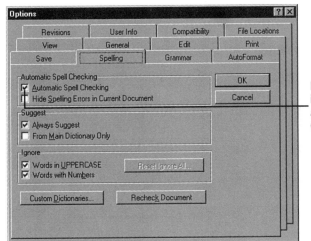

The Spelling dialog box.

Make sure this is checked for automatic Spell Checking.

About Word's Spell Checker

When Word for Windows 95 checks a document for spelling errors, it looks everywhere, including headers, footers, footnotes, and annotations. Also, if you repeat a word accidentally, or mis-capitalize it, Word will let you know with that red wavy underline.

You don't have to fix all of the wavy underlined words as they occur. Some people are paranoid and correct the words immediately, while others (real typists) never even look at the screen while they type. Still others like the red lines and do their best to fill a document with them.

After you finish your document (or reach a convenient stopping point), you can clean up all the misspellings. Those red wavy lines are like flags on a golf course, telling you Word has already found the mistake, compared it with its dictionary, and provided alternatives for you to choose from. All this happened while you continued to type or sip coffee.

You can manually start Spell Checking your document by pressing the **Spelling** button, pressing the **F7** key (the spelling shortcut) on your keyboard, or opening the **Tools** menu and selecting the **Spelling** command. If everything is hunky-dory, nothing much will happen, except that you will see a message box telling you that Spell Checker has finished checking your document. If your fingers moved a little faster than your brain, however, you may have a few misspelled words. If so, you will be presented with the Spelling dialog box.

Using the Spell Checker dialog box.

Press Ignore to leave your word alone.

Press this button to replace the misspelled word with the one found by the Spell Checker.

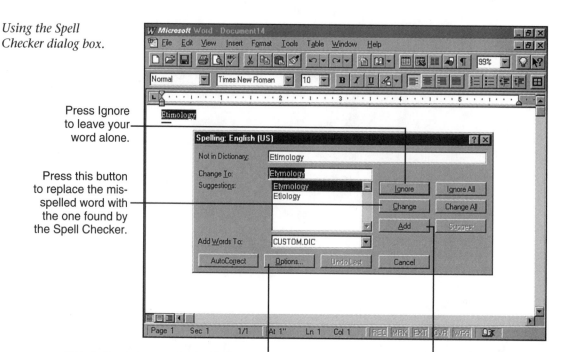

This button takes you to the Options menu, where you can turn on the automatic spell checking.

Press here if this is a real word and should be added to your dictionary.

Miscellaneous Corrections

Check This Out...

There are some interesting miscellaneous items that the Spell Checker will find. For instance, if two identical words are found next to each other, the second instance will be underlined, indicating that one of them should be deleted. But Word also knows that "had had" is often correct and leaves them alone (how about that?). Also, if any capital letters occur inside of a single word, the word is underlined for your inspection.

The Spelling dialog box displays the misspelled word and suggests alternative spelling. To correct the misspelling, select the correct word and click the **Change** button. If the word isn't in the list, you can type it in the Change To box. Or if the word is okay, you can click the **Ignore** button to skip over the word without making any changes. Word will immediately move to the next misspelled word, and you can continue the process until all misspellings have been corrected (or ignored). A dialog box will appear when the process is finished telling you that the process is finished. The following table gives you more information about what the options in the Spelling dialog box do.

Button Description for the Spelling Dialog Box

Action	Description
Correct the spelling of the word	If you agree with the suggestion in the Change To box, just click on the **Change** button. If you want to, you can type your own correction or select an alternative from the Suggestions list box.
Ignore or Ignore All	Click this button if your word really is a word, like names, acronyms, and products that often appear in documents. Word will no longer stop if it finds any more of these words existing in your document.
Change or Change All	Press this button if you want to change every word that's spelled a certain way in your document. It acts just like search and replace, and it's helpful if you accidentally misspell or mistype some words often.
Add	There's nothing more annoying than Word always telling you a common word, like your name or street address, is misspelled. To make these words a permanent part of the dictionary in Word, click the **Add** button.
AutoCorrect	This is an incredibly powerful tool that fixes mistakes as you make them. Common typing errors (like typing *teh* for *the* or *adn* for *and*) are changed instantly without wasting your time. If you have your own favorite misspellings, you can add them, along with the correct spelling, to this list for instant changing.
Delete the repeated word	If a word is repeated twice and it shouldn't be, click on the **Delete** button. You won't see this button unless Word encounters a repeated word.
Undo a previous correction	You can undo any of your last corrections in your document by clicking on **Undo Last**. This is great in case you click on the **Change** button only to realize that the last word was spelled correctly in the first place.

Wait! That Really Is a Word!

Many words you type are not included in the Word for Windows 95 main dictionary, like your name, address, abbreviations, or acronyms. You can ignore them or decide to add them to the existing dictionary.

To add the word to the computer dictionary, click the **Add** button in the Spelling dialog box. You can also click the right mouse button on a misspelled word to add the word to the dictionary (choose the **Add** command from the pop-up menu). From now on, any occurrence of that word will not trigger a red wavy line or the Spelling dialog box. Be extra careful adding words to the dictionary so you don't accidentally enter a mistake.

Creating Your Own Dictionary

Wondering where those words are stored when you click the **Add** button? It's a file called the *standard supplemental dictionary*, and it's stored in the Windows-MSAPPS-Proof folder (the file is named CUSTOM.DIC). You can view this file by opening the **Tools** menu, clicking the **Options** command, pressing the **Spelling** tab to bring it to the front, and pressing the **Custom Dictionaries** button. Finally, press the **Edit** button. You'll see an alphabetical list of all words you have added.

Since Word lets you add more dictionaries, you might want to create one yourself. Start with a new document. Type a list of the words that you want to add to the dictionary (acronyms, your name, and so on) and press the **Enter** key after each word. Click the **Save** button, and in the Save As Type box, click **Text Only**. In the File Name box, type a name for the custom dictionary, such as **My Business Dictionary**. Close the Word file so that it will be available the next time you check spelling. To use this new dictionary, you must click the **Add** button on the Custom Dictionaries dialog box, and locate the dictionary document you just created. It will appear just below the CUSTOM.DIC, with a check mark indicating all active dictionaries. Press the **OK** button and then close the Options dialog box. It's now working!

Oh yes, you can follow the same procedure to edit either the CUSTOM.DIC or your new dictionaries in case you accidentally add an incorrect spelling of a word. Just click the **Edit** button while you are in the Custom Dictionary dialog box. Word turns off the automatic spelling checker when editing custom dictionaries. Find the entries you wish to remove and delete them. Save and close this dictionary to save your changes.

The Magic of AutoCorrect

How many times do you mistype simple words? A common word is *the*, often mistyped as *teh*, or *and*, often typed *adn*. Technically, these aren't spelling errors because you know how to spell them; your fingers just got ahead of your computer. Word helps you by correcting these flaws on the fly using a feature called *AutoCorrect*. Plenty of entries have already been added for you.

To see what entries you already have stored in AutoCorrect, open the **Tools** menu and select the **AutoCorrect** command. Also notice that Word for Windows 95 automatically expands many "symbols" into real symbol characters. For instance, typing (**tm**) turns into the trademark symbol automatically.

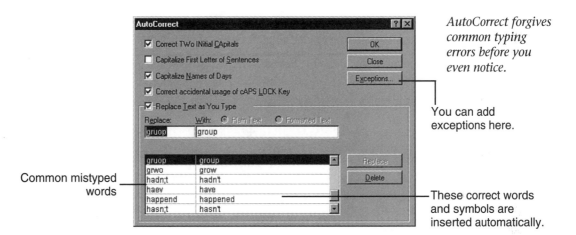

AutoCorrect forgives common typing errors before you even notice.

You can add exceptions here.

Common mistyped words

These correct words and symbols are inserted automatically.

Accidental usage of the caps lock key is automatically corrected with AutoCorrect. For example, when typing *tHIS* with the Caps Lock key depressed, Word will automatically change the typing to *This* and turn off the Caps Lock key.

AutoCorrect also supports an exception list for the "Capitalize First Letter of Sentence" rule. Word doesn't capitalize words that follow abbreviations from the exception list, and Word even watches as you type and automatically adds words to the list if you change an AutoCorrect action.

The Two Caps Feature Works Better The two initial caps rule is much smarter than previous versions of Word. It no longer mistakenly corrects CDs, PCs, or any other two initial capitals pattern which does not contain vowels. This really reduces the number of false "corrections."

There's more. You also can add an AutoCorrect entry during a spelling check. When a word you often misspell or mistype is identified, enter the correct spelling in the Change To box. To add the misspelled word and its correct spelling to the list of words and phrases that are corrected automatically, click **AutoCorrect**.

AutoText Will Save You Time!

You can use shortcuts to quickly insert frequently used text or graphics in your documents:

➤ If you store text and graphics as AutoText entries, you can retrieve them by clicking a button or pressing **F3**.

➤ If you store them as AutoCorrect entries, Word inserts them automatically as you type, which you learned about in the last section.

➤ If you store them in the *Spike*, you can collect text and graphics from various locations in one or more documents, and then insert them as a group in another location.

Check This Out...

Spike It!
Remember the Spike from Chapter 6? You can use Spike to remove several items from one or more documents and insert them as a group in another location. The Spike stores the items as an AutoText entry so you can insert the items repeatedly. When you collect text and graphics in the Spike, they appear in the same order that you added them to the Spike.

AutoText is a helpful way to save time typing out repetitive (or just plain long and boring) words. What kind of words? If you're a pharmacist you might get tired of typing the word for a bladder-controlling drug called pseudophonyhydroxidine. Wouldn't you much rather type PP and have the magic of AutoText expand it automatically to the correct spelling?

Before AutoText can be really useful to you, you first have to load it with the big words (or sentences or paragraphs) you use most often. Either find a document that already contains your big words or phrases, or start a new document and carefully type them. Don't forget to spell them correctly. Now select the text or graphics you want to store as an AutoText entry. To store paragraph formatting with the entry, include the paragraph mark in the selection. Open the **Edit** menu and choose the **AutoText** command. In the Name box, type the shortcut version you prefer, like pp or baffle. An AutoText name can have up to 32 characters, including spaces. Click the **Add** button and this entry will be stored and ready to use.

By default, Word makes the AutoText entry available to all documents. If you want AutoText entries limited to particular documents, you can specify a template in which you want to store the entry by selecting a template name in the Make AutoText Entry Available To box. To put the AutoText entries to work, just start typing your document as you would normally. When it's time to add the big word or phrase, just type the shortcut you stored in AutoText (like pp or baffle) right in your document and then press the **F3** key. The shortcut word will be removed and replaced by the actual big word or phrase it represents.

Using Your Thesaurus

It's right on the tip of your tongue. I can see it. But you can't, which is why you need a Thesaurus. Using big words can help you appear smarter than you are, and it sure helps when doing a crossword puzzle. Improving your vocabulary is a sign of higher intelligence in our species, so the next time you choose a word that doesn't exactly convey the meaning you want, try running it through the Thesaurus first.

To use the Thesaurus, just follow these simple steps. First select the word you want to look up, or move the insertion point anywhere inside the word. Then open the **Tools** menu and select the **Thesaurus** command, or press **Shift+F7**. Your word appears in the Thesaurus dialog box in the Looked Up drop-down list.

Click to look up another listed word.

You'll find opposite meanings here.

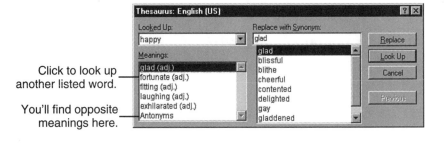

Use the Thesaurus when you can't think of the right word.

➤ If the word you selected is not found, enter an alternate word and click on **Look Up**.

➤ Choose from the synonyms listed in the Replace with Synonym (or Antonym or Related Word) list box.

➤ To change the synonyms listed, choose from general variations of the selected word that appear in the Meanings box. If the Related Words or Antonyms options are listed under Meanings, select either one to display additional choices.

➤ Look up additional meanings for the word displayed in the Replace with Synonym box by clicking on **Look Up**.

➤ Decide whether to replace the selected word. Click on the **Replace** button to substitute the selected word with the word displayed in the Replace with Synonym box, or click on **Cancel** to leave it alone.

➤ If one of the words in the left column is close but not exactly what you want, select it and click the **Look Up** button. The word's synonyms appear in the right column.

➤ If the word that you select has no synonyms, the Thesaurus displays an alphabetical list of words. Type a new, similar word or select **Cancel** to get back to your document.

Opposites Attract

Here's a tip for using the Thesaurus. On those rare occasions that you can't think of *any* words that mean what you want, don't give up! Try thinking of the complete opposite meaning. Quite often, the Thesaurus can take the opposite of what you mean and lead you back to what you really mean. (Work with me on this.)

The secret is in the word *antonym*, which we all learned at some point. It means the opposite, and how happy you'll be if it shows up as the last entry in the Meanings box! You guessed it; if you click on **Antonyms**, you'll get a list of opposite meaning words. Fancy that. Now you can be completely opposite in what you wanted to say.

But don't stop there! Now click on one of those opposite meanings and press the **Look Up** button. Does it have the word antonym listed? That's your ticket. Selecting the *antonym* of an *antonym* of the word you want often discovers the word that works. It's like two wrongs making a right! It's even easier than it sounds. Here are a few examples:

➤ If you can't think up a single positive description of your boss, try *stingy, lazy, cruel,* or *meatloaf,* and then choose **Antonym**.

➤ There seem to be more words describing laziness than whatever the opposite is. Why is that?

➤ Flipping back and forth between opposite meanings helps you enrich your vocabulary by exposing you to many more words than you would otherwise see.

If you don't find a word with antonyms immediately, keep trying. They aren't included as often as you might like them to be, but the words that include them are very delicious. *Delicious?!* Remember the lesson from the Spell Checker—don't use words unless you know their meaning. A real dictionary, and I'm talking about that fat book sitting on your book shelf, is still the very best tool available for helping you use words correctly. It lets you look up a word and see its definition. Neither the Spell Checker, Thesaurus, nor the Grammar Checker (which you are about to learn), can tell you the true meaning, and the proper usage, of any word.

Grammar Checker

The Grammar command checks your document for problems of a grammatical nature and suggests ways to improve your writing and to clarify your meaning. As an added bonus, it won't waste your time checking the grammar of misspelled words. It starts by running a Spell Check and has you repair the misspellings first.

To check the grammar in your document, open the **Tools** menu and choose the **Grammar** command. If Word finds something questionable, or just wants to annoy you, you will see a box offering some suggestions.

Grammatical Find and Replace Word for Windows 95 features new linguistic technology that understands the meaning of words and their different forms. You can now replace the word *buy* with the word *sell*, and you automatically replace all of the *buying* and *bought* with *selling* and *sold*. For more details, see Chapter 14.

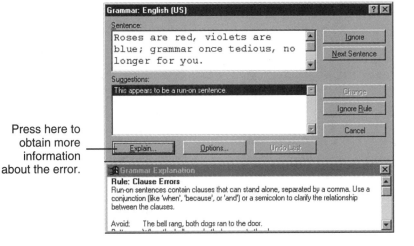

Press here to obtain more information about the error.

Pardon me, may I make a suggestion?

From here, you have these options:

➤ Accept a suggestion by selecting one of those listed in the Suggestions box and clicking on **Change**.

➤ Get more information about what's wrong by clicking on the **Explain** button.

➤ Make your own correction by clicking inside the document window and changing your text. To check the grammar in the rest of the document, click on **Next Sentence**.

➤ Bypass the suggestion by clicking on the **Ignore** button. You can bypass the entire sentence by clicking on the **Next Sentence** button instead. You can tell Word to ignore this "grammatical faux pas" for the rest of the document by clicking on **Ignore Rule**.

Check This Out...

Passive Voice A type of sentence that states what is done by (or to) the subject, rather that what the subject does. For example, compare "The race was won by our team" (passive voice) to the same phrase in active voice: "Our team won the race."

At the end of the grammar check, Word displays a short summary called *Readability Statistics*. It's like a final opinion, and it is very helpful. If you avoid criticism at all cost, you can choose not to display this information by clearing the **Show Readability Statistics After Proofing** check box (in the **Grammar** options), but then you probably wouldn't start the Grammar Checker anyway.

There's an important revelation in Readability Statistics that's worth looking at. It's how many sentences use the passive voice. They aren't wrong or bad, but passive sentences can be vague and confusing. Try to keep this number low (like zero).

Techno Talk

blah blah blah bla bl b

What's Your Readability?

After Word completes a grammar check, readability statistics are displayed, telling you what kind of people should be able to figure out what the heck you just wrote. Mighty intelligent people wrote formulas to figure this out, and since no one knows which is best, you can choose from all of them:

Flesch Reading Ease

This checks the average number of syllables per word and the average number of words per sentence. Scores range from 0 (zero) to 100. The average writing score is about 65. The higher the score, the greater the number of people who can easily understand your document.

Flesch-Kincaid Grade Level

This also checks average syllables per word and words per sentence, but the scoring indicates a grade-school level. A score of 8.0 means that an eighth grader would understand the document, and that's an average document.

Coleman-Liau Grade Level

This uses word length in characters and sentence length in words to determine a grade level.

Bormuth Grade Level

This also uses word length in characters and sentence length in words to determine a grade level, in case you need another opinion.

Business or Casual?

Maybe you're a bit annoyed that the Grammar Checker doesn't like contractions. That's great for a report to your boss (it also gives you more words and fatter reports), but who cares in a letter to Mom? If you still want to run the Grammar Checker but speed things up a bit, you can change the rules of the review. You can even make up your own set of rules, but for now the quickest solution is to choose between the two most common sets of rules.

Open the **Tools** menu and select the **Options** command. Click on the **Grammar** tab to bring it to the front. In the Use Grammar and Style Rules box, change the default from **Business** to **Casual** by clicking on it. Don't forget to change back, following the same procedure, if you want a more strict Grammar Checker for future documents.

Click here to change the default rules to Casual.

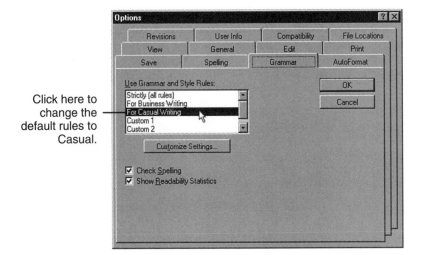

Toning down the Grammar Checker for casual use.

The Least You Need to Know

Writing a letter or report is hard enough. You focus on content, and Word will take care of the spelling and grammar, even helping you find better words with the Thesaurus. You learned that:

➤ Spell Checking is automatic (unless you turn it off); misspelled words are underlined with a red wavy line.

➤ Clicking the right mouse button on flagged words provides a shortcut menu with suggestions directly from the 125,000-word spelling dictionary inside of Word for Windows 95.

➤ To check the spelling of a single word, a selection, or an entire document, click the **Spelling** button on the Standard toolbar, or press **F7**.

➤ No longer must you waste time correcting simple typing errors, because AutoCorrect corrects the majority of them for you before you even notice. You can also add your own favorites to the list.

➤ You can create shortcuts for typing long and difficult words or phrases by using AutoText. Add AutoText entries by selecting the big word or phrase, opening the **Edit** menu and choosing the **AutoText** command. Give it a short name and press the **Add** button. Now, in any document, just type the shortcut name and press **F3** and your shortcut will be replaced with the real thing.

➤ To look up an alternative for a word, select it, and then use the Thesaurus by opening the **Tools** menu and choosing the **Thesaurus** command (or press **Shift+F7**).

➤ To check your document for grammatical errors, open the **Tools** menu and choose **Grammar**.

Chapter 17

Previewing and Printing a Document

In This Chapter

➤ Fast ways to print your document

➤ Printing just part of the document

➤ Printing several documents or multiple copies at once

➤ Printing envelopes

➤ How previewing saves paper

In a truly paperless society, we humans will overcome our need to convert trees into newspaper and phone books, we'll distribute our communications electronically, and one can only guess what we'll do in the bathroom. But in a paperless society, what will we wrap the dishes with during a move?

That time is still far in the future, so you're going to have to print your documents for others to read. That means you still need a printer, some paper, and a connection between your computer and the printer. And you might need some patience. We've come a long way since Gutenburg—but he never had to worry about portrait versus landscape or printer memory overruns.

Printing Basics

It's always a good idea to save a document before you print it so there is no chance of losing your latest changes in case you run into printer errors or other problems. Click on the **Save** button on the Standard toolbar, or open the **File** menu and choose the **Save** command (you can also press **Ctrl+S** to save the current document).

Printing the active document is easy if you want to print the entire document, and if you want only one copy of it. Later in this chapter, you will learn how to be more selective in what you're printing. But for now, let's start with the basics.

To print a document with the mouse, just click on the **Print** button on the Standard toolbar. The active document will start printing according to the print defaults—the standard settings that specify the details of printing just one copy of the entire document. If you want to print more than one copy (or less than the entire document), you'll need to use the **File Print** command described next.

Check This Out...

Kill That Print Job! The only trick to deleting a print job before it reaches your printer is *finding* it. After Word has finished preparing your document for the printer, it will be temporarily stored in a printer folder. To see the printer folder, double-click on the picture of the printer in your Windows 95 Taskbar (it shows up on the opposite end of Start when a print job is pending). When the dialog box opens, select your print job by clicking on it and delete it by pressing the **Delete** key.

To print the current document using the keyboard, open the **File** menu and choose the **Print** command (or press **Ctrl+P**). A dialog box appears when you use this command, allowing you to change the print defaults (such as the number of copies you want). In later sections of this chapter, you will learn what each of these options is for—but if you only want to print one copy of the entire document, press the **Enter** key and that's it!

Here are some other ways to quickly print a document:

➤ If the document is already created and is displayed through any means on the Windows 95 desktop, you can click and drag the document around the desktop, and drop it on top of any printer icon. It will print automatically. You can find your printer icons by pressing the **Start** button on the Windows 95 Taskbar, opening the **Settings** menu, and choosing the **Printers** command. A window containing your current printers will be displayed.

➤ If you've located your document through the File Find dialog box, you don't even have to open it to print it. Just click on it with the right mouse button and choose the **Print** command from the resulting pop-up menu.

Printing Only Part of a Document

Society's progress slows to a crawl when someone reprints a 350-page document just because a few words changed on a single page. Do you know anyone like that? Help them save the forests by teaching them the technique of single-page printing.

You can learn to print only certain pages in a document if you wish. For example, maybe you only want to print that impressive table on page 17, or maybe you need to reprint corrections on a single page of a large document (sure saves paper!). Here's what to do.

Paper Shortage?
If the printer runs out of paper during printing, a dialog box will appear and tell you so. Load more paper into your printer and then press the **Retry** button.

Open the **File** menu and select the **Print** command (do not use the Print button on the toolbar because it prints, by default, all the pages of a document). You will see the new and improved Print dialog box.

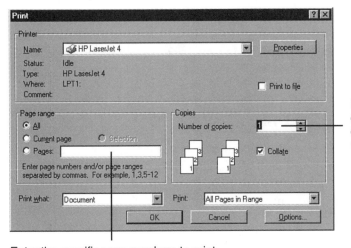

You can print only part of a document if you want.

Print more than one copy by changing this number.

Enter the specific page numbers to print.

You can print only the current page by choosing **Current Page** (or by pressing **Alt+E**) in the Page dialog box. Make sure you've actually moved to that page, however, or it's likely to print the first page of your document.

If you want a few pages printed from a large document and they are scattered throughout your document, you can do so as long as you know all of the page numbers you desire. In the Page range area of the Print dialog box, click to select the **Pages** option, and your

203

cursor will be placed in the position for entering your page numbers. Type a single page number (such as 7), a page range (for example, 37-42), or a combination of the two separated by commas (for example, 7,18,23-37,95-98,117). When you are finished, press the **OK** button, and your selection will print in the order you've typed them. Once again, it's a great way to save paper and wear and tear on your printer.

Printing Even Less Than a Page (Selected Text)

If you need to print only part of a page, or a graphic, table, or drawing appearing on a page, you can with Word for Windows 95. First, find the page containing the text or object you want to have printed and select the items using your favorite selection technique learned in Chapter 6. Now open the **File** menu and choose the **Print** command, or press **Ctrl+P**.

In the Print dialog box, you will find a new option called **Selection** in the **Print Range** area. Click to select that option and then press the **OK** button, and only the selected text will be printed. You can also print multiple copies by changing the number found in the **Number of Copies** box. If you happen to be making several copies of a many-paged document, you will probably want to click the **Collate** option. Collate means the printer will print the entire document, one after another, as many times as you desire. Without the collating option, the printer would print each page that number of times, and then move on to the next page, leaving it up to you to organize, or collate, your document copies.

Printing Multiple Documents at Once

If you need more than one copy of your document, Word can print it for you and save you time standing in the copier line. Start out by opening the **File** menu and selecting the **Print** command. (Do not use the Print button on the Standard toolbar because it only prints one copy of a document by default.) When the Print dialog box appears, type the number of copies you want under the **Copies** box. If you are using the keyboard, press **Alt+C** to move to **Copies**, and then type your desired number.

Watch It Collate!

Word for Windows 95 now uses animated graphics to explain how you can print multiple copies of a document. The animation appears in the Print dialog box, which you can open through the **File** menu with the **Print** command.

If you choose **Collate**, Word for Windows 95 will actually organize your printed mass by printing all of one copy first, and then all of the next. When you are completely finished, choose **OK**.

Printing Envelopes

Word makes it incredibly easy to prepare an envelope for a letter. The only thing you may find difficult is getting your printer to print the darned thing, so I'll give you some tips in a moment. First, the easy part.

➤ If you've included more than one address in your letter, start out by selecting the delivery address. If you didn't include an address in your letter (or if you included just the delivery address), that's okay—just skip this step.

➤ Open the **Tools** menu and select the **Envelopes and Labels** command (or press **Alt+T**, then E on your keyboard). When the Envelopes and Labels dialog box appears, if you didn't select an address earlier, you'll have to type one in the Delivery Address box.

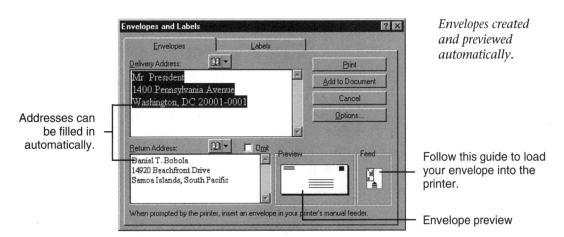

Envelopes created and previewed automatically.

Addresses can be filled in automatically.

Follow this guide to load your envelope into the printer.

Envelope preview

➤ Next, enter your return address by clicking in the **Return Address** box or by pressing **Tab**. (Your address may have appeared already; I'll explain how this magic trick was done in just a moment.) The first time you use this option, Word will ask whether you want to save the return address. Click on **Yes** or press **Enter** to save it. If you have special envelopes and you don't want to print a return address, then use the Omit check box. If you're using a keyboard, press **Alt+M** to check this box.

Two Ways to Print Multiple Copies If you have a printer that allows you to select the number of copies to print on some kind of control panel on the printer, you may want to use that option instead of having Word print the extra copies for you. You may find your printer is faster than Word is at this task.

➤ Before we print our envelope, let's check some of the options. Click on the **Options** button or press **Alt+O**, and the Envelope Options dialog box appears. If you want to, you can change the font for both the delivery and the return address. Click on the appropriate options, or press **Alt+F** for the delivery address and **Alt+O** for the return address.

Select different envelope sizes here.

Options for specifying fonts and envelope sizes.

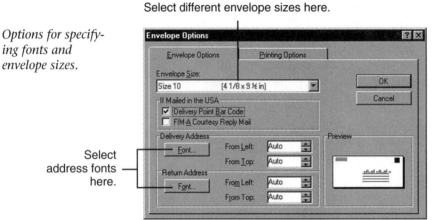

Select address fonts here.

➤ Finally, check the envelope size. Make sure that the correct size is selected in the Envelope Size box. To change sizes, click on the down arrow to open the list box or press **Alt+S**. Select an envelope size by clicking on it (or highlighting it with the arrow keys and pressing **Enter**).

Now you can stick an envelope in your printer, a process called *feeding*—a word that was probably coined shortly after a printer *ate* the first print job. Which way does the envelope go in? Follow the pictorial on the Envelopes and Labels dialog box. In the lower-right side, there's a box labeled **Feed**. There's a little picture showing the correct placement of feeding your envelope to your printer. If you still have trouble, refer to your printer manual or a local geek.

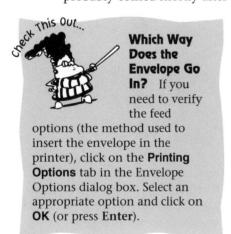

Which Way Does the Envelope Go In? If you need to verify the feed options (the method used to insert the envelope in the printer), click on the **Printing Options** tab in the Envelope Options dialog box. Select an appropriate option and click on **OK** (or press **Enter**).

You can print the envelope now, or you can print it later. If you want to print the envelope now, use the **Print** button (or the **Alt+P** key combination). Use the **Add To Document** button to print the envelope later, usually at the same time you print the document. To print just the envelope at some later date, print page 0 (that's right, zero) only.

Quick Tips for Printing Envelopes

Everyone likes to receive mail in envelopes with clear and distinct addressing, but nobody likes to stick envelopes in a typewriter to create them. They get all curled up, and it's difficult to keep them straight. Your computer printer can help. Most printers today have the ability to print addresses on envelopes, as long as you follow the directions included with your printer and your word processor.

If you have a laser printer:

➤ Unless you are very patient, you'll benefit from having an addition to your printer called an *envelope feeder*. If you don't have one, check your printer manual for instructions on how to feed an envelope through the straightest possible path in your printer, to avoid excessive curling and twisting.

➤ Check out the little Feed icon in the Envelopes and Labels dialog box. It shows you how the envelope is supposed to be inserted into your printer; whether it should be centered or against one of the edges.

➤ Most important of all, don't skimp on quality. Buy envelopes that are made for a laser printer. Other envelopes practically melt from the heat, and really gum up the works.

If you have a dot-matrix printer, you can print an envelope like this:

➤ Line up the left edge of the envelope against the left edge of the paper feed.

➤ Move the paper feed so the top edge of the envelope is even with the print head. Word will move the envelope up about half an inch before it prints anything, so don't worry that your address will fall off the edge.

Techno Talk
blah blah
blah bla
blah bl

Bar Coding Your Envelopes May Save Postage Costs

If your printer can print graphics, Word can print two types of codes on an envelope: the POSTNET bar code, which is a machine-readable representation of a U.S. ZIP Code and the delivery address; and the FIM code, which identifies the front of a courtesy reply envelope.

To print the POSTNET (Postal Numeric Encoding Technique) bar code, select the **Delivery Point Bar Code** check box in the Envelope Options dialog box. To print a Facing Identification Mark (FIM) in addition to the POSTNET bar code, select the **FIM-A Courtesy Reply Mail** check box. Word cannot print a Facing Identification Mark or POSTNET bar code if you use a daisy-wheel printer. It is expecting a laser printer.

Killing a Print Job (Make It Stop!)

Nobody ever prints a job accidentally, right? I do, and the great new features in Word for Windows 95 make it really easy to send too much to the printer. For instance, I often have many documents open at once, in a futile attempt to accomplish more work. Sometimes I forget if I've pressed the Print button, and press it again. Or sometimes my printer isn't turned on, and I accidentally print the same document four or five times (in frustration) before I realize it. Then I feel really dumb for about two seconds. Then I panic when I realize my printer is about to waste lots of paper printing those extra copies. There are several ways to delete those other undesired print jobs, and this section explains them.

Check This Out...

What's a Print Job?
The term *print job* refers to the collection of bits and bytes sent to the printer. It's actually more than just the words and formatting of your document. It includes control information unique to the type of printer you own, including details on print options chosen at the time of printing.

Watch the status bar at the bottom of the Word for Windows 95 screen the next time you print a document. For a short period of time, you will notice a little printer icon with pages flowing out of it. Each page is numbered, matching the document being printed. Word is processing your document in preparation for printing. There's nothing you can really do to stop this process, so let it finish. When your document is finished processing, the printer icon disappears.

If the little printer icon has disappeared, you know that Word has finished processing the document and has sent it to the appropriate print folder in Windows 95. It remains in the print folder until your printer is available to accept it, and then print it. While your print job sits in this folder, you have the opportunity to delete it if you wish.

To find and display your print folder, double-click on the picture of the printer in your Windows 95 Taskbar (it shows up on the right side of the Taskbar, next to the clock). When the dialog box opens, you will see a list of all documents scheduled to print. Click to select the name of your print job (most of the time, there is only one document in this list anyway, so it's easy). You can delete this print job by pressing the **Delete** key.

If your printer has already started printing the document when you ask to delete it, Word will display a message on your screen. It warns that the job may be in progress. Click the **OK** button because you want to delete the job anyway, regardless if a few pages have already printed.

What? It's Still Printing?

If your printer has lots of memory (meaning you paid a lot of money for it), you may find the print folder empty, even though you just sent the print job. That's because your printer picked up the entire thing and stored it inside the printer. Still want to stop that print job? Now you have two choices: the right way and the wrong way.

The wrong way is to turn off your laser printer. Sure, it erases that print job from memory, but it also fouls up the printer guts—stuck paper, loose toner, sticky mess—you get the idea. And you have to go inside the printer to clean it up. Once more for emphasis: *Don't ever turn off your printer while it's printing.*

The right way is to find and push the correct button on your printer (but not the power button). The Reset button is usually best and has fastest results. Press it to kill the print job. If you don't have a Reset button or if it doesn't work, you should take the printer off-line, and you must find the correct button on your printer to do this. It's usually a button labeled "On-line," which it is if the light next to it is turned on. Push the button to see if the light goes out (or turns a different color). The printer is now off-line. Off-line means the printer won't accept any more print jobs, and will also stop printing the current job. Soon. Be patient. It may continue to print a few pages, and that's okay. When it finally stops, you know it's safe to turn off your printer to get rid of any lingering evidence of your print job.

Look Before You Print: Using Print Preview

Before you print your document, you should look at it in either Print Preview mode or Page Layout view. These two viewing modes show you what your document will look like when printed, so you can make sure everything is the way you want it before you print. In Print Preview, it's a bit more difficult to make any last-minute text changes, so choose the viewing mode that best suits your needs. Lots of help on the different viewing possibilities can be found in Chapter 19.

To change to Print Preview mode, open the **File** menu and select the **Print Preview** command. You can also press **Ctrl+F2** to preview a document.

The purpose of Print Preview mode is to get a good visual feeling for what your document will look like on paper. Don't worry that the text is way too small to read. This is an artistic view. You can quickly find margin problems, pictures that should be moved, or columns that are too crowded. Press the **Multiple Pages** button to get an even more impressive view of a large document, by viewing how articles and graphics are balanced and flowing across pages.

View Ruler

Force the document to print on one page.

Toggle to Full Screen view.

Print your document.

Return to Normal view.

Preview before printing to avoid surprises.

Enlarge a portion so you can see it better.

View a single page

View multiple pages

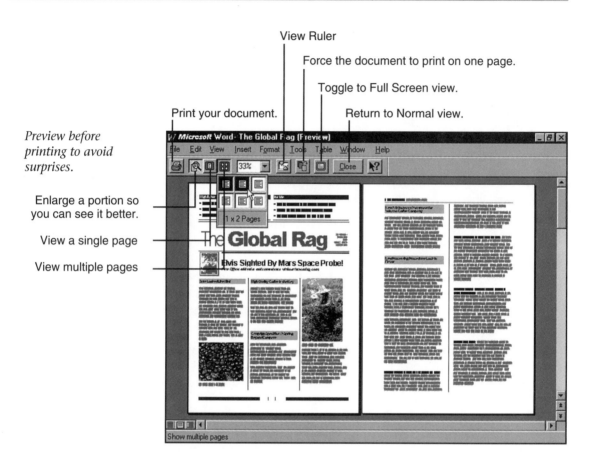

Shrink It to Fit! To reduce page count in a document by one so you can prevent a small portion of a document from spilling onto another page, click the **Shrink To Fit** button in the Print Preview screen.

You can do lots of interesting things in Print Preview, as you can see by the preceding figure. To print, just click the **Print** button. To edit text, click on the tiny magnifying glass, then click within the document. After you zoom in on the area you clicked, press the **Magnifier** button again— the cursor changes into a regular mouse cursor, ready for editing. Edit until you are tired, then click on the **Magnifying** button again—and the text area again—to return to regular Print Preview.

To return to whatever view you were using before you previewed, click the **Close** button. You can also change to any other view by clicking the appropriate button on the horizontal scroll bar.

Adjust Your Margins in Print Preview

A quick formatting adjustment is possible, and appropriate, in Print Preview mode. I say appropriate because it's the best way to see a whole margin before printing a document. If it needs a slight adjustment, you can make it instantly and see the results before you print.

With your document opened on the screen, move into Print Preview mode by opening the **File** menu and choosing the **Print Preview** command. Make sure the Rulers are displayed. You can display the Rulers by pressing the **View Ruler** button on the **Print Preview** toolbar. To move the left or right page margin, point to a margin boundary on the horizontal ruler. When the pointer changes to a double-headed arrow, drag the margin boundary back and forth a little. You will see the whole margin change on your screen. Drop the margin in the desired new location. Text will automatically flow on the page to accommodate the new space.

To move the top or bottom page margin, point to a margin boundary on the vertical ruler. When the pointer changes to a double-headed arrow, drag the margin boundary up or down. When you drop the pointer, you designate the new margin. Yes, even **Ctrl+Z** (or the **Undo** button) works in Print Preview mode in case things don't look as good after changing them.

Making a Printed Document Match What Appears on the Screen

You may ask yourself someday, "Why does my document print differently than it looks on my screen?" The industry buzzword for the desired phenomenon of printing exactly as it appears is called *WYSIWYG* (pronounced wizzy-wig). It stands for *What You See Is What You Get*, and it's usually what people want. So if your printed document looks different, you aren't getting WYSIWYG, and if this is causing you pain you might try to fix the situation with the tips offered below. Fortunately, Word for Windows 95 has almost perfected the technique for printing exactly what you see, but you may have to follow a few steps to confirm it.

Your screen display will most closely match the printed display when magnification is set at 100% in the Zoom dialog box. You can find the **Zoom Control** button on your Standard toolbar. It displays the current magnification, and it's easy to change to another magnification. You might want to change to a higher magnification when viewing small fonts, or change to a lower magnification when designing a page layout, or placing large graphics on a page.

To change the magnification, click the down arrow attached to the **Zoom Control** button on the Standard toolbar. The pop-down menu will provide a large selection of magnification sizes, just click on the setting you want and your screen will be adjusted automatically. Notice that one of the magnifications is not a percent, but is called Page Width. Choosing this option fits the margins of your page exactly to the size of your screen. It's often the best choice because it provides the largest viewing size without scrolling text off the left or right sides.

If you use *TrueType* fonts, Word for Windows 95 uses the same font to display text on the screen and to print (the screen fonts provide a very close approximation of printed characters). That's good because your printer will have to print the same as what you see. You can distinguish TrueType font names listed in the Font pull-down box on the Formatting toolbar by the TT symbol next to the name. Where do you get them? TrueType fonts are automatically installed when you set up Windows 95.

The other two types of fonts you may see are called *screen* or *printer fonts*. There's a little picture of a printer next to a printer font. These fonts are used only for on-screen display; the printer uses different fonts to print your document. If a matching font is not available or if your printer driver does not provide screen font information, Windows chooses the screen font that most closely resembles the printer font. That means there's a good chance you will not print what you see.

The Least You Need to Know

Sometimes getting your document to print can be irritating, but the whole process will go a bit smoother if you remember these things:

➤ Before you print, save your document by clicking on the **Save** button on the Standard toolbar.

➤ To print one copy of all pages of the document, click on the **Print** button on the Standard toolbar.

➤ Use the **Print** command on the **File** menu to print selected text or individual pages within a document. You can also use this same command to print multiple copies of your document.

➤ Use the **Envelopes and Labels** command on the **Tools** menu to prepare an envelope for your letter.

➤ Before you print your document, you may want to view it first, either in Page Layout view or in Print Preview mode.

➤ If you want to cancel a print job or change the priority of a print job, use the new high-performance Print Manager of Windows 95 to do it.

Chapter 18

Start Your Own Newspaper: Desktop Publishing Techniques

In This Chapter

➤ Fast and easy newsletters

➤ Creating columns like a newspaper

➤ Using WordArt and Draw

➤ How to create a drop cap

➤ Special character formatting

Read all about it! All the tips that are fit to print (the ones related to newsletters, anyway) are located in this chapter. And these features aren't just for newspapers alone—you'll find uses for some of these features in all your documents, especially formatting your text into columns, flowing text around graphics, and using some unusual character formatting tools.

Instant Newsletter Guaranteed!

You can't go wrong with a Wizard on your side. Although this entire chapter covers details about creating your own newsletter, here's an example that might be enough to satisfy your requirements. Word for Windows 95 comes with a *Newsletter Wizard* that steps you through the creation of something good enough to sell on the street corner.

Where's the Wizard? If you don't see the Newsletter Wizard, you can install it using the Setup program for Word for Windows 95. Choose the option to install **Wizards and Templates**.

Start a new document by opening the **File** menu and choosing the **New** command. You must use the *menu*, and *not* the **New** button on the Standard toolbar, to find the Wizard. In the File New dialog box, click the **Publications** tab to bring it to the front. Double-click on the **Newsletter Wizard**.

Answer these questions to customize your newsletter.

Instant newsletter success using the Wizard.

You can always move forward or backward with these buttons.

Working with a Wizard is kind of like ordering fast food at the drive-through. You don't see what's behind the wall creating your lunch. You get bombarded with lots of simple questions like, "Do you want lettuce? Tomato? Fries? Milkshake? Change?" All the answers you provide are used to create your meal, and determine how happy you are with that meal. Wizards do the same thing. They help you create a beautiful document by asking a few simple questions.

When the Wizard starts, you'll see an attractive finished newsletter in the Preview box. Your first question is if you prefer the Classic or Modern style. I haven't the foggiest idea, but since the **Classic** button is selected, it must be Classic. Click the **Modern** option and watch the change in your preview box. These changes are subtle, some parts moving around, but it is a different style. Click the **Next** button to continue to the next question. That's all there is to talking to your Wizard.

Continue answering the following questions. Notice that a default appears in all of them, so you can easily get through the process by pressing nothing more than the **Next** button.

➤ How many columns do you want?

➤ What's the name of the newsletter?

➤ How many pages do you think it will be?

➤ Would you like any of these options (Table of Contents, Fancy First Letters, Date, Volume and Issue)?

When you click the **Finish** button on the last Wizard dialog box, a completely formatted professional-looking newsletter will appear on your screen.

Fast and Simple Newsletter in Seconds.

Notice that Page Layout view is used to see columns.

With the formatting completed, you are left with the task of entering the contents of your newsletter articles. You can click directly in the heading of a column and type your headline, then click in the text area to type your news article. You never have to worry about paragraph formatting because it has already been created for you.

When you save your newsletter, it will be saved as a regular document, albeit one with loads of formatting. The point is that it's no longer related to the Wizard that created it. You can use the Wizard over and over again to create different newsletters.

If you always choose the same options in the Newsletter Wizard, you can save even more time by opening a previously created newsletter and saving it with a new name. Then you can simply make changes to it. Or if you want to get fancy, you can create your own custom newsletter template. The details for creating your own template are found in Chapter 21.

Doing Columns

Which would you rather read, a supermarket tabloid claiming that the president is Bigfoot, or *War and Peace*? Probably the tabloid, but not for the reason you may think (the president just isn't that hairy). Newspapers in general, along with magazines and newsletters, align their text in multiple columns on a page. Why? It's easier to *read* that way. You don't have to move your eyes as much, or turn your head, shoulders, or entire body to keep up with the text running across the pages of a book.

Creating Columns

Believe it or not, you are already using columns in your documents. It just happens to be one large column that stretches the width of the margins. At any point in your document, you can change the number of columns by creating a section. Without sections, your document will appear with a consistent number of columns throughout.

When you add columns to a document, the width of the columns is adjusted automatically so they fit between the margins. For instance, if you add three columns, the width of your paper is divided into three equal parts. You can also decide to create column widths that are uneven, if you want a different effect.

Check This Out...

Column or Table? A different type of column is the *parallel column*, which is just a fancy way of saying *table*. With a table, you read across (instead of down) several columns of text and numbers. If you prefer to have a table in your document, see Chapter 12.

The absolute fastest way to create columns on your page is with your mouse. Click the **Columns** button on the **Standard** toolbar. Drag to select the number of columns you want, and then release the mouse button. This method is a bit restrictive because you're limited to up to six equally-spaced columns (in portrait mode, or up to nine columns in landscape mode), but that's usually good enough for most people.

To learn more about what's happening, you should use the Columns dialog box to create your columns. There's hardly any limit to what you can do with columns when you create them this way.

Start by moving the insertion point to the section in the document where you'd like to change the number of columns. Open the **Format** menu and select **Columns**. If you prefer to use the keyboard, press **Alt+O** and then C. Select any of the preset column patterns by clicking on them, or by pressing the **Alt** key plus the underlined letter. As an alternative, you can enter the number of columns you want in the Number of Columns text box. If you need to create a section break so you don't affect earlier text, select the number of columns you want and then choose **This Point Forward** in the Apply To list box. You'll see a preview of your choices in the Preview screen. When you are finished, press **OK** and you will return to your document, now formatted in columns.

If you want to create columns of different widths, remove the check from the **Equal Column Width** check box by clicking on it (or press **Alt+E**). Now you can enter the width and spacing desired for each column. The numbers you enter are in the default unit of measure, in this case, inches. Try entering different numbers and watch the effect in the Preview box.

Editing Columns (Making Them Bigger or Smaller)

Your columns should be wide enough to have at least a few words on each line for readability. If you find you're averaging less than one, you do have a problem.

To change the width of your columns using your mouse, first expose your horizontal ruler. If your ruler isn't visible, open the **View** menu and make sure the **Ruler** is checked by clicking on it. To change the width of a column, drag the column marker on the horizontal ruler to the right or left, until the column meets your approval.

You can also use the keyboard to change the column widths. Open the **Format** menu and choose the **Columns** command. Press **Alt+I** to move to Width, and enter a new measurement. If column widths are even, the other columns will adjust automatically. If you are using uneven columns, use the **Tab** key to change the width of other columns. By pressing **Alt+S**, you can change the spacing between columns.

Drag a column marker to change width of column.

Changing a column's width.

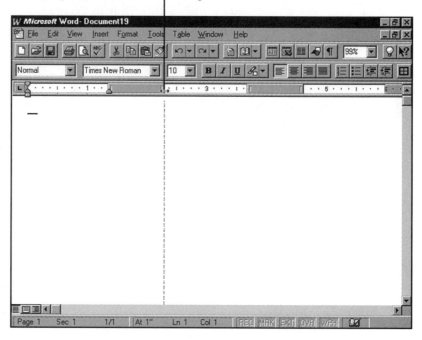

Viewing Your Columns

Each viewing mode displays columns a little differently, with each view offering its own advantages. You will learn more about different views in Chapter 19, but for now understand that the most common view won't do. At least when it comes to columns, the Normal view (most common all-purpose view) doesn't do a good job of displaying columns. You need to change your view.

To change to a better view for viewing columns, press the **Page Layout view** button on the horizontal scroll bar. You can also open the **View** menu and choose the **Page Layout** command.

Within either view, you can zoom in to get a closer look at text or zoom out to get a bigger overall picture of your work. Just click the **Zoom** box down arrow on the Standard toolbar and select a magnification from the drop-down list box. You can also zoom by opening the **View** menu and choosing the **Zoom** command.

In Page Layout view, columns appear as they will print.

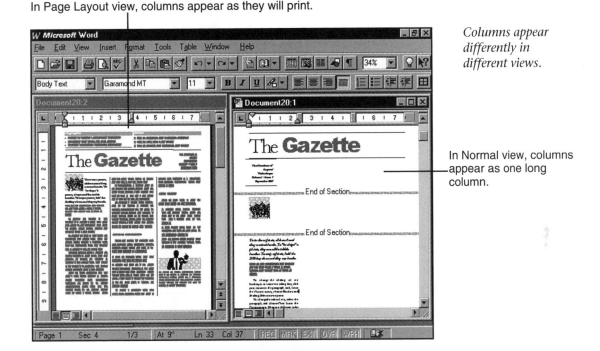

Columns appear differently in different views.

In Normal view, columns appear as one long column.

Dividing Your Columns with Lines

Sometimes it helps to keep those eyes where they belong. Truckers call it white line fever when you start hugging the middle of the road. Reading can be boring sometimes, just like driving, but instead of blasting the radio to stay awake (or improving your writing), you can draw lines between your columns of text to help contain them. It's especially helpful when your columns are close together.

Remember that you should be in Page Layout view when working with columns, and especially when creating these lines. Place the insertion point into the section where you want to add lines. Open the **Format** menu and choose **Columns**. Then click the **Line Between** check box (or press **Alt+B**). Using the **Apply To** box, select how much of the document you want to the line to appear in.

Vertical lines make your columns easier to read.

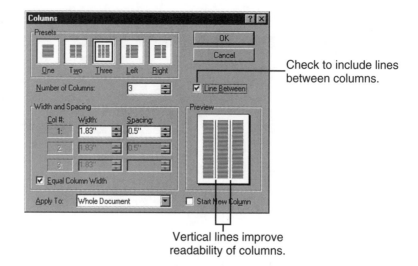

Check to include lines between columns.

Vertical lines improve readability of columns.

Other Ways to Draw Lines

The Line Between option will place lines between all the columns in that section. There is no way to place a line only between two columns in a three-column section using this option. You can always create a line yourself by using the Drawing toolbar and place it between just two of the columns. Word for Windows 95 does a decent job of creating newsletters and columns, but other products exist and specialize in the subject. Examples of these types of products are Microsoft Publisher, Ventura Publisher, or PageMaker.

Straightening Out the Ends of Those Columns

Take a look at the last page of your newly-columned document. When real newspapers or magazines can't fill a page, at least they balance the remaining text across the multiple columns. You can, too—and it's easy. Just insert a section break at the end of the document. Open the **Insert** menu and select **Break**. Under Section Breaks, choose **Continuous**, and then click the **OK** button.

You Want to Add Pictures?

Sure you want to add pictures to your newsletter or columns. The subject is so fascinating that it has its own chapter in this book! Turn to Chapter 11 to learn more about inserting graphics and pictures into any document, including newsletters.

You might also be wondering how to get text to flow around a picture or graphic. That's in Chapter 11, also. The secret is to make certain you create a frame to hold your graphic. Then text will flow around it. Without a frame, text skips entire rows that contain any portion of a graphic, so you're left with gaping holes everywhere except the want ads. They don't have pictures.

Playing with Your Words (Special Character Formatting)

Work hard. Play hard. Sleep in. Being the life of the party is hard work. So is coming up with ideas to make your words more interesting. The tools to accomplish this task, however, are easy to use and work quite well in Word for Windows 95. You'll now learn how to take your best stuff and make it even better.

Dropping Your Caps (but Not in Your Soup)

You've seen them all over the place, in magazines, books, and newspapers. Big letters. Really big. But only one, and it's the *first* letter of the *first* word of the reading. They have a name for this kind of thing. It's called a *Drop Cap*.

The Drop Cap used to be a special effect reserved for highly talented artists, editors, and monks. Now with Word for Windows 95, mere mortals can create them in a fraction of the time once required. Not much to learn here except how to choose the Drop Cap command from a menu.

To create a Drop Cap, move to the paragraph where you want to place it, then open the **Format** menu and choose the **Drop Cap** command. You can also press **Alt+O** and then **D**. In the Drop Cap dialog box, you can change the font and point size in the text boxes provided. Then choose whether you want it **Dropped** or **In Margin**. I never remember the difference, and that's why Word includes the great Preview box, so you can sample the choice before you apply it to your document. You can also change the number of **Lines to Drop** by clicking on it or by pressing **Alt+L**. This determines the size of the Drop Cap letter. You can even change the distance between the Drop Cap and the paragraph text by clicking on **Distance from Text**, or press **Alt+T**. Then press the **OK** button (or press **Enter**) to close the dialog box and gaze at your creation.

Staying Young and Playful with WordArt

Have you ever gotten so mad at a word that you wanted to twist it, stretch it, crunch it, or gut it all over your page? Relax, they're only words. Find another. Or if the idea appeals to you, use WordArt, which actually helps accomplish these tasks.

Fast and easy examples of WordArt.

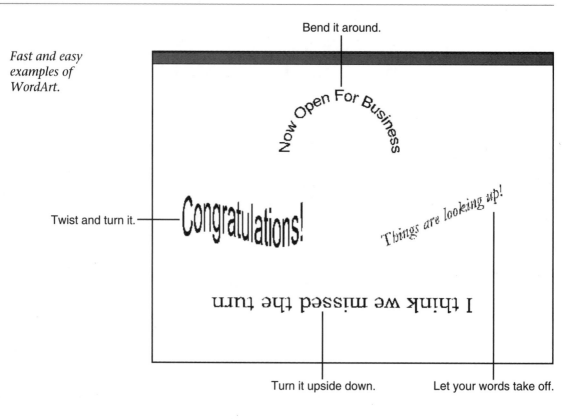

Bend it around.

Twist and turn it.

Turn it upside down.

Let your words take off.

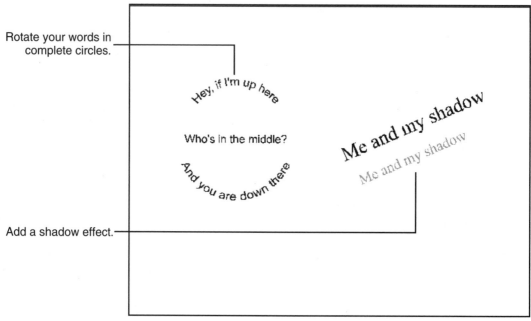

Rotate your words in complete circles.

Add a shadow effect.

WordArt is a tool that lets you manipulate words artistically, and it goes beyond the normal text attributes you learned about in Chapter 7. Take a look at some examples, and you will agree that they could have a place in your newsletter:

To give WordArt a try, place the insertion point where you want the creation. Open the **Insert** menu and choose **Object**. Scroll down the Object Type list until you find **Microsoft WordArt 2.0**. Click **OK**, and you will find sample text to get you started, along with a new toolbar.

Instead of explaining each toolbar button, it's probably better to just experience clicking each one and watching the effect on the sample text. Click in the text box and type your own text to see the real thing. When you are finished, click the **Update Display** button to see the WordArt object become part of your document. It's an object, however, and not text, so you manipulate it like a picture. Click on it once to make the handles appear. Drag the handles any way you want to change the shape and size of the text. Double-clicking the object brings back the WordArt toolbar in case you want to further enhance your art. Selected WordArt objects can also be moved around the screen and around your document. When you are finished, be sure to save your document.

Show Me Now! *Check This Out...* If WordArt doesn't update the display to reflect your choices, click on **Update Display** or press **Alt+U**.

Drawing Your Own Pictures

Word for Windows 95 comes with a Drawing toolbar you can use to create simple objects like lines, circles, and other shapes. You can also fill these objects with colors or patterns, and place them behind text or in the margins.

To display the Drawing toolbar, click on the **Drawing** button on the Standard toolbar. You can also open the **View** menu, select the **Toolbars** command, and select **Drawing** from the list. Press the **OK** button to close the dialog box.

Perfect Squares And Circles *Check This Out...* To create a perfect square or circle, hold down the **Shift** key as you drag the mouse.

Don't worry about the large number of buttons; you probably only need a few, but you should try many of them. Let your mouse float directly on top of these buttons, and the description of each button will appear. To use a tool, click on it. Then use your mouse to create the object or effect in your document. Click to establish the upper left corner of the object. Drag downward and to the right, and the object will form as you drag. Release the mouse button to create the object.

 **To use any of the first five drawing tools,** click on it first. Move to the drawing area and click to establish the first point. Move to the second point and click. Move to the third point (if appropriate) and click, and so on.

 To change the style of a drawn line, click on the **Line Style** tool and select an option. You can even do this after an object is created—simply click on the object to select it, then click on the **Line Style** tool to change its border. You can change the color of the border with the **Line Color** tool.

 To change the inside color of an object, click on the **Fill Color** tool. If you've already drawn the object, simply select it, and then use the **Fill Color** tool to change its color.

 To select multiple objects, use the **Select Drawing Objects** button. Click and drag over several objects to round them up in your selection.

 To place an object on top of another one, just drag it on top. If there's more than one object in a stack, use the **Bring to Front** tool to bring an object to the top (called the *foreground*).

 To push an object under another one, click on the object and then click on the **Send to Back** tool.

  To place an object under text, click on the **Text to Front** tool. To place an object over text, drag it on top or click on the **Text to Back** tool.

Entering Strange Characters That Aren't on Your Keyboard

Sometimes you need to enter a character that isn't on your keyboard, such as the trademark symbol, the cents sign, or an umlaut. Word for Windows 95 makes it easy to insert these symbols wherever you need them. Just open the **Insert** menu and choose the **Symbol** command (or press **Alt+I** and then **S** on the keyboard).

In the dialog box that appears, double-click on any symbol to insert it into your document. If you want to insert additional symbols, simply repeat the process. To close the dialog box, press **Esc** (Escape key) or press the **Close** button.

Boxing Your Words, and Shading Them Well

Warning labels had trouble in the 1950s and 1960s. Nobody was reading them. Dying continued to be the major cause of death around the world. But then, almost like magic, someone decided to draw a box around a warning label. People started reading them. Lives were saved. And now you can do the same (draw a box, that is—not save lives).

You don't need a warning to draw a box. You can draw a box around anything. It will call attention to whatever is inside the box. Need more attention? Shade your box, or else wear baggy lime-green pants and cluck like a chicken.

Drawing a Box around Your Words

Start easy. Write some words first. Then box them up. You won't find the word *box* anywhere, however, because Word refers to them as *borders*. Borders are lines placed on any (or all) of the four sides of a text paragraph, the cells in a table, or a graphic like a picture or a chart.

Placing a border around text or a graphic is fairly easy. Start by selecting the text or table cells using your favorite method (all of the methods are described in Chapter 6). A graphic (a picture or a chart) can be selected by clicking on it.

After making your selection, open the **Format** menu and select **Borders and Shading**. On the left side of the dialog box, you see a make-believe page with two paragraphs. The choices you make in this box will be reflected in this little page as a sample. If you want to add a box (a border around all four sides), click on **Box** under Presets. To get rid of a box, click on **None**. Really upscale boxes have a shadow effect, giving your words a three-dimensional appearance. You can try it by clicking **Shadow**. If you don't have a mouse, you can do the same with the keyboard by pressing **Alt** plus the underlined letter of the option desired.

If you do nothing more than click on **Box** and press **OK**, you may be disappointed. Sure, you'll get a box, but the line quality may have you shopping for something better. You can choose a better line for yourself right inside this dialog box. Clicking on any of the sample lines will demonstrate how that line will look in the sample page. If you like what you see, press the **OK** button. If not, try another line type. Or, you can try another line style.

Easier Than Ever to Make Horizontal Borders!
Horizontal borders can now be created quickly with a secret shortcut in Word 7. Just press three or more special characters in a row and then press the **Enter** key, and a perfect horizontal border will appear. The special symbols are === (equal), —— (dash), or ___ (underline).

There's a Border Toolbar That Might Be Easier If you want to apply borders and shading to a lot of areas within your document, use the Borders toolbar. To display the toolbar, open the **View** menu, select **Toolbars**, and then select **Borders**. You can also click the *right* mouse button while pointing to any displayed toolbar, and select **Borders** from the list.

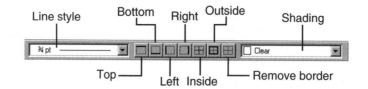

The border toolbar buttons.

Maybe you're itching for a partial box, one without a top or bottom, or maybe without a left or right side. You can do this with the same dialog box. Just click on the side you don't want in the **Border** area. For example, to get rid of the bottom of the box, click on the bottom border line. You'll notice that when you do this, the arrows marking both ends of that border will disappear. These arrows indicate which borders have lines. You can even click between paragraphs to add a border between them. When you're through making your selections, click on **OK**.

Shading Really Important Boxes

Too many boxes scare away sanitation workers. You should avoid them in your document, also. But if you really need to have several, and still want to call special attention to one or more of them, try *shading*. In fact, forget about how many boxes you may have; shading is so great that you can do it anywhere!

It's important to understand that shading is the background color of your text. You'll want to know that in case you plan to include a picture or two because any picture existing in a shaded area will disappear on you. It's still there, of course; it's just hidden behind the shading.

Carefully select the text or table cells you want to shade. The shading will occur exactly where you highlight (unlike boxes, which were still square, even if a paragraph was indented). Then open the **Format** menu and select **Borders and Shading**. Click on the **Shading** tab or press **Ctrl+Tab** to bring **Shading** to the front.

Use the **Shading** box to select the percentage of gray that you want. If your letters are small, choose a lighter percentage, like 10 percent. Larger letters can withstand larger percentages to become more striking and yet remain visible. The result is really determined by the type of printer you have and how well it handles shading; therefore, you may need to experiment until you get the results you like. Use a font with clean, crisp lettering, such as Arial, or apply bold formatting for better results. Now press the **OK** button to return to your document and witness the shading of your selection.

Headlining with Fancy Titles

It's probably time to put a *banner* on this thing and go home. A banner is a *headline* or a major title across the top of a page. It's usually on the first of your document. If you already tried this on a multiple-column section, you may have been frustrated if you couldn't figure out how to spread the title over the multiple columns. The answer is coming up.

Banners should be fancy. If you haven't used any of the fancy character formatting capabilities of Word yet, now is the time. How else will you capture the attention of your audience, unless they see a startling and teasing title like *Elvis Seen with Mars Probe* or *Pumpkin Crushes Building*?

Type the words first. Short and interesting. They will become your heading text, which can span multiple columns. Now change to Page Layout view (open the **View** menu and choose the **Page Layout** command). Now select the heading text, using your favorite selecting technique learned in Chapter 6. Click the Columns button on the Standard toolbar and drag to select a single column. Your heading will appear in what's basically a single column above multiple columns.

Next click the **Font Size** box, also on the **Formatting** toolbar (in fact, all of these tools are found on the **Formatting** toolbar, so you will get to know them well). Pick a large number, like 26 or so. If the text flows to the next line, it's too big; try something a little smaller. Although you can justify this text to spread evenly across the page (using the **Justify** button), it's better to choose the proper size with natural font spacing.

Oh, yes; next is the choice of the actual font. Click the **Font** box to see the many fonts you can choose from. Scroll down the list and try different fonts to see what's available. Make sure your text is selected before trying this, or else you won't see much. You should be able to find a font that matches your mood or style. Don't forget the basic font attributes of **Bold** and *Italic* that can also help the appearance. You may even want to shade the background, put a border around it, or both, using the skills you learned earlier in this chapter.

Adding a Caption to a Picture or Table

Adding a caption to a figure allows you to make a simple statement that summarizes your point. Adding a caption to a figure or table is easy. Start by clicking on the object to select it. Open the **Insert** menu and select the **Caption** command. Select the type of label you want from the **Label** list. You'll see a label such as "Figure 1" appear in the **Caption** text box. If you want to add something more, just type in the space after the label. Click the **OK** button (or press **Enter**) when you're done, and that figure will have a caption.

Adding captions can help clarify pictures or tables.

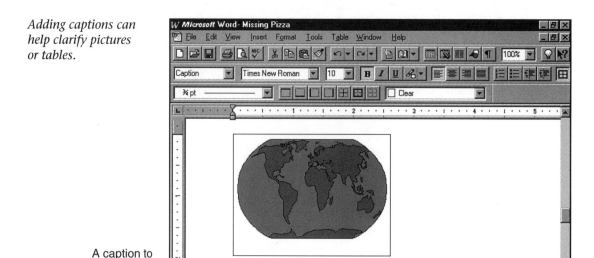

A caption to summarize the figure.

Figure 1 Our New Sales Territory

Using the **Numbering** button, you can change the numbering system of your figures to include chapter numbers, for example, or create your own label, by using the **New Label** button. You can even create automatic captions when you insert certain items into your document that increment automatically. Just click on **AutoCaption** or press **Alt+A** and click an item to select for automatic captioning.

Callout and Touch That Figure

You can also add a note of explanation for a figure or table using another tool called the *callout*. The callout tool is a button on the **Drawing** toolbar. To display the Drawing toolbar, click the **Drawing** button on the **Standard** toolbar.

To add a callout anywhere inside your document, press the **Callout** tool button on the **Drawing** toolbar. Now move to your document area and click at the point where you want the callout line to begin, then drag to create the callout. Enter your text and click outside the callout box when you are finished.

To add a border or change the callout style, click on the **Format Callout** tool on the **Drawing** toolbar and select your options. To change the angle of the callout, click on the text box and drag it to a new location. To change the size of the text box, click on a corner of the box and drag it to its new size. You can also change the color of the callout line and the text box border by using the **Line Color** tool.

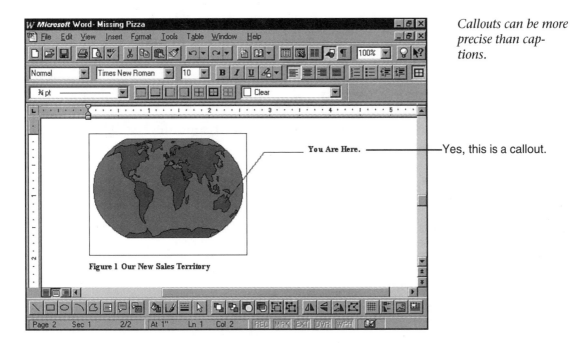

Callouts can be more precise than captions.

Yes, this is a callout.

Printing Your Newspaper

You can publish yourself with little effort or cost, and the quality will equal or exceed many professionally produced newsletters for which people pay good money. Just compose your thoughts in columns with pictures, boxes and borders, give it a title, and send it to the laser printer. If you want to impress garden vegetables, you can also use a dot-matrix printer.

Previewing Prevents Paper Cuts

Good thing that in the last chapter you learned how to preview a document before you print it. Desktop publishing is one of those things that you can't get a sense for until you see the whole page. Maybe it's too crowded, unbalanced, and confusing, and that's what life is like—but your document doesn't have to be. Take a good visual browse at it before you print to catch the bigger mishaps.

Changing Your Margins in Print Preview

It's very common in desktop publishing to change margins based on the amount of space your words take up. While you are in this print preview state, remember the easy way to change margins. All you do is drag a margin handle to its new location (point at the margin handle, then press and hold the left mouse button as you move your mouse). As you drag, you'll see an "invisible" guideline to help you get it right. When the margin is set, release the mouse button, and the text will flow automatically.

The Least You Need to Know

If you ever need to make your document look more interesting, this is the chapter to review. Here are some of the highlights:

➤ Newsletters are easiest to create using the Newsletter Wizard. Find this wizard by opening the **File** menu and choosing the **New** command. Click the **Publications** tab to see the Newsletter Wizard, and double-click the icon to start it.

➤ To create columns in your document, press the **Columns** button on the Standard toolbar and drag to select the number of columns you desire.

➤ To create special effects with text, use WordArt, which is available as a button on the Standard toolbar.

➤ You can create simple drawings for your documents using the Drawing toolbar in Word. Click on the **Drawing** button to display the toolbar, then click on a tool and drag to create an object.

➤ To insert a special character into your document, open the **Insert** menu and choose the **Symbol** command.

➤ Create a callout for a table, graph, or figure by clicking on the **Callout** button on the Drawing toolbar.

Part 4
Customizing Word to Work for You

You aren't a default kind of person, are you? Sure, standard settings minimize pain for most people, but they can also slow you down at times. Who picked 1.25 inch margins, anyway? And I'm allergic to Times New Roman! And get those blasted toolbars out of my face so I can see what the heck I'm typing!

Shh, relax. Breathe deeply. Find your happy place. Call your therapist. Then take action. You can grab your computer by the power cord and threaten it, or you can follow these tips for getting the most out of Word for Windows 95.

Chapter 19

We Can Fix That View

In This Chapter

➤ Changing views of your document

➤ Why graphics appear different in different views

➤ Making your work area larger

➤ Assistance for WordPerfect users

➤ Working with outlines

➤ Creating a document using Outline view

There's nothing more frustrating than having your words or graphics too small to see, or so large they extend beyond the edges of your computer display. Or page numbers! You swear you put them in there; why can't you see them? And graphics that seem to move without warning, or print differently than they appear on the screen. How can you possibly feel comfortable learning about special features in Word (like page numbers or footnotes) when you have trouble even seeing them?

This chapter should calm your fears. How you view your document is up to you. Word provides many alternatives for you to choose from, based on your viewing convenience or the need to perform a particular function. If you've only experienced one view in Word for Windows 95, your eyes are in for a treat.

Changing Your View on Documents

Here's an important point before we start: Your document doesn't change just because you change your view of it. Why have more than one view? To help you and your computer perform at their best, depending on the task at hand. The only reason to change the view of your document is to help you see parts of it better, or work with it in a different manner. There is a suggested document view for each of the tasks you are trying to accomplish, whether it's editing (Normal view), reorganizing (Outline view), manipulating graphics or pictures (Page Layout view), or preparing to print (Print Preview). There's even a special view for performing tasks like working with outlines, or creating something called a master document.

Let's take a peek at each view available to you in Word for Windows 95.

The Ever Popular, but Boring, Normal View

When you install and open Word for the first time and create a document, the text region you see on your screen is called the *Normal* view. It's called Normal because there's nothing special about it, except that it works well for just about all of your word processing needs. Use Normal view for general-purpose typing and editing of documents, and for moving around in them. It's also great for formatting. If you were to interview everyone in the world using Word for Windows 95 at this very instant, you would find almost all of them using Normal view.

To confirm that you are in Normal view, or to change to it if you aren't, open the **View** menu and choose the **Normal** command. Or if you prefer magic buttons, look at the buttons down in the horizontal scroll bar. Take your mouse pointer and hover over them to see the description appear in a pop-up box. The one farthest to your left is called **Normal view**, and pressing this button takes you to Normal view.

Help! There's a Line Down the Left Side of My Screen!

Relax, that line means you're exposing the Style Area of your screen, and you can get rid of it when you finish using it. Open the **Tools** menu and choose **Options**. Click the View tab to bring it to the front. Near the bottom left part of this dialog box, you will see the Style Area Width box. Type the number **0** (zero) into the box and press the **OK** button. The Style Area will be gone from your screen.

Normal view is great for everyday typing.

The Normal view button

Changing Your Units

To set the default unit of measurements that you type in dialog boxes and on the horizontal ruler, open the **Tools** menu and choose the **Options** command. Click the **General** tab to bring it to the front. Near the bottom of this box, you will find a place to enter your default unit of measure. Click the **Measurement Units** box to select the standard unit of measurement you prefer from the drop-down list.

Page Layout View Shows More

When you go to insert graphics and pictures into your document, you will discover that Normal view has some limitations. And sooner or later, you're going to want to know what's hiding in your margins. Normal view doesn't display your document margins, or the header or footer regions, and that's where the page numbers are hiding. Word decided to create a special view for showing you these things, and it's called Page Layout view.

Page Layout view presents your document as it will look on a sheet of paper. You can see the edges of your paper, and you no longer see page breaks, because you actually see two sheets of paper, and where your words stop on one and start on the other. Page Layout view is great for working with graphics, headers and footers, and newspaper columns. You can see everything as it will look when you print it, and still make changes to your document.

Click on the **Page Layout view** button on the horizontal scroll bar, or open the **View** menu and select the **Page Layout** command.

Page Layout view reveals the margins.

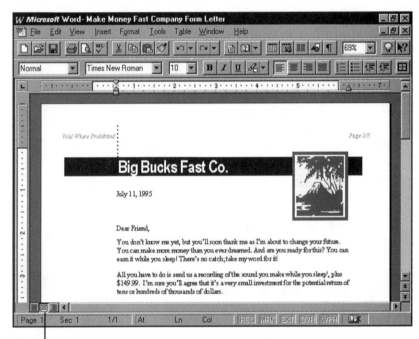

Page Layout view button

Speeding Up Scrolling If You Have Pictures

Techno Talk

To increase the speed of scrolling through graphics-ridden documents, open the **Tools** menu and choose the **Options** command. Click the **View** tab to bring it to the front. Now click the **Picture Placeholders** to place a check in the check box. Press **OK** to return to viewing your document. Now Word displays a box to represent each graphic in the document, which is as fast as text to display.

Working in the Master Document View

If you want to divide a long document into separate files (such as a book with several chapters), you can use the Master Document view. I don't recommend sitting in this view for long, but it does contain a relatively easy way to split a single document into two separate sections or documents.

Open an expendable document on your screen. *Expendable* means you don't care if it gets screwed up, and you won't sue the publisher of this book if something bad happens. Open the **View** menu and choose the **Master Document** view. Pretty ugly, huh? Looks aren't everything. Place the insertion point somewhere in the middle of your document. Now press the **Create Subdocument** button on the **Master Document** toolbar. A box will appear around a portion of your text, and what's inside is called the *subdocument*. Everything outside of this is called the *master document*. To save the new master document and all of its subdocuments, open the **File** menu and choose the **Save As** command. Enter a name for your master document. Word automatically assigns a name to each subdocument based on the first characters in the subdocument heading.

> **Viewing What Does Not Print** To view special characters on your screen that do not print, make changes to your View options. Open the **Tools** menu and choose the **Options** command. Click the **View** tab to bring it to the front. Select the check boxes for the characters you want under Nonprinting Characters.

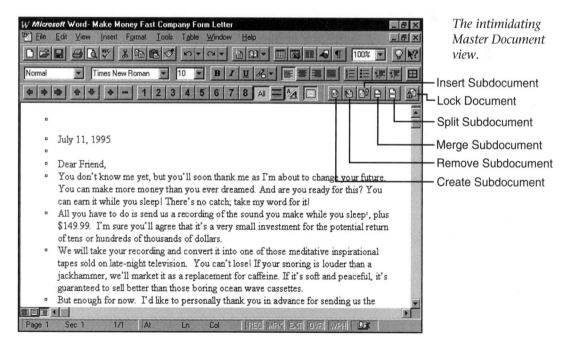

The intimidating Master Document view.

237

Don't Forget Print Preview

Print Preview, like Page Layout view, displays *everything* as it will print. Print Preview can be viewed by opening the **File** menu and choosing the **Print Preview** command. You can also press **Ctrl+F2** to view Print Preview.

Although you can use Print Preview to make editing changes, it's very difficult. Most of the text will appear much too small to accurately edit, although you can use the **Magnify** command to zoom in on something.

You can find more details on Print Preview in Chapter 17.

Zooming In and Out of Your Document

In all views, you can adjust the page display as if you were holding a magnifying glass to the screen. Things can look bigger, and things can look smaller. You can choose from several standard magnifications, or make one up yourself. Click on the **Zoom Control** button in the Standard toolbar. A drop-down list will appear, containing the following options:

But I Want 178.5% To choose another viewing size not listed in the **Zoom Control** drop-down list, such as 178.5 percent, just click in the Zoom Control box and type the magnification you desire.

200, 150, 100, 75, 50, 25, 10   Select a percentage, and the page will be reduced or enlarged to that proportion of its normal size. For example, if you select **200**, the page will appear twice its normal size. Choose **50** and it will appear half its normal size.

Page Width   Choose this option to see both margins of your document on the screen. Your text will fill the screen from side to side, and it's considered the most comfortable view setting for most people.

Whole Page   This option lets you see your entire page reduced to fit on the screen. You must be in Page Layout view to see this option.

Two Pages   You can see two pages at once, helpful for placing pictures in a newsletter, for example. You must be in Page Layout view to see this option.

Tips on Making Your Workspace Larger in Word for Windows 95

If you find yourself constantly squinting at your screen with bloodshot eyes, why not give yourself a break? Here are some tips on how to make documents easier to see on your computer screen.

➤ Run Word for Windows 95 full-screen (see Restore, not Maximize button, in Title bar).

➤ View only a single document at a time.

➤ Hide any toolbars you don't need. Most people can get along fine without the Ruler or Status bar (or even the scroll bars).

➤ Adjust Zoom control to maximize your comfort level.

➤ Switch to Full Screen View.

Full Screen View

To see only your document on the screen without rulers, toolbars, or other screen elements, you can switch to Full Screen view. It's the best way to increase your work area to the fullest extent. To remove all Word paraphernalia (I mean everything) from your screen, leaving only your text area, open the **View** menu and choose the **Full Screen** command.

The first time you use this command on a document, you will still have a small unidentified object on the screen. That's your panic button. It's supposed to be a little button with an icon of your screen, and when you press it you are returned to Normal view. If you want to get rid of even this strange object (after all, it's still blocking your view of *something*), close it by pressing the small Close button (marked with an X) in the tiny Title bar of this varmint. Now your screen is completely void of any reminder that you live in the Microsoft world of Word for Windows 95.

```
properly, and Word for Windows 95 is running with a document
open, you may find nothing else on the screen but your document.
No toolbars, no menus, no scroll bars; nothing but document. You
probably requested this state of consciousness; and it's popular
once you are familiar with Word because it allows the largest
viewing area of your document. It's called Full Screen View.
    If you want to experience this for yourself, open the View
menu and click the Full Screen command. All of the parts of Word
you've come to know and love will disappear. You are left with
nothing but your document. And yet you have all features
available to you, if you remember the keys to get there. For
example, press Alt+F and you will see the File menu, or Ctrl+P to
print your document.
    You may see a little icon on your screen
```

The Full Screen view panic button.

Press here to return to Normal view.

(c) The Least You Need to Know
[lh]
[lh]
[lh]

No need to panic here, either. You can get out of Full Screen view by pressing the **Esc** (escape) key on your keyboard. Incidentally, you can still access all of the Word commands while you are in Full Screen viewing mode if you can remember the shortcut key combination. For instance, **Alt+E** still drops down the Edit menu from nowhere, and the hot-key letter (or your mouse) can execute any of the commands.

Changing Your Default Colors in Word

The color of your work area is a very personal thing, and as creatures of habit we depend on them. Most of us had a word processor in the past that displayed white text on a blue background (and *real* old-timers remember green on black). In other words, color. With the advance of technology, we now have black and white. Black letters on a white background (that's much harder for your computer to do, if it's any consolation) is the current rage, but before you drag out that old PC-XT or Kaypro, try changing the *default colors* in Word for Windows 95.

You have lots of color choices in Word for Windows 95. For the background, you can choose between white and blue. For the text, you can choose between, well, nothing. You don't get a choice for your text color—if you pick the blue background, you get white text. Otherwise, the text is black. Viva la Word!

Open the **Tools** menu and choose the **Options** command. Click the **General** tab to bring it to the front. Find the Blue Background, White Text box and click it to insert a check mark. When you press the **OK** button, your screen will be magically transformed.

Creating and Viewing Outlined Documents

The final view in our discussion is called Outline view. You may not be interested in creating outlines, but this view can also be used on existing documents, to assist you in organizing and rearranging the contents.

To change to Outline view, open the **View** menu and choose the **Outline** command. You can also press the **Outline View** button located on the horizontal scroll bar. Notice that you are given an outline toolbar, which is available only in Outline view, containing buttons for everything you could possibly dream of:

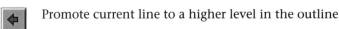 Promote current line to a higher level in the outline

Demote current line to a lower level

Demote line and remove any heading styles

Move current line up (to an earlier position in the outline)

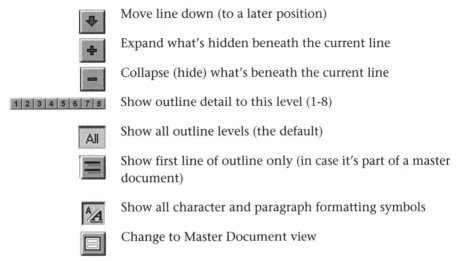

Move line down (to a later position)

Expand what's hidden beneath the current line

Collapse (hide) what's beneath the current line

Show outline detail to this level (1-8)

Show all outline levels (the default)

Show first line of outline only (in case it's part of a master document)

Show all character and paragraph formatting symbols

Change to Master Document view

Creating and organizing the typical outline hierarchy is easy using the tools provided on the **Outline** toolbar. To make any heading less important (called *demoting*), place the cursor *anywhere* in the heading and press the **Demote** button in the Outline toolbar (or press the **Tab** key). The heading moves to the next level and the corresponding heading style (the *character formatting*) is applied. Likewise, to *promote* any heading to a higher level, place the cursor *anywhere* inside the heading and press the **Promote** button (or press **Shift+Tab**). Once again, the corresponding heading style is applied. If you prefer to use the mouse instead, you can drag the plus and minus symbols (appearing in front of each line of text) up or down, throughout your outline.

Reorganizing your outline at any time is made easy using the mouse. To move any heading to a different location, double-click to select the heading and then drag it up or down throughout your outline. Any demoted headings below the heading you move automatically move with it (and stay organized). You can also press the **Move Up** or **Move Down** buttons with the cursor anywhere inside a line to move it up or down throughout your outline.

The **Expand** and **Collapse** buttons can be used to either show or hide more levels of detail in your outline. Use these when you want to see more levels of detail with a smaller region of your outline. If the plus sign exists to the left of any given line, it means there is a level of detail hidden beneath it. You can click

Where's the Outline Toolbar? You can display the Outlining toolbar only in Outline view. If you are already in Outline view and the toolbar is not displayed, click **Toolbars** on the **View** menu.

If you hide the toolbar in outline view and then switch to a different view or to a different document window, Word will automatically display the toolbar when you return to the document in Outline view.

241

either the plus sign to the left of the line, or the **Expand** button (they serve the same purpose), to see the levels immediately below. Clicking the minus sign (or the **Collapse** button) on a higher outline level will hide all levels underneath it.

You can condense your entire outline to see only the major headings by pressing one of the **Show Headings** buttons on the Outline toolbar. Pressing the **1** button will display only the first-level headings, which are the highest. Pressing the **2** button will display both the first-level and the second-level headings. The default is **Show All**, which displays all the headings.

When you're satisfied with the organization of your new outline, you can switch to Normal view to add detailed text, graphics, headers, footers, page numbers, and so on. Or you can stop here and send it to someone else to fill in the details.

What Happened to My Formatting?

Don't worry, in Outline view your original formatting is safe and sound; Word is temporarily using outline *styles* to help clarify the structure of your document. Your original formatting will return when you change to another view. If you happen to be using heading styles (see Chapter 20), you may not see a change at all. Each heading level in Outline view corresponds to one of the heading styles that comes with Word.

Quick Formatting Tips in Outline View

➤ Outline formatting is displayed automatically. To display the outline as plain text, click the **Show Formatting** button (it toggles formatting on and off) on the Outlining toolbar, which is available only in Outline view.

Prefer A, B, C or 1, 2, 3?
You can change the labels used in your outline instantly. Open the **Format** menu and choose the **Heading Numbering** command. You'll see sample drawings of the different numbering schemes available. Click the one you like and press **Enter**.

➤ Paragraph formatting is not displayed. Word temporarily indents paragraphs to reflect the heading levels. The displayed indentation does not affect the actual format of the document, and the indentation is removed when you switch from Outline view.

➤ The commands for formatting paragraphs, including the ruler, are not available. You can apply styles, although you might not be able to see the style formatting until you switch from Outline view.

➤ To insert a tab character, press **Ctrl+Tab**. Pressing the plain old **Tab** won't work in Outline view, because it's used to demote a heading to a lower heading level (pressing **Shift+Tab** promotes it).

➤ If you really, *desperately* want to see the actual formatting of a document while working in Outline view, you can split your document window. You can use Outline view in one pane and Page Layout view (or Normal view) in the other pane. Any changes you make to the document in Outline view are instantly visible in the second pane.

Quick Selecting Tips in Outline View

Feeling lost in Outline view? Here are some tips to keep you moving on the right path:

➤ Select a heading, subheading, or body text by clicking the Plus symbol, or double-click in the selection bar to the left of the heading.

➤ To select *only* the heading (without the subordinate parts), click in the selection bar to the left of the heading.

➤ To select a paragraph, click the Dot symbol, or click once in the selection bar to the left of the paragraph. The entire paragraph will be selected.

➤ You can select multiple headings or paragraphs by clicking in the selection bar and then drag to include more headings.

Reorganize an Existing Document in Outline View

Outline view can also be used to help you reorganize existing documents. For instance, say you want to move a summary section from the back of your report up to the front. Yes, you can use cut and paste, but you can also use Outline view, which might make large documents easier to manipulate. Also, if you happened to format topic headings with the built-in heading styles, you can easily rearrange the text by dragging the headings in Outline view.

Open your document and switch to Outline view by opening the **View** menu and choosing **Outline** (or press the **Outline** button on the horizontal scroll bar). Paragraphs are identified with at least a minus symbol, and can also be dots and plus symbols. To move text to a different location, drag these outline symbols (plus, minus, and dot) up or down through your document. As you drag, Word displays a *horizontal* line. Release the mouse button when the line is where you want to move the text.

Who Changed My Margins?
When you print from Outline view, Word uses temporary margins of 1.25". Actual margin settings are not affected and will be used when you print from other views. Why does Word do this? I don't know.

To change a heading level, drag the outline symbols left or right. To promote a heading to a higher level, or to change body text to a heading, drag the outline symbol to the left. To demote a heading to a lower level, or to change a heading to body text, drag the outline symbol to the right. As you drag, Word displays a *vertical* line at each heading level. Release the mouse button to assign the text to the new level. Word applies a consistent heading style to the heading, or applies Normal style to body text.

The Least You Need to Know

Your document won't change just because you change your view of it. But changing views can help you see your document better, or work with it differently, by following these tips:

➤ Use Normal view for normal editing tasks. Click on the **Normal view** button on the horizontal scroll bar, or open the **View** menu and choose the **Normal** command.

➤ Page Layout view is great for working with graphics, headers and footers, and newspaper columns. You can see everything as it will look when you print it, and still make changes to your document. Click on the **Page Layout view** button on the horizontal scroll bar, or select **Page Layout** from the **View** menu.

➤ Want to see something close up? Select a larger number from the **Zoom** drop-down list found in the **Standard** toolbar, or use the **Zoom** command on the **View** menu.

➤ Creating an outline can be an easy way to organize your thoughts and make a large document easier to write. You can visit **Outline** view by choosing the **Outline** command in the **View** menu (or click the **Outline view** button on the horizontal scroll bar).

Styles of the Rich and Famous

You want your documents to look good, right? So do I. By now you've had a chance to try some of the formatting features of Word. You may have developed likes and dislikes of formatting and how you want your paragraphs to look. You're developing your own *style*, and Word for Windows 95 wants to help.

Help? Lots of beginners run and hide when the word *style* is mentioned. So what is it about this subject that keeps people away in droves? Well, the droves may be more interesting, but you can learn ways to create documents in your own style more easily and consistently by using styles.

Nothing in this chapter is mandatory. You can lead a productive life in Word without ever learning about styles. But give them half a chance and see if you're not tossing a heading or two around very soon.

What Is a Style?

You can see for yourself. Take a full-page peek at two pages and decide for yourself which has a better *style*.

You can recognize style when you see it.

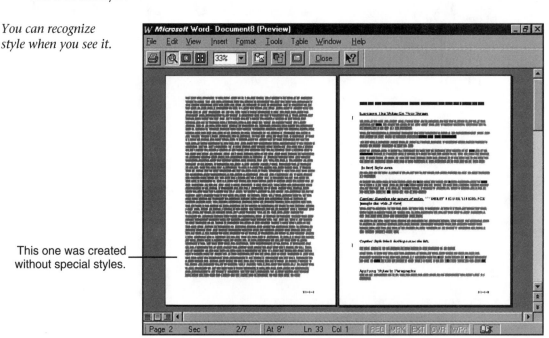

This one was created without special styles.

The page on the right looks better because the paragraphs are formatted. Without using styles, this appearance could be obtained by manually inserting extra lines between paragraphs, indenting them, and applying various other formats. How long does that take? A few seconds for each, multiplied by the number of paragraphs you create in your lifetime. There's a better way.

The page on the right was created by using a single style, one of hundreds you can find or create. At the end of each paragraph, the **Enter** key ignites the power of the style which takes care of spacing, indenting, formatting, and so on, placing you at the start of a new paragraph.

Styles are combinations of character, paragraph, and other formatting all saved in one easy-to-remember name. This goes beyond the bold, italics, or underline formatting that you give to individual words. Think of styles as a broader collection of interesting details brought together to become the default formatting of what you type.

Exposing the Styles on Your Screen

When the insertion point is placed in a paragraph, the style you are currently using appears in the Style box on the Formatting toolbar. If a character style is applied to a word, its style will appear in the Style box when the insertion point is placed *within the word*. To keep you from straining your neck looking up at that Style box all the time, you can show the paragraph styles right next to each paragraph in your document. To do this, turn on the **Style Area**.

To display the Style Area on your screen, open the **Tools** menu and choose the **Options** command. Click the **View** tab to bring it to the front. Look for the **Style Area Width** box and replace that zero with a positive decimal number. You can just type over it, or click the up/down arrows to increase or decrease the width. A number like .5 will do just fine. Now press the **OK** button and look at your screen.

Is it a Style or a Template?
What *is* the difference between a style and a template? Basically, a *template* is made up of several *styles*. A single *style* is a collection of paragraph and character formatting used in a document. A collection of styles can be saved as a template. Read more about templates in Chapter 21.

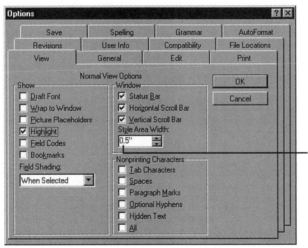

Exposing the secrets of styles.

Enter the width of the style area column for viewing.

Style labels leaking out on the left.

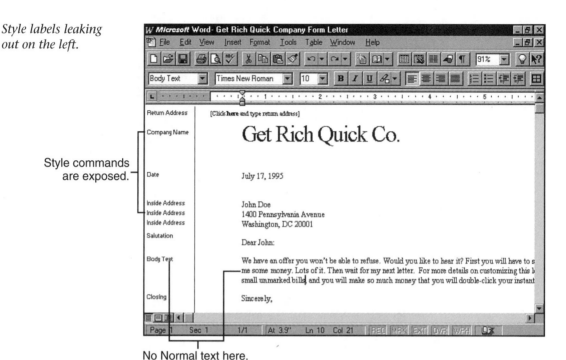

Style commands are exposed.

No Normal text here.

The extra margin to the left displays the style applied to each paragraph on the screen. Don't forget to close this style area after exploring it, unless you really enjoy seeing this stuff. To close this impressive exposure to the style area of a document, open the **Tools** menu, choose the **Options** command, and click the **View** tab if it's not already in front. Enter a **0** (zero) in the box **Style Area Width** box and press **OK**.

Applying Styles to Paragraphs

With that introduction out of the way, and before you think styles are too complicated, let's apply a style to a paragraph.

Find a boring paragraph and place the insertion point anywhere inside the paragraph. Select several paragraphs if you want to format multiple paragraphs at one time. If it's your first time, however, you may want to start with a very small, perhaps single-line paragraph, so you can see the whole thing. Using your mouse, click the down arrow in the **Style** box on the **Formatting** toolbar. All of the currently available styles can be seen and selected from this drop-down scroll box. Click one of them, such as the **Heading 1**, and watch your paragraph jump into action and transform itself into something that looks like a major heading of a magazine article.

Try another style. Click on the drop-down **Style** list and choose **Heading 2**, and then **Heading 3**, for example. Keep trying different styles to get a feel for how styles convert your paragraph into impressive, consistent formats that can improve the look and feel of your document.

Now press the **Undo** button on the **Standard** toolbar, or press **Ctrl+Z**, which is also the **Undo** command, and watch your paragraph change to the previous style. You can always undo an applied style, so don't be afraid of experimenting with them!

I Want More Styles! If a style you want to use isn't listed, press the **Shift** key, then click the same down arrow. A box will appear displaying all of Word's built-in styles, instead of the mere sampling you usually see.

Copying Styles from One Paragraph to Another

If you have a paragraph that looks really good and you want to copy that formatting to another paragraph inside your document, you can use a helpful feature of Word for Windows 95, even if it has a silly name. It's called the *Format Painter button.*

You can also copy styles from one paragraph to another with the **Format Painter** button. For our first experiment, let's copy the formatting of an attractively styled single paragraph (called Spiffy) to another single paragraph (Ugly). Start by selecting Spiffy using your favorite selection technique. Mine is triple-clicking anywhere inside Spiffy, and Spiffy doesn't mind. Now press the **Format Painter** button on the **Standard** toolbar. Now Word has committed the style to memory, at least temporarily. Now go hunting for Ugly. When you find this paragraph, just click anywhere inside of it. Ugly will be magically transformed into Spiffy.

To copy a style you really like to several paragraphs, select the preferred paragraph and this time *double-click* the **Format Painter** button. Now you can go click on as many paragraphs as you wish, and they will all have your preferred style applied to them. When you want to stop this activity, press the **Esc** (Escape) key to end the repetitive style applications.

Creating Your Own Style

You can create a style from scratch right now that will not harm your document or your copy of Word for Windows 95. Start by typing a short sentence and pressing the **Enter** key at the end. In Word's mind, it's now a paragraph. Now make some formatting changes to it. Apply some simple formatting, just to get started. For instance, change the alignment by clicking the **Right-Align** button on the **Formatting** toolbar. Maybe change the font or the size of the font. When you finish making changes to the formatting, select

Longer Style Names
Style names can now be as long as 256 characters, including spaces, so you can really explain what your new creations do, and remember them better the next time you need to use them.

your paragraph. This selection represents something good enough to become a style. And styles have names, so you have to think up a name. Names are given when you define a new style.

To define a new style, make sure your paragraph is selected, and then click on the **Style** box in the **Formatting** toolbar (or press **Ctrl+Shift+S**). Type in a name for this style, and you can enter a name up to 256 characters long, including spaces. Now press the **Enter** key. A style is born.

A Hands-On Introduction to Styles Using AutoFormat

If you are new to the whole subject of styles, there's a quick way to jump in and immerse yourself. It's called the **AutoFormat** command. The **AutoFormat** command *sounds* like a miracle worker—*garbage in, beautiful document out*, right? Not so, my friend. A better suited phrase for AutoFormat is *garbage in, garbage out*. And that's good enough, because it gets rid of the garbage most of us (who don't use styles) put into our documents as we create them.

Take a look at your **Style** box in the **Formatting** toolbar. Does it say Normal? Does it *always* say Normal? If so, then you aren't making use of styles. The **Normal** selection is the epitome of boring text. Now let's find the garbage produced by using nothing but the Normal style.

How do you separate paragraphs to make them look better on your page? Most people press **Enter** twice. In the Style world, that second **Enter** is considered useless, and therefore, garbage. How do you indent the first line of your paragraph? Sure, you are to be congratulated for moving up from the **Spacebar** to the **Tab** key, but both are considered unnecessary (garbage) when using styles. Do you create numbered or bullet lists manually? Do you always center the page heading on the page, and make it bold or underlined? All of these formatting tasks chew up your valuable time needlessly.

Training Wheels: AutoFormat While You Type and Watch

In your mind, **AutoFormat** probably exists as a command on the **Format** menu that is applied *after* you create a document, right up there with Print and Save. That's correct; your mind has tuned into the default setting of the AutoFormat command. But there's more! Try something really different using AutoFormat.

With AutoFormat, Word for Windows 95 analyzes each paragraph within your document (even as you create it) to determine its purpose (such as a heading, a bullet or number list, regular text, and so on), and then applies an appropriate style from the current template.

Open the **Tools** menu and choose the **Options** command. Click the **AutoFormat** tab (by golly, it has its own tab!) to bring it to the front. Click to select the option **AutoFormat As You Type**. Notice the box labels in the dialog box change from merely Apply and Replace to Apply As You Type, and Replace As You Type. Go ahead and click to select the **Headings** box, also. Now start a new document and have some fun.

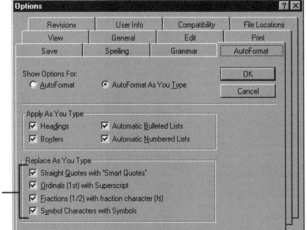

AutoFormat while you type.

These options don't change for either mode of AutoFormat.

Type the title at the top of your page as you would normally, and then press **Enter** twice. How about that? Word watches you press **Enter** twice and determines the text is important enough to become a style heading, and it picks a style called Heading 1. It also gets rid of the spare blank line above your insertion point.

Now press three underline symbols (_) and press **Enter**. An instant underline appears across the entire page! Actually, you always have this feature regardless of AutoFormat, and it even works with the equals symbol (=) and hyphen (-). I just threw it in here for fun. Now back to work learning about *styles*.

Use the **Tab** key to begin your second short sentence and press **Enter** twice. AutoFormat kicks in, and you are pleasantly surprised with a *Heading 2* style applied (you must be using a Tab stop on your ruler for this one to work).

Keep going. Start a list by typing something like: **1) My first option** and press **Enter**. Instant numbered lists! AutoFormat presumes you will want a 2 next, and gives it to you, also removing any spaces or tabs you may have included between the number and your text. Not a bad way to create numbered lists in a hurry. As long as you include a closed parenthesis or a period (some form of punctuation) after the first number, AutoFormat is activated and adds new numbers and applies an appropriate style for you. To make it stop, just press **Enter** again, and you'll be returned to normal text waiting patiently for your next command.

You can also create quick bulleted lists this same way. Type an asterisk (*****) or the letter **o** (the one after n) and a space, then type some text and press **Enter** once. The asterisk or letter **o** will be converted to bullet symbols automatically.

Fun, huh? You don't have to know any more about styles if you want to plug away like this. But these styles that you include can be combined and saved.

New Styles Don't Travel

If you just created a new style and plan to use it tomorrow in a new document, you're about to discover something that people don't like about styles. The style you have just created exists in one place—your document—and you have to do a little more work to free it up to help you with other documents.

When you create a style, it's initially available for that document only. If you want to make a style available for more documents (or if you want to make changes to the Normal style affecting more than one document), you must add that style to a *template* (which you will learn in the next chapter). A template defines the whole working environment for a document, such as its margin settings, page orientation, and so on. The template also controls which menu commands are available, and what tools appear on the toolbars.

Changing an Existing Style

There are two ways to change a style, and you may find them both easy. Keep in mind that any changes you make to the Normal style affect *all other styles in this document*. So as a rule, keep changes to the Normal style to a minimum. Stick to changing other styles until you get comfortable with your power.

Pick a paragraph that has the style you want to change, something other than Normal style (you may have to create or apply one first). The style name should appear in the **Style** box. Make a change to the style of this paragraph and then select the paragraph. Now select the same style name from the **Style** box and press **Enter**. Word will ask you if you want to redefine the style. Click on **OK**. If you decide not to change the style, click on **Cancel**.

The second way to change an existing style is to use the Style dialog box. Open the **Format** menu and choose the **Style** command. Select the style you want to change from the list. Now press the **Modify** button (or press **Alt+M**), and then press the **Format** button (or press **Alt+O**). Choose the part of the style you want to change. Line spacing, for example, can be found in the **Paragraph** command. Make the changes you want in any of these areas, and then press the **OK** buttons to back your way out. Press the **Close** button to return to your document from the Style dialog box.

Using the Style Dialog Box

You can also create and modify existing styles using the Style dialog box, which contains every possible paragraph formatting function under the sun. It's useful to take a peek at it to give you an idea of the wealth of formatting options available. Open the **Format** menu and choose the **Style** command. You will see the Style dialog box.

You can sample styles in the Preview box.

Bold names contain font and paragraph formatting styles.

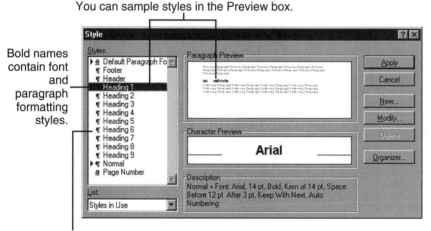

The Style dialog box helps you create and save styles.

Regular names contain character formatting styles only.

Notice the different Styles listed, including descriptions and a preview box for each one. Some names appear in bold, while others appear in normal text. Styles in bold contain both font and paragraph formatting. Regular style names contain only character formatting. You can edit or create new styles here, but with so many options it's easy for beginners to get lost. Close the Style dialog box by pressing the **Cancel** button, or by pressing the Close button in the Title bar.

Are You Really Interested in How Normal Style Works?

Up until now, every paragraph you've typed has started its life in the Normal style: Times New Roman 10-point font in a left-aligned paragraph. All other styles are based on the Normal style, so if you hate Times New Roman font, all you have to do is modify the Normal style to use some other font before you create any new styles.

Changing your Normal style can, and often does, change the rest of your styles. Whether or not the change affects another style in that document depends on what Normal attributes the other style has. For example, suppose you create a style called *Title* that is centered, specified at 24-point size, and used the same font as Normal style (Times New Roman). The size of these fonts do not match, so if you change the size of your Normal font, your Title font will not change. But the *font* used in your Title matches the Normal style, so your Title *will change* if you change the Normal font to something other than Times New Roman.

When you create a style, you usually start with the Normal style as a model. Therefore, any formats that you change will no longer be affected by subsequent changes to the Normal style. Formats that you leave at Normal's default *will change* if you change the Normal style. Got it?

The Style Gallery

The *Style Gallery* is a fun place to play and learn. It's basically a workshop where you can experiment applying various format styles to your documents. To get to this playground, open the **Format** menu and choose the **Style Gallery** command. You will see one of the largest dialog boxes Word ever dreamed up. A list of styles is on the left, and a preview of what they look like is on the right. If you are the curious type, this is a great place to experiment with the different styles and see how they change your document.

If you aren't the curious type, it can still be helpful to press the **Example** button. This way you will see a preview of the style effect on a finished sample document instead of your own text.

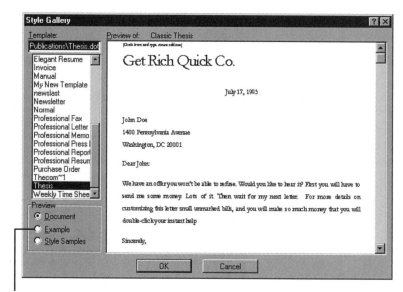

The Style Gallery playground.

Click Example to see a sample complete document.

Press the **OK** button when recess is over to return to your document. Any style changes you discover and apply will remain with your document, as long as you save your document before closing it. Press the **Save** button to enjoy this style tomorrow.

The Least You Need to Know

Styles exist to capture good paragraph formatting and make it available to other paragraphs. You can write home about some of these style tips learned in this chapter:

➤ You can tell what style is applied to each paragraph by displaying the Style Area (open the **Tools** menu and select the **Options** command). Choose the **View** tab to bring it to the front and then change the Style Area Width setting to 1 (or .5 to save space).

➤ To copy a paragraph's style to another paragraph, select the paragraph whose style you want to copy, click the **Format Painter** button, then click within the paragraph to which you want to copy the style.

➤ To create a style yourself, format a paragraph the way you like it and leave the insertion point somewhere inside it. Type a name for this style in the Style box on the Formatting toolbar, and press **Enter**.

➤ To make changes to a style, change a paragraph with that style, and then select it. Make sure the style name is correctly displayed in the Style box on the Formatting toolbar, then press **Enter**. Click on **OK** to confirm that you want to make these changes to the style.

➤ To save a style to the current template, open the **Format** menu and select **Style**. Click on **Organizer** or press **Alt+O**. Under the In..., select the style you want to add to the template, and click **Copy** or press **Alt+C**. Click on **Close** or press **Enter** to close this dialog box.

Chapter 21

Templates: Worth Their Weight in Megabytes

In This Chapter

➤ What is a template, and why should you care?

➤ Changing your documents template

➤ Using Word's custom templates

➤ Creating, editing, and saving your own templates

➤ Meet the Wizards

Computers have been promised to make our life easier. Yeah, right; I'd like to get my hands on the neck of that salesperson. But the promise has been delivered in a key feature of Word for Windows 95 called *templates*, and if this is news to you, this chapter is guaranteed to make you happy. That is, of course, if creating beautiful documents in a fraction of the time (so you can get home earlier) makes you happy.

Introducing Templates

Creating any document takes time, especially if you want it to look good. There are lots of tedious steps. You type the date, enter the addresses and the salutation, and maybe create headers and footers (such as a company logo or a page number). Maybe you change the margins, paragraph formatting, or add borders or lines to improve the appearance.

When you use a template, most of this groundwork is already done for you, so you can focus your attention on the words you want to say. You don't have to start a document from scratch.

What Is a Template?

Think of a template as a blueprint for the text, graphics, and formatting of a document. Templates in Word for Windows 95 are predesigned, ready-to-use documents into which you put your own information. You order a template, and the template automatically creates the foundation for your document. Those tedious details, like margins, dates, salutations, and so on, instantly appear on your screen. All you do is type the words of your memo or report. When you're finished and it's time to save your work, you provide a name and your creation is stored as a regular document. The template you chose is safe and sound for the next time you want to use it, and it will be just as helpful the next time.

Word for Windows 95 includes 28 professionally designed templates for you to use. This includes templates for letters, memos, fax cover sheets, reports, newsletters, press releases, resumes, and an assortment of other common documents.

Templates can be changed, and you can change them. Templates can also be created, and you really should consider taking your most common document type and saving one as a template to make your life easier the next time. Before we get too daring, let's test drive an existing template.

Using a Template for the First Time

Take a look at all the templates Word has to offer by opening the **File** menu and choosing the **New** command. Unfortunately, pressing the **New** button on the Standard toolbar will not allow you to access the stored templates so you have to choose **New** from the **File** menu.

With the New dialog box open, notice the list of tab titles across the top. This is how Word organizes the templates so you can find the one you want faster. Click the **Letters & Faxes** tab to bring it to the front. What you see are all templates, waiting to be chosen.

Double-click the **Contemporary Letter** to start using it. Be sure that **Document** is selected in the Create New box near the bottom. Your screen will fill with an interesting preformatted letter just waiting for you to fill in with your own information.

Click in any of the areas you would like to fill out, and start typing. The text you enter is formatted automatically for that part of the letter. Click your way through the rest of these text fields to complete the letter. When you're finished, press the **Save** button (or open the **File** menu and choose **Save**). You are given a chance to save this completed letter as a regular document—it's no longer a template.

Press these other tabs to see
more ready-to-use templates.

Click on a template and press
this button to preview it.

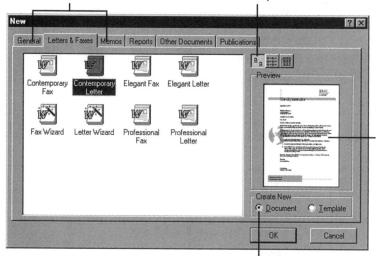

*Templates are the
fastest way to create
a great-looking
document.*

The preview lets you
quickly browse through
existing templates.

Be sure Document
is selected to use a
template.

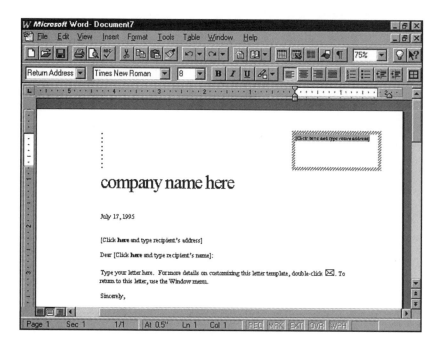

*Templates guide you
to perfectly format-
ted documents.*

So remember, opening a document with a template does not change the template. Your new document is simply an automatic copy of the template's styles and any text it already has.

Creating Your Own Template to Store Your Styles

You probably have documents you already use as unofficial "templates." Maybe it's a weekly report that you open and change a few words, then save it as a new document. Whenever you open, copy, and adapt the contents of an existing document, you're using that document as a template. Protect your time investment by formally saving these documents as templates.

The easiest way to create a new template is by saving an existing document as a template. To create a new template based on an existing document, open the **File** menu and choose the **Open** command. Locate and open the document you want.

Before making any changes, save your work. Open the **File** menu and choose the **Save As** command. In the File Name box, type a name for the new template. In the Save In box, open the Templates folder (it should be labeled Templates). If you want the template to appear in a particular template group, open that folder. In the Save As Type box, click **Document Template**, and then click **OK**. Congratulations! You've just created your own template, and now you can customize it.

Add the text and graphics you want to appear in all new documents that you base on the template, and delete any items you don't want to appear. Don't forget to make the changes you want to the margin settings, page size and orientation, styles, and other formats. When you finish, click the **Save** button, and your customized template will be saved.

Where Should You Store Your Templates?

Save your custom templates in the appropriate folder inside the Templates folder, such as the Letters and Faxes folder, or the Memos folder (the Templates folder is found in the same folder where you installed Word). Templates that you save in the Templates folder or any of its folders appear in the New dialog box when you open the **File** menu and choose **New**. Any documents that you save in the Templates folder (or below) also act as templates.

You can add a folder to the Templates folder to store your custom templates. When you first save the template, click **Create New Folder** in the Save As dialog box. Templates in the new folder appear on a separate tab in the New dialog box. To list a template on the General tab, save the template in the Templates folder, not in a sub-folder.

You should always save your new templates in this standard Word Template folder, which is the default location that appears when you click the **Save File As Type** text box and choose **Templates**.

If you choose to store your template anywhere else, you can, and it will still work and act as a template. But to use it next time, you will have to remember where you put it.

Create Your Own Tab in the New Dialog Box

You can create a tab that appears in the New dialog box by creating your own new folder within the Template folder. During the Save As, locate the template folder. Now press the **Create New Folder** button. A default name is provided, which you can change by typing over it. Name your folder and store your new template inside. The next time you see the New dialog box, your template will be listed right with the others.

What Should You Include in Your Template?

As you learned in the previous chapter, *styles* are a collection of paragraph and font attributes that you store under a single convenient name. Chapter 20 also taught you how to use existing styles and also create styles of your own. If you want to save these styles so they can be used together over and over again, you should create a document template to hold them. And you just learned how to do that, so the timing is impeccable.

You can store more than just styles in a template. Templates can contain any commonly used text to save you time and energy from retyping each time you create a document. One of the most common templates people create is the fax cover sheet. It contains the standard information about your company, addresses, the headings of From: and To: along with the return fax number. It can even include graphics. Whatever you put inside, be sure to keep it general enough so it applies all the time and no time is wasted changing an entry before using it.

Protect Your Originals If you happen to click any of the templates in the New dialog box with the right mouse button, be careful not to choose the Open command. The original template is opened for modification, and you might accidentally change the original. Always use the **New** command to create new documents based on templates.

Another Quick Way to Put the Date and Time in Your Document

You can quickly add the current date and time into any document or template. Start by placing the insertion point at the desired location you want the date and time to appear, then open the **Insert** menu. Choose the **Date and Time** command and you will see the Date and Time dialog box, and it's loaded with just about every imaginable format used to display dates and time. Scroll through this listing until you find the format you prefer. Click on your choice and then press the **OK** button and the current date and time will be placed into your document.

Also, if you are interested in having your document always reflect the *current* date and time, be sure to click the **Update Automatically (Insert as Field)** check box at the bottom of this dialog box. Now when you select and place the date and time in your document it is inserted as something called an intelligent field, which means it will always look at the clock built into your computer, and display the current date and time right in your document, constantly changing it as needed to remain accurate.

Modify an Existing Template

Once you have created your own template, it's not too difficult to follow the same procedure for modifying an existing template. A word of warning: don't change the Normal template. You can prevent an accident like this by first opening up a different template and making sure it's open.

Open the **File** menu and choose the **Open** command. Open the template you want to modify (if there aren't any templates listed in the Open dialog box, click **Document Templates** in the **Files Of Type** box). If you don't find any, try looking in the Templates folder. If you need help finding the Templates folder, you can learn some good searching tips in Chapter 23.

Now go ahead and make changes. Change any of the template's text, graphics, styles, formatting, macros, AutoText entries, toolbars, menu settings, and shortcut keys. When you have finished, press the **Save** button. The template will be saved with your changes, ready to provide customized service in the future.

Once again, any changes to the template's content and formatting are reflected in any new documents you choose to create from this new template; existing documents aren't affected.

Copying Your Favorite Styles into a Template

If you have a style you are particularly proud of, but it's part of a document you don't want to make a template, you can still grab a copy of that style and include it with your new template. You can copy styles between templates and documents by following this procedure.

Open the **File** menu and choose the **Templates** command. Click the **Organizer** button and take a close look at what is being displayed in the Organizer dialog box. On the left side is a template. On the right side is a template. You use this dialog box to copy things from one template to another. Sound reasonable? Most importantly, you change the template you're seeing in either the left or right side, to control exactly which templates you want to work with.

To change the current template on either side, press the **Close File** button underneath it. The button will change to an **Open File** button. Press it and use the Open dialog box that appears to find the template you want, and press the **Open** button to have it appear in the Organizer dialog box. Follow this procedure until you have the template that you want to copy from on the left, and the template you want to copy to on the right.

Now click to select any style items you want to copy in either list, and press the **Copy** button appearing in the dialog box. To select a range of items, hold down the **Shift** key and click the first and last items. To select non-adjacent items, hold down the **Ctrl** key as you click each item. When you have finished making changes to your template, press the **Close** button on the Organizer dialog box. Your style changes will be saved.

Take your choice of any style in any document or template.

Copy your choices to your own template or document.

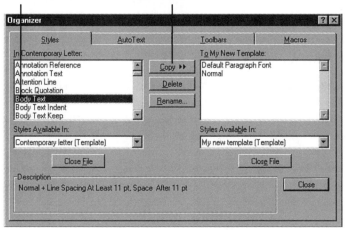

Feeling lucky? Try copying a favorite style to your template.

What's Normal About the Normal Template?

Remember the *Normal style* from the last chapter? Remember how important and sometimes confusing it is? Well, there also exists a *Normal template*, and the same rules apply. It's a good idea to leave the Normal template alone.

The Normal template is a general-purpose template for any type of document. When you start Word or click the **New** button, Word creates a new blank document that is based on the Normal template. It's possible, but not advised, to modify this template to change the default document formatting or content.

Word also uses the Normal template to store the AutoText entries, macros, toolbars, and custom menu settings and shortcut keys you routinely use. Customized items that you store in the Normal template are available for use with any document.

Nice Documents Word Can Create for You

In addition to templates, Word includes several wizards to save you time in creating many common types of documents. For example, you can use the Letter Wizard to create personal or business letters. If you installed the prewritten business letters provided with Word, the Letter Wizard can also help you prepare letters for a number of common business situations.

To create one of the documents in the listing below, open the **File** menu and choose the **New** command. Then select an appropriate template or wizard that can be found in any of the categories. If you plan to create several documents, and you would like them to contain similar formatting styles, choose templates with the same description in their name, such as Professional, Elegant, or Contemporary. For example, if you use the Professional Resume template, use the Professional Letter template to create a cover letter in a similar style.

If you don't see the template or wizard you want in the New dialog box, rerun the Word for Windows 95 Setup Program to install it.

Here are the categories that already exist to help you create common documents with the least amount of work:

- ➤ **Letters & Faxes** Business letters in several styles, personal letters, and fax cover sheets.

- ➤ **Memos** Three different styles (simple and elegant to contemporary or professional) of memorandums.

- ➤ **Reports** Three different styles of casual and professional reports.

➤ **Publications**   Brochures, directories of names and addresses, manuals, newsletters, press releases, and theses.

➤ **Other Documents**   Agendas for meetings, award certificates, calendars, invoices, legal pleadings, purchase orders, resumes or curriculum vitae, and weekly time sheets.

Whizzing Your Way Through with Wizards

Wizards take the idea of templates one step further. What if you had an assistant that could help you one step at a time in the creation of a complete and customized document, using information that you supply? That's how a wizard can help you. Templates sit back and make you do much of the work of creating a document. Wizards jump into action and actually create, or at least get started creating, the contents of your document. You just have to add your customized text to the appropriate locations.

Yes, Word for Windows 95 includes ten automated Wizards for creating letters, memos, fax cover sheets, newsletters, resumes, calendars, tables, meeting agendas, award certificates, and legal pleading documents.

Using a Wizard is like hiring a contractor to build your house. You don't want to know all the details about construction—you just want a kitchen over there and a fireplace over there. And you don't want to be bothered by too many questions because then you start second-guessing yourself. You just want it done.

There's nothing wrong with using a Wizard to help you complete a task. Some people think it's cheating, or it couldn't possibly look as good as a document created from scratch, or what would the world be like if all our documents looked the same, and so on. If you have any of these hang-ups, stick with templates, but the rest of you keep reading.

The Wizard helps you quickly create a completely formatted document. All you have to do is add the words. The formatting of the finished document is not set in stone; you can change any bit of it by modifying the styles of the document, or even the template, that the Wizard bases the document upon.

Ready to try and whiz through the creation of a document? Open the **File** menu and choose the **New** command. Click the different category tabs to bring a selection of Wizards to view. They live side-by-side with their template friends. If you are interested in creating a spectacular newsletter, you should click the **Publications** tab and choose the **Newsletter Wizard**. Click the **OK** button, and the wizard will kick into action.

You may see a single dialog box or many dialog boxes during the "wizarding" that ask you for general information about what you're looking for. Don't pressure yourself! Casually click each option button appearing on the right, and you will see and understand what it does by watching the Preview box included for each decision. When you are ready to move to the next step, press the **Next** button. You can step backwards also, right up to the very end, to change any of your previous requests. (Try doing that with your house contractor.) At the very end, you will see a **Finish** button. Push it. You will land in the middle of a completely formatted document awaiting your content. You can save it at any time, and you will have to give it a name and a folder to live in.

The Least You Need to Know

Good templates are worth their weight in megabytes. Make use of them, following these tips from this chapter:

➤ Templates are predesigned, ready-to-use documents into which you put your own information.

➤ When you create a new document, select the template you want to use in the Template list box.

➤ You can create a template based on a document by opening the **File** menu and choosing the **Save As** command. Enter the name for the template, then select **Document Template** under Save File As Type.

➤ Beginners should use Wizards! Experienced beginners should use wizards! Wizards create completely formatted custom documents instantly. You can find your Wizards by opening the **File** menu and choosing the **New** command.

Chapter 22

Managing Your Documents and Your Health

In This Chapter

➤ Managing your documents from the File Open dialog box

➤ Renaming and deleting documents

➤ Comparing documents for changes

➤ Bringing documents back from the dead

➤ Automatically saving your work in case you forget

➤ Taking work home using the Briefcase

If you happen to enjoy word processing as a hobby, or have been locked in your office for years, your computer is probably chock full of documents. Each one is taking up space, and they might be scattered all over the guts of your computer. It's easy to get lost and sometimes run out of space on such a busy computer, which can cause premature aging, weight loss (or gain), and severe frustration. This chapter describes ways to organize the storage space inside your computer and clearly identify what you create, so you'll be more relaxed the next time you need to find something.

Filing Documents in a Folder?

Folders vs. Directories The folder concept introduced with Windows 95 makes it easier to think about how we store documents. Users of previous Word versions will recognize the Folder as nothing more than a directory that can have a long name.

When you print your documents, where do you store them? In piles on your desk, the floor, or in a file cabinet? Where is it easiest to find them? Many people think storing documents in neatly labeled and organized folders makes it easy to find in the future. They find the correct folder, and the document is sure to be in there.

The same now goes for documents in Word for Windows 95. The people at Microsoft went so far as to call the document storage area *folders* and present them as icons of little manila folders. Folders always appear the same, and you can store folders inside of folders, providing the ability to create any type of hierarchy you can think of.

Managing Documents Right from the Open Dialog Box

Managing files in previous versions of Word, as well as other word processors, was a real pain. You had to switch to DOS to do things like erasing and renaming files. And before folders, we were limited to directories with 8-character names. But you don't care about all of that now because it's in the past. All of those problems have been fixed.

Now you can create, name, rename, and remove documents and folders, all in one place, whenever you need to. This has to rank right up there as one of the real joys in life. See for yourself. Open the **File** menu and choose the **Open** command to display the Open dialog box.

Click the Name bar to change the sorting order.

Complicated searching is possible by pressing this button.

Managing your documents from the Open dialog box.

You can rename or delete a file right here.

Enter searching criteria here.

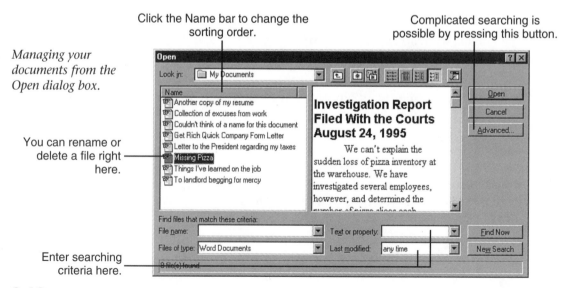

The new File Open dialog box makes it easy to manage documents right from here. Using the right mouse button, click on the document and choose a command from the pop-up menu. A summary of the most useful commands is listed here:

➤ **Find** You can enter simple or advanced searches, and the whole topic of searching is detailed in Chapter 23.

➤ **Sort** You can sort this list by clicking the Name bar.

➤ **Name** Your documents can have names as long as 255 characters, so use them.

➤ **Rename** To rename, you just double-click on the name and edit it right where it is, without opening it.

➤ **Delete** To delete a document, select the document and press the **Delete** key. You'll be asked to confirm that it's what you really want.

➤ **Print** One or more documents can be printed without even opening them.

Recovering Deleted Documents

If you accidentally delete a document that you need back, you'll be happy to hear that it hasn't really been deleted—yet. Windows 95 uses the Recycle Bin as a temporary storage area until you decide that it's time to "take out the trash" and empty it. Open the Recycle Bin by minimizing applications until you can see the Bin icon on the Windows 95 Desktop. Double-click the icon to open it, or click on it with the right mouse button and choose the **Open** command.

Find your documents on this list and click them once to select them. Open the **File** menu in the Recycle Bin and choose the **Restore** command to fully recover every aspect of the original document. It won't be any worse for wear.

Changing the Default Folder in Word

Now that you know how to create and use folders, you might want to change the default working folder in Word for Windows 95. This is the first place Word looks for documents, and it's the same place Word stores your documents if you don't specify a folder.

Bring 'Em Back Alive If you accidentally delete a file in Word, look in the Recycle Bin. A double-click will bring it right back to you.

Open the **Tools** menu and choose the **Options** command. Click the **File Locations** tab to bring it to the front. In the File Types box, click **Documents**. Press the **Modify** button. Now you are ready to provide the new folder location. Click the folder you want for the working folder, or click the **Create New Folder** button to create and name a new folder.

Old-Timers Only: Care to See the Complete DOS Path?

If you come from the land of DOS, you might think the folders are "cute" but you want to see where the files are *really* stored. You can actually get the full DOS filename and path to appear in the Title bar of your applications by following these instructions. Open My Computer or Windows Explorer and click the **View** menu, and then click **Options**. Click the **View** tab to bring it to the front. Make sure the option for displaying the full MS-DOS path is checked. Press **OK** to save and close the Options dialog box. But is this progress?

Specifying a Folder for Recovered Documents

While we're on the subject of specifying folder locations, there's another one you should be concerned with. It's the folder for recovered documents, and it plays a big role in disaster recovery.

What disaster? How about a power failure while you're in the middle of making hundreds of changes to a thousand-page document? Any time your computer becomes incapable of saving your latest changes, for whatever reason, you can lose your work.

But there's hope! You can specify a folder location for recovered documents. With one of these specified, Word will always save your work in this directory, even changes you make that haven't been saved yet. So when the power comes back on, there's a better chance that more of your work is recoverable.

To specify a location for recovered documents, open the **Tools** menu and click the **Options** command. Click the **File Locations** tab to bring it to the front. In the File Types box, click **AutoSave Files**. Press the **Modify** button. Now enter the name of the folder in which you want Word to store recovered documents. Press the **OK** button (or press **Enter**) to save your location setting and close the dialog box.

Documenting Your Documents

When you start a new document (or any time thereafter), you can add document summary information, which will make it faster to recognize and easier to locate later on. With the Summary option, you can record the document's title, author, subject, keywords, and comments.

To add summary information to a new document, open the **File** menu and choose the **Properties** command. Click on the **Summary** tab to bring it to the front. Complete as many or as few of the summary fields as you like and then press **Enter** or the **OK** button. Save your document to save this new summary information.

There are plenty of statistics kept on every document that you might be interested in. They're stored in the **Statistics** tab.

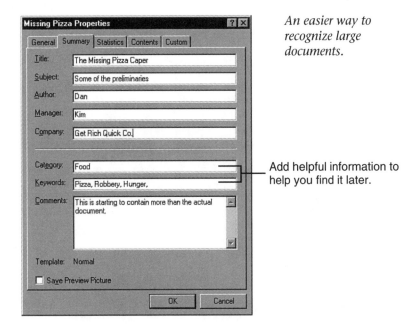

An easier way to recognize large documents.

Add helpful information to help you find it later.

You can also search on any of this summary information when it's time to try to find a lost document. These summary entries are among the fastest options for searching. Not many people religiously fill in summary details for documents, often because they aren't responsible for managing their computer files, and it can take a bit more of their precious time.

Comparing Versions of Documents

Sometimes you find a document on a diskette that has the same name as a document on your computer's hard drive. How can you tell which is the document you really want? Some people look at the date on the file, but a later date doesn't always mean the better document. No, a better way to solve the mystery is to compare the two documents and actually see the difference. But is there a way to ask your computer to look at both and tell you what the differences are? Yes, in Word for Windows 95, that feature is called *Revisions*, and you have several varieties of the feature to explore.

Make sure that the documents you are comparing have different filenames. If the documents have the same name, make sure they are in different folders. Start by opening the latest version of your document. To start comparing, open the **Tools** menu and choose the **Revisions** command. Click on the **Compare Versions** button to open the Compare Versions dialog box, which looks exactly like the regular File Open dialog box.

Find the other document you want to compare and double-click the name of the document to start the comparison process. Comparisons can take many seconds, even minutes, so be patient. When the comparison is completed, you will see a single document on your screen with all differences between the two documents fully identified. You can save this as a new document, or discard it after reviewing the change. Lawyers use features like this often to determine if any changes have been made to a contract.

Comparing two documents with the Revisions feature.

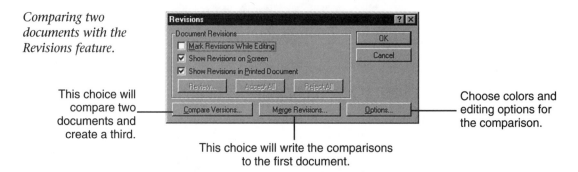

This choice will compare two documents and create a third.

This choice will write the comparisons to the first document.

Choose colors and editing options for the comparison.

Creating and Reading Annotations

If you give your document to someone else and ask for her opinion, she may decide to use Word for Windows 95 and put the Annotations feature to work. Using annotations, you can insert comments anywhere you like inside a document, and they won't print or change the formatting in any way. Annotations provide a way for reviewers to add their comments to the document without actually changing it. Annotations are formatted as hidden text, so they won't print.

To annotate your document, open it and place the insertion point in the location you want to add a comment. Open the **Insert** menu and choose the **Annotation** command. You can also use the **Alt+Ctrl+A** key combination. You can type your message (it will automatically be spell checked) and press the **Close** button to save it. A small set of initials will appear, representing the initials of the person creating the annotation.

You won't see an annotation, at least not in Normal view, because it's not really part of the document. But you can view annotations by changing your view of the document. Open the **View** menu and choose the **Annotations** command. Annotations will be revealed in the lower half of your screen. Each annotation will be identified by the initials of the author. If you want to see only the comments from a particular reviewer, select that person from the reviewer's list by clicking on it (or by pressing **Alt+R**). When you finish reading the comments, click on the **Close** button.

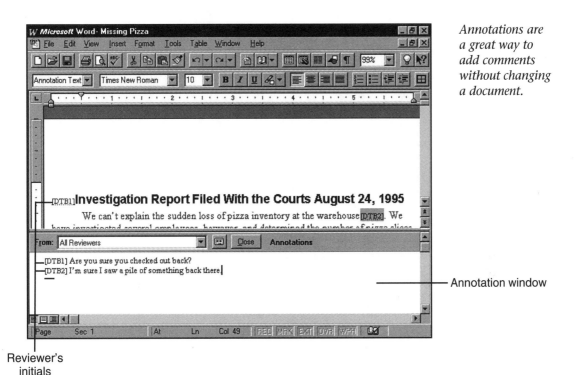

Annotations are a great way to add comments without changing a document.

Annotation window

Reviewer's initials

To locate the next annotation, scroll through your document or open the **Edit** menu and select the **Go To** command. In the Go To What box, click on **Annotation**, or press **Alt+W** and select it from the list. Click on **Next** or press **Alt+T**, and you'll find the next annotation in the document. You can also click on **Previous** (**Alt+P**) to move to a previous annotation.

To delete an annotation, make sure you are in Annotation view so you can see it. The annotation fields will be visible in your document when you are in the proper view. You must select the annotation field in your document first, before deleting it; the backspace or delete key alone won't cut it. You can also click in the Annotation part of your split-screen and delete your message there.

If you really want to print your document and the annotations, open the **File** menu and choose the **Print** command. Click on the **Options** button and under Include with Document, use the Annotations check box. If you are interested in printing the annotations only, select **Annotations** in the Print What list on the Print dialog box, and then press the **OK** button.

> **Viewing Annotations Without the Window**
> You can also view annotations by first displaying the hidden codes. Do this by pressing the **Show/Hide** button on the Standard toolbar. The annotation fields will be visible. Double-click on any of them, and the Annotation text will become visible.

273

Techno Talk

blah blah
blah blah
blah bl
b

What Did You Say?

More and more computers these days are classified as *multimedia*. That means, for one thing, that the computer can produce real sounds, not just beeps. If you have one of these machines, and if you have a microphone attached to your computer, you can even *record* your own voice annotation. Click the **Record** button in the Annotation window, speak your words of wisdom, and press the button again. The words won't be translated into text, but you will hear the recording if you click on the annotation. Remember, however, that you will have to have sound equipment on your computer if you want to hear the annotation.

Placing Identifiers in Your Printed Documents

You may find that it's easier to manage your documents if they all contain some type of characteristic identifier on them, something you can see at a glance and know where it comes from. For example, if you have lots of documents piled up on your desk and want to know if any given document is current enough to give to your boss, wouldn't it be helpful to have the actual print date appear in small letters at the bottom of the first or last page? It could save you from always having to print another copy.

There are lots of examples and requests for these kinds of identifiers, such as:

➤ Name of the person who made the last change to the document

➤ Revision number of the document

➤ Current page number and total number of pages in a document

➤ Total number of words and characters in a document

➤ Date the document was last printed

These interesting factoids belong to a group called *Fields*, and these happen to be intelligent fields. The good news is that you can place them anywhere you want in your document. Find a good spot in your document and place the insertion point there.

Now add these to your document. Open the **Insert** menu and select the **Field** command (or press **Alt+I**, then **E**). In the Field dialog box that's displayed, you could scroll through the Field Names list until you find an item you want, but it could take years. Click on one of the categories of fields, like **Document Information**, in the Categories box. Now you'll see a much smaller list of the more interesting items. Some fields also have additional options. Press the **Options** button if you want any special formatting applied to the intelligent field, such as capitalization or all uppercase.

Click on a field of your choice and press **Enter** (or click the **OK** button), and the field is inserted into your document.

You can't edit these fields like normal text because they are playing by different rules. If you don't like them, it's best to get rid of them completely instead of trying to edit them. To delete an inserted field in your document, select it first and then press the **Delete** key.

Intelligent Field? You Decide An intelligent field is text within a document (like the current date) that is updated automatically when a change occurs.

Save Options

Make sure you take the time to protect yourself. It can save you endless hours of pain in the unfortunate instant when disaster strikes—or when you're just too tired to remember to save your stuff.

Protect Yourself with AutoSave

When the AutoSave feature is active, your document is periodically saved to disk. That's good; it prevents a disaster in case you forget to save your document and something bad happens to your computer. The AutoSave feature isn't the same as pressing Ctrl+S or the Save button to save your document. Instead, Word makes a secret backup copy every so often. In the event of a power failure, for example, you can recover your work from this backup copy, even if you never saved your document at all.

To turn on AutoSave, open the **Tools** menu and choose the **Options** command. Click the **Save** tab to bring it to the front. Click on the **Automatic Save Every** box to put in an **X** if there isn't already one there. Then enter the backup time interval in the Minutes text box. For example, I type **7** to have Word for Windows 95 back up any open document every 7 minutes. If the power isn't very stable where your computer is plugged in, you might want to have an even lower number, like 5 or even 1 minute as your backup interval. Now press the **OK** button to return to your document.

After a disaster hits, the smoke clears, and you turn on your computer again, start Word for Windows 95. If you had a document open when the lights went out, Word will automatically open the backup copy and tell you it has been restored. You may not recover all of your document, but certainly most of it will be there. Since your computer thinks of this document as the backup copy, you will have to name it again when you save it, overwriting the previous document. That's okay to do, because the previous document is less likely to have the last changes you made before your disaster. The backup copy did have these changes.

A Word or Two About Fast Saves

Avoid them. Okay, maybe I'm being overly critical, but the concept of Fast Save still causes pain if you share documents with others. The purpose of the Fast Save is to keep you moving along quickly when a save occurs, so only the *changes* you make to a file are saved. For instance, if you open an existing document, make one change, and press Save, only the change is saved. And if you make lots of changes, the size of the document you save becomes much larger than if Fast Save is turned off.

Okay, you don't have to take my advice, take it from Microsoft itself. If you click for help on the **Allow Fast Saves** button, you get the message saying that Fast Saves are great, but turn it off when you are finished with your document so you can do a *full save*. Okay, what's your interpretation?

Why bring this subject up at all? Because the default setting is to have Fast Saves turned on. To turn them off, open the **Tools** menu and choose **Options**. Click the **Save** tab to bring it to the front. Click the **Allow Fast Saves** check box to remove the X in the box. Press the **OK** button to return to peace and serenity with your documents and Word for Windows 95.

Using Passwords to Protect Secret Files

You can place passwords on Word documents that require that anyone wanting to open the document must have the password. A dialog box pops up on the screen when you attempt to open a password-protected document, asking for the correct password. If the correct password isn't provided, access to the document is denied.

You can set passwords by opening the **File** menu and choosing the **Save As** command. Click the **Options** button and then click the **Save** tab to bring it to the front. Near the bottom left of the dialog box, enter a password in the Protection Password box. Above all, remember this password. There is no method available in Word that allows you to "look into" a file and read its password.

Also understand that passwords are case-sensitive. Check to see whether the CAPS LOCK key is on *before* you type a password, or retype the password to make sure that you didn't mistype it.

Using Briefcase to Keep Documents Up-to-Date

If you want to work on files at home or on the road, you can use Briefcase to help keep the various copies of the files updated.

To use Briefcase, you drag files from shared folders on your main computer to the Briefcase icon on your portable computer. When you are finished working on the files on the portable computer, reconnect to your main computer, and click **Update All in Briefcase** to automatically replace the unmodified files on your main computer with the modified files in your Briefcase.

The files on your main computer are automatically revised; you do not need to move the files you worked on out of Briefcase or delete the existing copies.

Create Your Own Briefcase
If you don't have a Briefcase on your Windows 95 desktop, you can easily create one. Move your mouse cursor to an empty spot on the Desktop and click the right mouse button. This opens the pop-up menu. Click on the **New** menu option and then choose the **Briefcase** command. A new briefcase will appear on your Desktop.

Keeping Work and Home Files Synchronized

Follow these steps to maintain a single and correct version of your document at work, and at home, by carrying it on a diskette.

Start by inserting a floppy disk into a disk drive on your main computer. Copy the document to your Briefcase. The easiest way is to open the **File** menu, choose the **Save As** command, and select the **My Briefcase** in the Save In box. You can also drag the document to the My Briefcase icon on your desktop, if you prefer. Still another way is to right-mouse-click on your document name (no matter where you find it) to reveal the pop-up menu, then click on **Send To** and choose the **Briefcase** command.

Now move the Briefcase to your diskette. The easiest way is to click the right mouse button on the briefcase and choose the **Send To** command. Send it to the option **3 ½ Floppy**. Don't forget; your diskette should already be in there. Now your document, or documents, will be on diskette.

Take the diskette wherever you want, and you can continue to work on your document. Take it home, use it on your portable laptop, give it to your secretary. To work on a document, place the diskette into that computer and use Word for Windows 95 to open the document from the diskette. Save the document when the editing is finished.

When you are ready to synchronize the files, reinsert the floppy disk containing Briefcase into a disk drive on your main computer, and then double-click the **My Briefcase** icon. On the Briefcase menu, click **Update All**.

But What If You Don't Want Them Synchronized Anymore?

You may decide that you want to keep an earlier version of a document on diskette, and don't want to accidentally synchronize it in your main computer. You want to break the relationship between the document on your diskette and the document in your main computer. This is called a *split*.

Open the My Briefcase on the desktop. Click the document you want to split. Open the **Briefcase** menu and choose the **Split From Original** command. That's all you have to do. After you split a document file from its original, it is labeled an *orphan* and stops being updated. Splitting separates the relationship between the copy of the document file inside Briefcase from the copy outside of the Briefcase.

The Least You Need to Know

Word for Windows 95 offers several features to help you manage your files better. You just have to learn how to use them. Some of the better ones are reviewed in this chapter, including these highlights:

➤ File Open makes it easy to rename and delete files. To rename, you just click on the name and edit it right where it is, without opening it. To delete, just press the **Delete** key and confirm that it's what you really want.

➤ Make your printed documents easier to identify. To add a date or other intelligent field to your document, open the **Insert** menu and select the **Field** command, and then choose from the hundreds available.

➤ Use the **Insert Annotation** command to insert comments into someone else's document. Use the **View Annotations** command to view comments added to your document by others.

➤ Use AutoSave to periodically save your documents, in case you forget. Open the **Tools** menu and choose the **Options** command. Click the **Save** tab and check the **Automatic Save** box, and enter a small number (like 5 or 10) of minutes.

➤ You can take work home with you using My Briefcase feature of Windows 95. Dragging documents to and from the Briefcase is controlled by your computer, ensuring you always work with the latest version of your document.

Part 5
Troubleshooting Word for Windows 95

Yes, for those of you venturing beyond Chapter 2, here's where to go when it breaks—or won't even get started. Error messages have been known to cause lost documents, lost jobs, lost hair, and world hunger. Let's put an end to problems before they put an end to us. Fight back! Look it up! Take a peek at the next few chapters created especially to assist you in solving the most common problems you're likely to face in Word for Windows 95.

Chapter 23

Finding Lost Things (Documents, Toolbars, and Your Mind)

In This Chapter

➤ Looking for documents in all the right places

➤ Finding a document by name or date

➤ Using Word for Windows 95 Document Search features

➤ Finding a document when you only know a word it contains

➤ Finding hidden toolbars and menus

It's tough enough to find your car keys in this day and age—you don't need the extra headache of a complicated search for a particular document. Thank goodness Word for Windows 95 provides the kind of searching tools we've been asking for since the industrial age began. Too bad it can't find my car keys.

Finding Lost Documents

Finding lost documents isn't as bad as it used to be. For example, can you imagine searching through hundreds of files on the subject of hamburgers? Before Word for Windows 95, documents were limited to names with only eight characters, and it took way too long to preview them. Without a clear descriptive name, you were forced to open each, one at a time, to see if you recognized it. It could take days.

Now you can have names of up to 255 characters; more than enough to fully describe and recognize a document. And you can browse the entire contents of your document quickly, inside the Preview box, without wasting time opening the document. And if you still haven't found the document you are looking for, you can search to your heart's content using some powerful tools. You can search for documents by words (or fragments of words) used in their names, or by words that are stored inside of a document (the actual contents of the document). And you can search for documents on diskettes, your own computer, or even on other computers connected to your network.

Using File Open

All the searching capabilities you need to find documents are now included in the Open dialog box. This includes the capability to browse, perform simple searches, and perform very complicated searches, all in one screen.

To begin your search for a document, open the **File** menu and choose the **Open** command (or you can press **Open** on the **Standard** toolbar). Take a look at some of the new buttons available on the Open dialog box.

Starting your search by deciding where to look.

Look on diskettes you may have.

Look on your computer's hard drive.

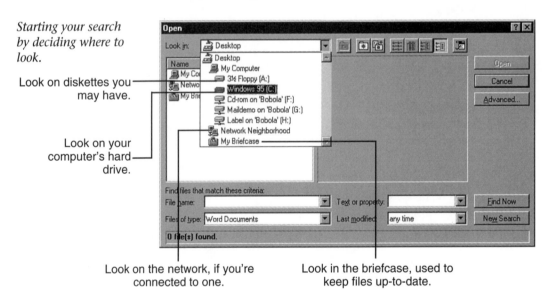

Look on the network, if you're connected to one.

Look in the briefcase, used to keep files up-to-date.

The start of a search for any document usually begins with the Look In box at the top of the Open dialog box. On the right side of the attached box is a down arrow, which reveals a drop-down list when you click it. Click the **down arrow**. This list contains all the possible places your computer can search for your documents.

You can search these locations:

➤ **Desktop**, which refers to your entire computer.

➤ **My Computer**, which represents all disk drives including network drives connected to your computer.

➤ 3 ½ **Floppy (A:)**, which represents your diskette drive.

➤ **CD-ROM Drives**, if you have any available.

➤ **Network Neighborhood**, which means you can search on any other computer on the network (if you have permission).

➤ **My Briefcase**, which is a special folder for storing documents that you often copy to diskette. There's more detail on the Briefcase in Chapter 22.

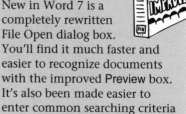

New and Improved Opens Today!
New in Word 7 is a completely rewritten File Open dialog box. You'll find it much faster and easier to recognize documents with the improved Preview box. It's also been made easier to enter common searching criteria by selecting from a list.

By double-clicking on any of these icons, you can dig deeper into the folder levels to find your documents. For example, double-clicking on My Computer reveals all the disk drives connected to your computer. Double-clicking any of these icons displays files and other folders that may be stored inside them.

Up One Level

If you open the Open dialog box and don't immediately see the document you want, it just means your document is stored somewhere else. Documents are usually stored in folders, and the Open dialog box can only display one folder at a time. Your computer has lots of these folders. So it helps to get comfortable moving around these folders and looking inside of them.

A folder can contain documents and other folders. When you double-click on a folder, you go *down* into it, and see the documents and folders that might be stored inside. You can continue to go down further by moving into folders inside of folders. It doesn't take too long before you want to back out of this adventure, and it's called moving *up* a folder, or level. You can continue to move back up, one level at a time, until you are back where you started. That's how you can move around in Word, and Windows 95, to find things you are looking for.

To make it easy for you to move around this way, a very important, and new, button is included in the Open dialog box. It is called the **Up One Level** button. Press this button once and you will move up a folder level. Press it again and you will move up another, and so on, until you are at the top level of your computer. It's kind of fun once, and then it gets boring. Let's continue.

Now, doesn't it seem kind of weird that there isn't any Down One Level button? You actually don't need one because every time you double-click on a folder, you are going down one level, into that folder. They only had to invent the Up One Level button so there would be an easy way to climb up out of wherever you dig yourself into!

Knowing this folder structure, you should feel more comfortable trying to explore folders to search for things. It's not absolutely necessary that you know how to jump up and down levels this way, but you'll be able to quickly find the majority of your documents this way. And it's much faster to perform a sophisticated search (which we'll learn shortly) if you start in the general vicinity (the folder level) of where the file is located.

Your Favorite Hiding Spot

Two other new buttons on the Open dialog box can help you store and find documents: the Look in Favorites and Add to Favorites buttons. This Favorites folder could become your *favorite* place to store the documents you create.

To find out if the document you want is in the **Favorites** folder, just click the **Look In Favorites** button. You can also create folders inside of **Favorites**, and you probably should if you plan to store more than a handful of documents here. Organize your documents by storing them in several logical folders, and name the folders so you will recognize them, such as Weekly Reports, or Client Contracts, and so on. It will be much easier to find what you're looking for in the future.

Exactly where is this mysterious Favorites folder stored? It's usually stored in the default Windows folder, but you really don't have to worry about it. Just be comforted in the fact that Word for Windows 95 knows where it is, and you can build your own structure of personal folders starting in Favorites. And since the File Open dialog box has a button called Look In Favorites, doesn't it make sense to store your documents here?

Looking on Diskettes

Lots of people save their documents to diskette—with good reason. There's a lot of comfort in the fact that you can carry the documents wherever you go, on a single diskette that's easy to protect. It's much rarer these days, but computer hard drives have been known to "crash," which means they lose all the documents (and everything else) stored on them. But if you have all your documents *backed up* to a diskette, you can take them to any computer and continue working. Oh, joy.

In the previous chapter, you learned how to save your files to diskette using the Briefcase feature of Windows 95. But you may have other diskettes full of documents from months or years ago, and these documents were copied to the diskette manually. Now it's time to review how you can find documents stored on a diskette. Diskettes can store lots of documents—maybe 10, 20, or more, depending on the size of the documents you create. And some people own thousands of diskettes (imagine how many documents you may have floating around out there on diskettes). So it becomes very important to be able to sort through the contents of a diskette quickly. Here's how to quickly scan a diskette for the document you are looking for.

Place your diskette containing documents into the diskette drive of your computer. Press it in all the way until you hear or feel a solid click that tells you it's in securely.

Open the **File** menu and choose the **Open** command (or press **Ctrl+O**). Near the top of the dialog box, you will see the Look In text box. On the right side of the attached box is a down arrow that reveals a drop-down list when you click it. So click it. This list contains all the possible places your computer can search for your documents. Click on the **3 ½ Floppy** to display the contents of your diskette. The documents will be displayed in the Name box.

If you have folders on the diskette, you can double-click them to look inside, and then press the **Up One Level** button to return to where you started.

If you don't see any documents, it could mean that the files stored on diskette were not created with Word for Windows 95; and in that case, your best bet is to view all possible file formats on the diskette. To view all types of files on diskette, click the down arrow connected to the Files of Type box near the bottom left of the Open dialog box. In the drop-down text box that appears, scroll to the top of the list and choose **All Files**. This option will allow you to see the name of any file, no matter what word processor may have created it. You might also see lots of other files that aren't documents at all, and it's best not to waste too much time on them. Be sure to check once again in any folders that might be included on your diskette.

If a quick browse of the diskette failed to locate the document you're looking for, you may have to apply some searching criteria and have your computer go look for it by itself. This feature of Word is covered next.

Searching All Over for Your Documents

Still can't find your document? It's time to get creative. Word allows you to throw in some curious information to assist in the search for a document. Do you know when it was last used? Can you guess at any part of the name or summary information? Do you know any words that might be inside the document? It might be enough to locate your document.

You can specify any additional search criteria you want in the bottom of the Open dialog box. You can type the name of the document in the File Name box, if you know it; or you can type partial names, and it's no longer necessary to use the wildcard character * (asterisk) at all. Just type as much of the word as you know (for example, just type gold to search for any document name containing the word *gold* anywhere in its name).

Now you must tell the computer where to search. To search all subfolders from where you start the search, click the **Commands and Settings** button (near the top right of the Open dialog box), and then click **Search Subfolders**.

To display the folders that contain the files found, click the **Commands and Settings** button again, and then click **Group Files By Folder**. Otherwise, you'll see only the names of the files found, and not the folders containing them.

With your search criteria entered, click the **Find Now** button. The search may take a few seconds, or longer, depending on your search criteria and the size of your computer's hard drive. If you ever want to stop a search, just press the **Stop** button.

If the search works well, and you want to use it again in the future, you'll find it at your fingertips. To use an existing saved search to find the files you want, click the **Commands and Settings** button in the Open dialog box, click **Saved Searches**, and then click the name of the search. Your original entries are loaded and ready for you to press the **Find Now** button.

The following is a summary of options (in the Open dialog box) for finding files:

➤ **File Name**   If you happen to know the name, type it here so searches through folders won't display anything but the document you're looking for.

➤ **Files of Type**   To specify the type of file you want to open, like a Word document or WordPerfect, or any other type of document.

➤ **Text or Property**   To locate all files that contain specified text, either in the file contents or as a file property, such as the title, enter the text in the Text Or Property box. For example, to find only files that contain the phrase "fresh hamburger," type **"fresh hamburger"** in this box. You must enclose what you type in quotation marks (" ").

➤ **Last Modified**   To find all files that were saved during a specific time period, like any files created in the last day or week.

Using Advanced Searching Features of File Open

If the list of files found does not contain the file you want, you can specify even more detail in your search criteria. In the Open dialog box, click **Advanced....**

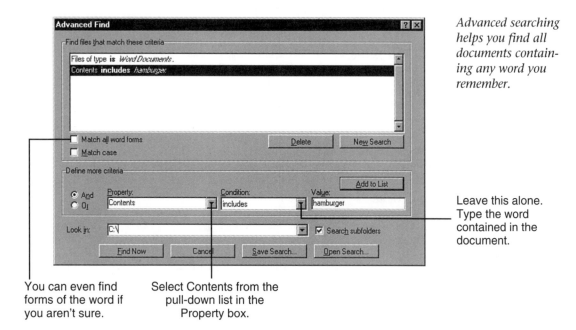

Advanced searching helps you find all documents containing any word you remember.

Leave this alone. Type the word contained in the document.

You can even find forms of the word if you aren't sure.

Select Contents from the pull-down list in the Property box.

This dialog box looks intimidating, and it is sort of, but it's worth the investment of learning a simple and important search feature. See the Property box? Click the arrow to expose the pull-down list of possible properties to search on. If you ever bothered to enter the summary information when previously working with a document, you can quickly find those documents now, and you'll be pleased that these properties are among the fastest things to search for. For example, if you filled in the Company or Keywords fields (or any of the other fields) in the Properties dialog box for any documents you have created, you can now perform searches like finding all documents related to XYZ Company.

If you want to try a more complicated search, give this a try. If you ever want to find a particular word inside of a closed document, no matter what the word or where the document might be, follow these steps.

In the Advanced... Find dialog box, click the **Property** down arrow to display the list of choices. Find the word **Contents** and select it; it will appear in the Property text box. Leave the Condition box alone, as long as it has the word Includes in the box. Now click in the **Value** box and type the word you are looking for. Once the boxes are filled in, press the **Add to List** button. You will see a sentence describing your search in the display box.

Before starting the search, you may want to narrow down or expand it with further available options. Click on **Match All Word Forms** if you want to find similar forms of a word (for example, choosing this option on a search for the word "sell" will also locate documents containing the words "selling" and "sold." Or you might want to click **Match Case** if you are certain of the case of letters in your word search. Also, be sure to put a check mark in the Search Subfolders check box if you are interested in checking the folders beneath the current one.

When you are ready to go, click the Find Now button. This type of searching takes significantly longer than other types, so be prepared to wait many seconds or minutes, again depending upon the complexity of your search and the number of documents it has to look at. During the search the Find Now button turns into the Stop button, which can stop a search in progress if you've changed your mind.

After a successful search you may want to save your searching parameters for the next time you need to search. You can save your search criteria by pressing the **Save Search** button and providing a name for your search.

Finding Hidden Toolbars

One day you may look up to the Standard or Formatting toolbar to execute a familiar command, and it won't be there! The entire toolbar may be gone! You can either celebrate or try to get it back. You probably don't need any help celebrating, but here are a few tips to bring it back.

First of all, realize that the toolbar really isn't gone; it has just disappeared temporarily from view. Whether it was intentional or accidental, there's no need to worry because you can bring it right back. Just open the **View** menu and select the **Toolbars...** command. If you don't even see your menu bar, there's still no need to panic. Have faith and press the combination keys **Alt+V**, and the **View** menu will pop down from nowhere.

Choose the toolbars you want to see.

Standard and Formatting are the most common choices..

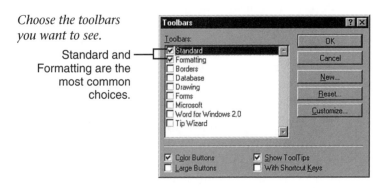

288

Now you see the Toolbars dialog box, and it lists all the available toolbars that can be placed on your screen. Just click the box to add or remove the checkmark that designates if you see it or not. You can choose to see all of them, but the screen would be so crowded that you wouldn't have any room left to write. The standard Word screen usually has the **Standard** and **Formatting** toolbars checkmarked, so start with those.

Waking Up and Finding Your Ruler Turned into a Monster

If you find that your ruler has changed into a toolbar full of strange symbols like arrows, numbers, and math symbols, it doesn't mean your ruler has been impeached. You are simply in the Outline viewing mode of Word. To find out more about using this toolbar, review Chapter 19 ; otherwise, to get rid of it, open the **View** menu and choose either **Normal** or **Page Layout**.

Missing Buttons on Your Toolbar?

There's no need to look on the floor. If any of your toolbars are missing buttons, especially ones you want, you can always bring them back.

You can also customize your toolbars to contain exactly the buttons you want. It's a good idea to stay away from the feature about to be described because you can accidentally remove a button, change button order, or put so many buttons on a toolbar that they extend beyond your display. But you can peek and cause no harm.

Open the **Tools** menu and choose the **Customize** command. In the Customize dialog box, you will see three tabs: Toolbars, Menus, and Keyboard. These are important screens because they define how you see the features of Word for Windows 95. Click on the **Toolbars** tab to bring it to the front, if it isn't already.

Before you make any changes, look near the bottom of this dialog box for the Template box. Since toolbars are saved inside a template, you should make sure you aren't changing the Normal template. Click the drop-down box to select another template, or type in a new name for a new template now.

In the Categories list, you see names for each group of buttons classified by function. The buttons grouped in that category are displayed in the Buttons preview box. For instance, the Table category has 18 buttons for creating tables (and you only have one on the Standard toolbar). You can customize your own toolbars by dragging and dropping any button onto any toolbar.

Once you see how easy this is, you may be tempted to change all of your toolbars. That's not recommended. I suggest you create a new toolbar and keep all of your changes limited to that single toolbar. Then you can always return to the original toolbars if someone else needs to work at your computer.

What to Do When Everything Is Hidden

Assuming your computer is turned on and functioning properly, and Word for Windows 95 is running with a document open, you may find nothing else on the screen but your document. No toolbars, no menus, no scroll bars; nothing but document. You probably requested this state of consciousness; and it's popular once you are familiar with Word because it allows the largest viewing area of your document. It's called Full Screen view.

If you want to experience this for yourself, open the **View** menu and click the **Full Screen** command. All of the parts of Word you've come to know and love will disappear. You are left with nothing but your document. And yet you have all features available to you, if you remember the keys to get there. For example, press **Alt+F** and you will see the **File** menu, or **Ctrl+P** to print your document.

 You may see this little icon on your screen. Then again, you might not. If you do see this icon, you can press the **Full Screen** button and restore visibility to all of Word for Windows 95.

If you are the curious type and click the **Close** button on this full screen icon, it disappears for good. Permanently. The next time you change to Full Screen view, you will no longer see this icon. There's only one escape—and that's Escape. The Escape key always works in Full Screen view to take you back to seeing all of Word for Windows 95.

The Least You Need to Know

I still haven't found my car keys, but I have found every document that contains a reference to them. Lucky me. Lucky you, too, if you gleaned some of these tips from this chapter:

➤ You can find any document you want by using the features provided on the Open dialog box. Open the **File** menu and choose the **Open** command, or press **Ctrl+O** to see it.

➤ Get in the habit of searching different levels of folders when trying to locate files. Use the **Up One Level** button in the Open dialog box to help you get around.

➤ You can search for files on diskette, on CD-ROM, and even on other computers attached to a network you might be on, by choosing the appropriate source in the Look In box. You can even apply advanced searching criteria to help you find documents hiding in these locations.

➤ By clicking the **Advanced...** Find button on the Open dialog box, you can perform such searches as finding any or all documents that contain the word "buy" or any form of the word "buy," including "buying" and "bought."

➤ Hidden toolbars can be exposed by opening the **View** menu and choosing the **Toolbars** command. To make a toolbar visible, click its entry in the toolbar list.

Chapter 24

Exterminating the Editing and Formatting Bugs

In This Chapter

➤ Common problems and how to solve them

➤ When you need help with editing

➤ Solving formatting bugs before they drive you crazy

There's nothing worse than being stopped dead in your document because some unknown bug has reared its ugly head, and you don't have a clue how to proceed. This chapter is here to help with some of the more common tribulations that plague innocent souls.

This chapter does not expose any "bugs" in Word for Windows 95, but rather the irritating details you might have overlooked. They're grouped vaguely into categories to help you locate answers faster, but it might help to scan them all, since the toughest problems are the hardest ones to describe or categorize.

Sentence and Paragraph Problems

Here are some of the most perplexing issues facing the human race, at least as they apply to sentence and paragraph formatting using Word for Windows 95.

Getting Rid of Those Dots Between Your Words

One day you may find your document is full of dots and other strange symbols. And to your surprise these symbols don't show up on paper when you print the page. What gives?

At least they don't print.

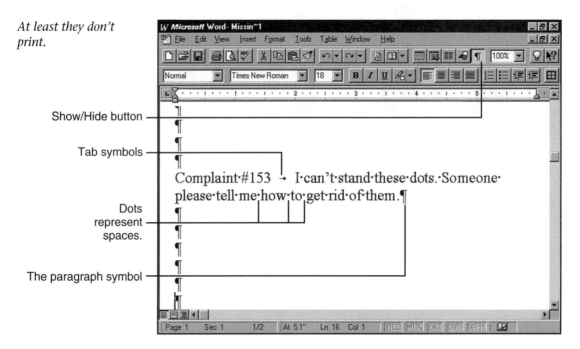

The symbols you are viewing are called *nonprinting characters*, and they serve a good purpose. They represent the places you pressed the Spacebar, Enter, or Tab keys. You are able to see them now because your Show/Hide button on the Standard toolbar is depressed. Cheer up! This button is a toggle, and pressing it again will hide all of those symbols on your screen.

You may want to use this button someday—on purpose. It's helpful to reveal the details of styles and alignment (example: is that really a tab or just several spaces?).

My Words Are Really Large, but They Don't Print Large

What you see may be deceiving. Take a gander at the **Zoom Control** button on the **Standard** toolbar. If it shows a number greater than 100%, then you are viewing something larger than real life. Click the **Zoom Control** button and select something smaller, such as **100%** or **Page Width** to get a better idea of the true size of your words.

If you really want to make your words larger on the page, you need to adjust the font size. Select the words you want to shrink by using your favorite selection method from Chapter 6, and then press the **Font Size** button on the Formatting toolbar and choose a large point size for your characters. The bigger the number, the larger your text.

Another quick way to confirm how your page actually looks before you waste paper printing it is to open the **File** menu and choose the **Print Preview** command. You will see the entire perspective of your document displayed on the screen, to give you a quick warning if something is way too big or small.

What Happened? Where Am I?

If your fingers or mouse ever slip when trying a command in Word, you may find yourself lost, because an unknown event occurred. That's why the **Shift+F5** key combination was born (at least we think that's why). This command takes you back to the previous spot of your document where you last worked, and things should look more familiar (at least it should be; you were just here a second ago). If you don't like where you land, you can press **Shift+F5** again to go back again.

Also remember the **Undo** key (or **Ctrl+Z**). By undoing whatever that mistake was, you might recognize the territory once again and return to that comfortable state of word processing bliss.

Stop Word from Replacing My So-Called Mistakes

If you happen to work for the ACN Corp., or any other of hundreds of companies with acronym names that happen to appear on the "misspelled" list in Word's AutoCorrect, you're probably irritated that it always changes to CAN Corp. Instead of turning AutoCorrect off altogether, just remove that entry from the AutoCorrect listing. Open the **Tools** menu and choose **AutoCorrect**.

Now delete the AutoCorrect entry you no longer want Word to correct automatically. In the list under the Replace box, click the entry you want to remove and press the **Delete** key.

To turn off the AutoCorrect feature, clear the Replace Text As You Type check box.

My Document Is All Locked Up!

Sometimes a Word feature appears broken because it has no affect on your document. Check to see if your document is protected. When you protect a document for revision marks and annotations, or when you protect a form, you make some commands unavailable. To restore access to all Word commands, open the **Tools** menu and choose the

Unprotect Document command. If the document is protected with a password, you must know the password before you can remove protection from the document.

AutoFormat Didn't Do Squat to My Document!

This frequently starts to happen as you begin to explore styles. The **AutoFormat** command on the **Format** menu applies styles only to text that is formatted with the Normal or Body Text style. If you have changed some or all of your document to different styles, nothing will happen when you run AutoFormat.

If you want to remove all previous formatting so AutoFormat will work, click **Options** in the AutoFormat dialog box, and then clear the Styles check box. Your document will revert to the Normal template, and AutoFormat can run and should make a difference.

Why Did My Text Formatting Change When I Cut Text?

Believe it or not, the paragraph mark stores the paragraph style for the text preceding it. If you select text that includes a paragraph mark and then use the **Cut** command, the remaining text will take on the style of the *next* paragraph.

My Mouse Must Be Dying—It Keeps Selecting Text Everywhere

Mice do die, but that's not a symptom. The Extend Selection mode is probably turned on. This is a mode that allows you to select different portions of text. It's not that popular, and your fingers can accidentally land you in this temporary mess. When this mode is active, the letters EXT appear bold on the status bar. To cancel the Extend Selection mode, double-click on the EXT box on the Status bar at the bottom of the screen. Or you can press **Esc** (Escape key), and then click anywhere in your document. People forget about the "clicking anywhere" part of the solution.

I Can't Select or Change My Bullet or Number Character

That's right. You cannot select the automatic numbers and bullets added by Word. But you can change the appearance or character used for the bullets or numbers. Here's the scoop:

➤ **To Modify Bullet or Number Formats**   Select the paragraphs that have the bullet or number format you want to change. Open the **Format** menu and choose the **Bullets And Numbering** command. Click the tab for the type of list you want to modify. Press the **Modify** button and change any of the format options you want. If you want to modify a multilevel list, you have to do it one level at a time.

➤ **To Remove Bullets or Numbering**   To remove a single bullet or number, click before the bullet or number and press the **Backspace** key.

To remove many items, select the bulleted or numbered items you wish to change. To remove bullets, press the **Bullets** button on the Standard toolbar. To remove numbers, press the **Numbering** button on the Standard toolbar.

I Only Wanted One Line Bulleted, Not All of Them

When you add automatic bullets and numbers to items in a list, Word adds bullets or numbers to each selected paragraph. If you press the **Enter** key at the end of each line of a paragraph, you'll get a bullet or number on each line. If you really want the paragraph broken into shorter lines, use **Shift+Enter** (instead of Enter) to return to the next line.

To clean up this document, you must delete the paragraph marks at the end of all lines (except the last line). The numbers or bullets will disappear.

Where Did My Page Numbers Go?—I Can't See Them

What view are you looking at? Word does not display page numbers in Normal view; they are best displayed in Page Layout view. To view page numbers, click the **Page Layout view** button to the left of the horizontal scroll bar.

If your view is correct but you still don't see the page numbers, they may be overlapped by other text. The page numbers are inserted in frames, which can be positioned in the same location as other text in a header or footer. To avoid overlapping text, position the other frames outside the header or footer area, leaving the page numbers visible.

Getting Rid of a Really Tough Page Break

Sometimes you may end up with a page break in the middle of your document that you don't want. But no matter what you try, you can't seem to delete it. What went wrong?

You may have applied paragraph formats that affect the document's pagination, such as Page Break Before, Keep With Next, or Keep Lines Together. Select the paragraphs surrounding the unwanted page break, open the **Format** menu and click the **Paragraph** command. Click the **Text Flow** tab to bring it to the front. If the Keep Lines Together, Keep With Next, or Page Break Before check boxes are selected, clear them. Then you will be able to delete the Page Break.

Otherwise, you may have created a section break and selected the Next Page, Even Page, or Odd Page option, which contains a page break. Click the section immediately following the section break, and then open the **File** menu and choose the **Page Setup** command. Click the **Layout** tab to bring it to the front, and then click **Continuous** in the Section Start box. You will now be able to delete the Page Break.

Too Many Hyphens?

Hyphenation is an automatic feature that splits long words at the end of a line to make the text fit better on the page. The default setting is to have it turned off, and no words are hyphenated. It's generally believed that hyphenation tends to slow down your pace of reading. But if you like to play with columns, it's a good thing to turn on.

Whether you want to turn it on or off, you can do so by opening the **Tools** menu and choosing the **Hyphenation** command. The Hyphenation dialog box will also let you be somewhere in between on and off. Try adjusting the Hyphenation Zone, which is the distance from the right margin that determines if a hyphenation will occur. Or you can make newspaper columns more readable by changing the number listed in the Limit Consecutive Hyphens To: box. Change the zero to a 3, for instance, to ensure your reader will get a visual break on the forth line. Be sure to press the **OK** button to save your changes and return to your document.

Font Problems That Can Cure Insomnia

This portion represents some of the more common font problems plaguing our world today. Some of these are closely related to printing problems, so if your font problem is on the printed page, you may also want to refer to the next chapter on Printing Paranoia.

Revealing the formatting codes.

Click with the Help pointer to see the formatting details.

Click any character.

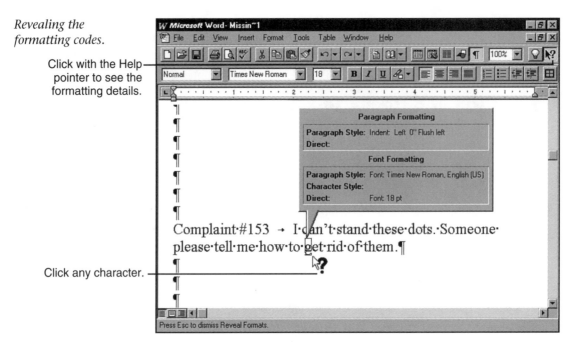

Don't forget, the easy way to see the details of any font code is to click the Help Arrow/Pointer in the Standard toolbar, which turns your insertion point into a question mark floater, and then click on top of any character to reveal formatting information.

My Font and Font Size Boxes Are Empty

Empty boxes on the Formatting toolbar just mean that you have selected two or more paragraphs that have different formats, and Word can't display the different settings at the same time. You can, however, select a font or font size with two or more paragraphs selected, and the entire selection will receive the new font or size.

The same applies to the Ruler. On the horizontal ruler, dimmed indent and tab markers show the settings for the first paragraph in the selection. To apply a format to several selected paragraphs that have different formats, you can still adjust the ruler settings, click toolbar buttons, and select dimmed or blank options in the Paragraph dialog box.

My Subscripts and Superscripts Have Been Chopped Up

If your subscript characters appear cut off, adjust the *position* of the subscript. Select the subscript text, then open the **Format** menu and choose the **Font** command. Next click the **Character Spacing** tab. Decrease the points in the Position By box to adjust the lowered text until the subscripts can be seen clearly.

If your superscript characters appear cut off, increase the *line spacing*. Open the **Format** menu and choose the **Paragraph** command to open the Paragraph dialog box. Click the **Indents And Spacing** tab, and then click **Exactly** in the **Line Spacing** box. In the At box, type a point size that is a few points larger than the font size used in the paragraph. Do this a little at a time until the superscript is clearly visible.

Printed Text Looks Different from the Text on My Screen

First check to see if you are displaying a draft font on your screen. Open the **Tools** menu, click **Options**, and then click the **View tab** to bring it to the front. Make sure the Draft Font check box is not checked. If it is, click on it to uncheck it, and your problem has been solved. You were viewing a replacement font used to quickly move about the screen. If that wasn't the problem, keep reading.

The font used in the document might be a *printer* font that is not available on the connected printer, so the printer substituted its own font. Change the font in your document to a TrueType font, which will print as closely to the screen display as possible, or change the font to a font available on your printer.

Finally, the font used in the document might be a printer font which *is* available on your printer but which doesn't have a matching screen font. Windows will substitute a TrueType font to display the text on the screen. For better consistency between the screen display and the printed document, change the fonts in your document to TrueType fonts.

If you want to find out if your document is formatted with a font that is not available on your printer or computer, start by opening the **Tools** menu and click the **Options** command. Click the **Compatibility** tab and then click **Font Substitution**. If the substituted font is listed as Default, then Word uses the font that best matches the size and appearance of the missing font.

Problems of Style

Styles act goofy enough to drive anyone insane. If this is your first encounter with Styles and you're having a bit of difficulty, don't feel bad. Review some of these more common problems and solutions.

Style Gallery Didn't Keep the Template with My Document

Sorry about that. The Style Gallery command does not change the template attached to your document; it just allows you to copy styles from other templates to your document. To attach a different template to your document, use the **Templates** command on the **File** menu.

Same Style—Looks Different. What Gives?

You may have two paragraphs that have the same style, but they look very different. The Style function is not broken; this problem relates to something outside of Styles.

Some paragraphs might have been formatted manually by pressing buttons on the Formatting toolbar (such as Bold, Italic, or Underline) or with the **Font** or **Paragraph** commands located on the **Format** menu. To remove any of this manual formatting, select the paragraph (including the paragraph mark) and then press **Ctrl+Spacebar** to remove character formatting and **Ctrl+Q** to remove paragraph formatting. Now they will look the same.

My Style Just Changed for No Reason

Sure it did. Let's review what can appear to be a "no apparent reason." Remember learning that all documents are based on the Normal style? The Normal style is the base style for many of Word's built-in styles, as well as for styles you may have modified or created.

If you redefine the Normal style or any other base style, other styles in your active document might change. For example, if you change the font in Normal to the Century Gothic font, Word will change the font for the styles used in footnotes, headers, footers, page numbers, and other text you might not have thought about.

If you don't want a style to change when you change the base or Normal style, make certain that your style is not based on another style. To do this correctly, open the **Format** menu and click **Style**. Click the style you want to modify in the Styles box. Click the **Modify** button and then click **(no style)** in the Based On box.

Annoying Picture and Graphics Problems

Ugly pictures and graphics are annoying, and there's nothing I can do to help but recommend that you don't use them. If you have pretty pictures, however, and are having difficulty working with them, I can help. Here are a few of the more common graphics problems you may run into, along with some no-nonsense solutions. Some of them are even proven to work.

I Inserted a Graphic, but Only Part of It Is There

The line spacing in your document may be set to an exact amount that is smaller than the height of the graphic. Generally, line spacing varies depending on the font and point size of the text in each line. If a line contains a character that is larger than the surrounding text, such as a graphic, Word increases the spacing for that line. However, if you specify an exact line spacing on the Indents And Spacing tab that is too small to accommodate large text or graphics, the graphics or text will appear clipped. To see the entire graphic or text, increase this line spacing.

Start by selecting the graphic, then open the **Format** menu and click the **Paragraph** command. Click the **Indents And Spacing** tab to bring it to the front. In the Line Spacing box, click **Single**. If you select **Exactly** in the Line Spacing box, be sure to increase the measurement in the At box to the height of the graphic.

I Can't See the Frame I Just Created for My Graphic!

It's there, have faith. You can only see a frame that contains graphics when it's *selected*. To select a frame, click the objects that are in the frame. Or click in the general vicinity of where you created the frame. Remember, you must be in Page Layout view to see frames. You can change to this view by opening the **View** menu and choosing the **Page Layout** command, or by clicking the **Page Layout view** button near the bottom of your screen at the left end of the horizontal scroll bar.

Where Did My Graphic Disappear To?

This could be caused by a few things. Here are some of the possible causes:

➤ Did you just do something wild and crazy? Is there a chance that you deleted it accidentally? If so, you can still press **Ctrl+Z**, or the **Undo** button on the **Standard** toolbar to bring back a graphic that was accidentally erased.

➤ The Picture Placeholders option may be on. This option improves scrolling speed by displaying each graphic as an empty box. To turn this option off, open the **Tools** menu and click the **Options** command. Click the **View** tab to bring it to the front. Clear the Picture Placeholders check box, and your graphic will once again be visible.

➤ The graphic you want to see may be a drawing object. Drawing objects are not visible in Normal, Outline, or Master Document view. To view, draw, and modify drawing objects, you must be working in Page Layout view or Print Preview. Open the **View** menu and choose the **Page Layout** command.

Why Can't I Edit My Graphic?

If your graphic happens to be something called a *bitmap*, you may have a bit of difficulty editing it. Any image that is a bitmap cannot be ungrouped and modified with the tools on the Drawing toolbar. You can still add borders, shadows, labels, and callouts to bitmap images. If you really need to edit your bitmap, you can use another graphics application that specializes in bitmaps, and then insert it into your Word document.

The Least You Need to Know

This chapter covers many miscellaneous problems that are common to working with Word for Windows 95. If you have a problem, don't forget the basics:

➤ Remember that the **Undo** button, or **Ctrl+Z**, can usually get you out of a bind.

➤ You can reveal the formatting codes of any character by first pressing the **Help** button on the Standard toolbar, dragging the question mark cursor to the character, and clicking on top of the character. The pop-up box contains the details of formatting.

➤ Many problems only appear to be problems because of the view on your screen. You can change your view by opening the **View** menu and choosing **Normal** or **Page Layout** for the most common views.

➤ When in doubt, call for help. In Word for Windows 95, the number to call is **F1**, or you can open the **Help** window and shout for one of the help commands.

Chapter 25

Printing Paranoia

In This Chapter

➤ Getting yourself out of a print jam

➤ Installing a new printer

➤ Common printing problems and how to solve them

➤ Faxing documents in Word

What good is Word for Windows 95 if you can't print your document? You'd have to buy a really long extension cord to drag your computer around to the people who need to read your documents. Save your money and review the answers to the most common printing issues—from setting up a new printer to clearing paper jams. And if you still can't print, at least you'll learn how to fax your document to your audience, directly from your computer.

Setting Up a New Printer

If this is the first time you are trying to print on your computer, or if you have just purchased a new printer, then you have to make sure your computer recognizes the printer. This task has been made much easier in Windows 95, if that makes you feel any better.

Press the **Start** button on your Windows 95 Taskbar. Choose the **Settings** command and then choose the **Printers** command.

Adding a new printer in Windows 95.

Double-click this icon to start the Printer Wizard.

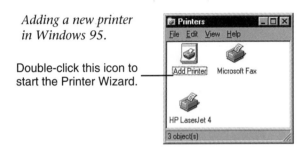

By double-clicking the **Add Printer** icon, you start a process called the Print Wizard. You are asked questions like "Is this a network printer or is it attached to your computer directly?" Answer the questions the best you can, and then click the **Next** button to proceed.

You will get the chance to identify the type of printer you have. Look for the name brand, like HP or Epson, and provide it when asked. Next you will need the model of your brand, and most of them will be listed. Choose your brand and model from the list and continue by pressing the **Next** button.

If your printer came with a diskette, you will probably need to use it. This diskette contains something called *drivers*, which is the code your computer needs to talk to your printer. If your printer can't find any code to run the printer you've selected, it will ask if you have a diskette. Place the diskette into your computer diskette drive and press **Enter**. The Print Wizard should be able to find the required code from the diskette, and continue the process of installation.

When you have finished, request a sample print page to test everything. Celebrate wildly if a printed page comes out and you can actually read it. But if you have problems getting this sample page printed, you need to perform more investigation, covered next.

Solving the Most Common Printing Problems

This brief list describes some of the more common printing problems you are likely to run into. Don't forget the basics when troubleshooting print problems—including good attachments of the printer cable, making sure everything is turned on, the printer is on-line, and the printer cable is plugged into your computer correctly.

Clearing a Paper Jam

If your document decides to take an off-ramp inside your laser printer, you will experience the thrill of a paper jam. To get the paper flowing again, open the cover of your laser printer and look, don't touch, for the snagged document. If you can safely reach it without touching any of the printer parts, do it; otherwise, wait for these hot parts to cool down. Grasp the paper firmly and gently pull it out.

Watch out for loose toner, too. This black dust spreads like the plague on your skin to your clothes to your lunch. Don't touch it if you can help it, and that includes the printing on the page you just yanked out (the toner may not have been burned into the paper yet).

When you close the lid of your printer, things should resume normally, but you probably have to reprint that last job (or maybe just a page or two).

If you happen to have a dot-matrix printer and the paper jams, turn off the printer. Rewind the paper knob to back out the paper from the printer. Be careful not to pull too strongly on the paper or it will tear, and then you'll have to take it apart to clear the jammed paper. Call for help, or see if there's a help section in your printer manual.

Here are some things you can do to prevent paper jams from ever occurring:

➤ When loading paper, remove any pieces that have even the smallest folded corner or crease. These tend to snag on the parts inside your printer.

➤ Make sure nothing is obstructing the path of your paper going into, or coming out of, your printer.

➤ Always use high quality paper. Cheaper paper tends to be dusty, and the dust gathers into dustballs inside, which can stand in the way of progress.

➤ If you want to print transparencies, you can, but be sure to buy the high-temperature type that can withstand the heat of your laser printer. Otherwise, it will melt inside and really gum up the works.

➤ The same goes for printing labels. It's even more important to purchase high quality labels because they're sticky to begin with. Buy a name brand, like Avery, and make sure the package mentions use in laser printers.

What to Do When Nothing Prints At All

When you follow all the rules and push all the right buttons, but still nothing comes out of the printer, do you have the right to beat on it? No—people will start to wonder about your childhood, and beating doesn't help anything come out of the printer any better or faster. And pressing the **Print** button fifty or sixty times will only add to your misery later.

Start solving this problem logically. First check cable connections; quite often a cable is just loose, and jiggling it around may get things started. Unplug a loose cable and plug it back in firmly. Read any error messages on the printer and see if they point to a likely cause. Blame your assistant if the printer wasn't turned on in the first place.

Now tell me about that print job. Do you have any large or detailed graphics inside? These are notorious for causing long printing delays—but they're only delays, and the job will ultimately print. Have patience.

Does history teach you anything at all here? When was the last time that printer actually printed? If it's been a while, maybe the printer does have a problem. Turn it off and on and run a self-diagnostic, instructions of which can be found on the printer or in the printer manual.

Well, At Least Part of My Document Printed

It starts out harmless enough, as you glance at a freshly printed document. But as you look closer, you notice some part of your document is missing. Where did it go, and how can you get it back?

➤ **If your graphics are not printing** You may be printing in draft mode. To print the borders and graphics in the document, open the **Tools** menu and click **Options**, then click the **Print** tab. Clear the Draft Output check box.

➤ **If only a partial page prints** Open the **File** menu and choose the **Print** command to make sure that you have selected to print all of the document, not just selected pages or text. Also check that you are using the correct orientation for your document, landscape or portrait. If the setting is correct in your program, check the properties of your printer to make sure the setting is correct there, too.

➤ **A header or footer didn't print** You may have placed the text in the nonprinting area of the page. Check your printer manual to see how close to the edge of the paper your printer can print. On the **File** menu, click **Page Setup**, and then click the **Margins** tab. Under the From Edge box, enter a larger value. If Word displays a message stating that a margin is outside the printable area of the page, click the **Fix** button.

Printing Font Problems

Take some initial steps to make sure your printer is set up correctly to print special fonts. If your printer uses a font cartridge, make sure that it is installed correctly in your printer, and make sure that the correct font cartridge is selected. Also check to make sure the Font settings in both your computer and the printer are capable of printing the font. Then review some of the other more common font symptoms:

➤ **No fonts printed**   It is possible that your printer does not have enough memory to print the document you are working on. If your document has complex graphics or numerous fonts, try printing a smaller portion of the document.

➤ **The wrong fonts printed**   Check to see what kind of fonts you are using in your document. You should use TrueType or printer fonts; screen fonts won't necessarily look the same printed as they do on your screen.

➤ **Really weird symbols printed**   They are likely called PostScript output. Click the **Details** tab on the Printer's File Properties and make sure you have the correct printer driver specified. To print a PostScript file, you must have a printer that supports PostScript.

Printing Is Really, Really Slow

If it's taking a lifetime to print your document, and you have a gut feeling that you're not going to live that long, try to investigate the cause. If you're printing tons of graphics, you may just have to wait because graphics are the most difficult things for a printer to print.

➤ **Check memory**   The more memory your printer has, the faster it will print. Check the memory settings in your printer properties and make sure they are correct.

➤ **Try printing a different resolution**   If your printer supports multiple printing resolutions, try printing in a lower resolution.

➤ **Make sure spooling is on**   Open the Printers folder and click the printer you are using. Open the **File** menu and then click **Properties**. Click the **Details** tab, and then click **Spool Settings.** Make sure spooling is turned on.

Why Aren't My Borders Printing?

Check the printing options in Word. Open the **Tools** menu, click **Options**, click the **Print** tab, and then clear the Draft Output check box. Next, on the **Table** menu, click **Gridlines**. If the borders disappear, they were gridlines, not borders. Word displays table gridlines on the screen but does not print them. To print the lines between cells, you have to add borders.

The easiest way to apply borders is to use the **Table AutoFormat** command on the **Table** menu, which automatically applies predefined borders and shading to a table.

You can also use the Borders toolbar or the **Borders And Shading** command on the **Format** menu to create custom borders and shading.

What to Do When the Print Command on the File Menu Is Dimmed

Your printer may not be selected, or the printer driver may not have been installed properly. On the Windows **Start** menu, click **Help**. Click the **Index** tab, and then search for printer drivers, installing.

If your printer is already selected, select a different printer to see whether the command becomes available. If the **Print** command is still dimmed, try reinstalling your printer driver according to the instructions in Microsoft Windows Help.

Why Do I Get a Blank Page at the End of My Printed Document?

Some blank paragraphs may have spilled onto the last page. To view paragraph marks, click the **Show/Hide** button on the Standard toolbar and see if any remain past the end of your document. If you see paragraph marks without text on the last page of your document, delete them. If you're printing to a network printer, see whether the printer has a form feed option. A blank page is considered the normal form feed at the end of a print job. Ask the network administrator to turn it off.

If You Need More Help with Your Printer

If printing has got you down, I strongly recommend using the Printing Troubleshooter available in the Word for Windows 95 help facility. This Printing Troubleshooter helps you identify and solve printer problems. Just click the appropriate buttons and try the suggested steps to fix the problem. It even asks you if the problem has been fixed as a result of its suggestion, or should we try the next likely solution on the list?

Open the **Help** menu and choose the **Help Wizard** command. Type your plea for help using words like, "Please help me troubleshoot this stupid printer." The key words to include are *print* (or printing or printer) and *troubleshoot*. Check out Chapter 4 for more information about Word's Help.

Changing Your Printer and Faxing

What's that? What does *faxing* have to do with *printing*? The answer is that both are very much related to one another, and that's good news for you. In the past, if you wanted to fax anything from your computer, you had to install special software and follow special rules about faxing. You can forget about all those hassles, because Windows 95 and Word provide a simple fax process.

A printer takes information from your computer and turns it into a printed page. A fax machine takes a printed page and turns it into something that flows over phone lines. Today's computers often have a fax machine built right in, and all you do is plug it into your telephone line for as long as it takes to send your fax. So how do you tell your computer to send your document to the fax machine, instead of the printer? By changing your printer, of course!

You don't have to understand it, just do it. Create your document in Word, and when you are ready to fax it, open the **File** menu and choose **Print**. Near the top of the Print dialog box, you will find the Name drop-down text box. Click the down arrow to the right of this box to see the printers you can choose from. If your computer is equipped with a fax/modem, you are likely to see the Microsoft Fax option in this list. If you don't, you can try to install it (see installing printers earlier in this chapter), or it means you don't have the equipment needed to fax. With **Microsoft Fax** selected, press the **OK** button and watch your computer come to life.

If it's not already set up, you will see the Compose New Fax Wizard dialog box, ready to help you through the fax process, from start to finish. Answer the questions the best you can and include a phone number. Make sure you connect the phone cable from your fax/modem in your computer to your telephone wall outlet.

If the Fax Wizard already set up your computer, selecting Microsoft Fax as the printer won't be as exciting, but you can still be excited because your document is ready to fax. Just press the **Print** button (or open the **File** menu, choose **Print**, and press the **OK** button). Your document will be transformed into outer-space sounds that travel the phone lines to your destination.

Don't forget to change your printer back to a real printer before you decide to print your document again. This mistake will cause an increase in your phone bill, instead of your toner bill.

Selecting a Network Printer

If your computer happens to be connected to a network, there's a good chance you have access to *many* printers. Maybe some are full-color or higher resolution, and you want to try them. You can select a network printer the same way you selected your own printer, or the fax in the previous example.

Open the **File** menu and choose the **Print** command. Find the Name box, and its pull-down arrow, near the top of the Print dialog box. Click the pull-down arrow and choose the name of your network printer. Press **OK** to print your document, and it will be sent to that printer.

If you can't find your network printer, and you are certain that it really does exist, you can try to set it up yourself. Press the **Start** button on the Windows 95 Taskbar. Choose the **Settings** command and then the **Printers** command. Double-click the **New Printer** icon to start the Print Wizard. You must know the brand and model of the network printer you want to use, or else your print jobs will come out looking miserable. Have this information handy so you don't panic.

The secret to the simplicity of this is an early question the Print Wizard will ask you. It wants to know if the printer you are installing is a network printer, or a local printer (which means a printer cable is connected between your computer and the printer). When you choose Network, the wizard analyzes your network connection, finds the printer, and sets up your connection with very little input from you. In my book, the fewer the questions the better, especially when conversing with your computer. During the last part of the installation, you are asked if you want to make this the default printer for all of your programs. It's a definite advantage to do this if that's your primary printer; you won't have to keep opening your File menu to select the different printer.

The Least You Need to Know

Printers are great when they're working. But sometimes they stop working, and so does your business. This chapter described methods for solving certain printing problems which can be performed by humans, including these tips:

➤ Setting up a new printer is almost fun when using the Print Wizard. Press the **Start** button on the Windows 95 Taskbar, select the **Settings** command, and choose **Printers**. Double-click to start the Print Wizard and answer all the questions to the best of your knowledge.

➤ Printer jams can occur if your printer is abused or you are using cheap paper, among other things. To clear a print jam, turn off the printer, open the cover, and carefully find and remove the stuck paper without touching any hot components.

➤ When in doubt, press the Help key (**F1**) to find the Answer Wizard, and enter **Print Troubleshoot** in the search area. Many printing problems can be solved through this method.

Moving Around in Word with the Keyboard

In This Chapter

➤ Quick ways to move around inside Word for Windows 95

➤ Getting to know your keyboard

➤ Weird keys—Who needs 'em?

➤ All menu commands have keyboard equivalents

➤ The top ten keyboard commands

This chapter is dedicated to the hard-core keyboard users, mousers need only browse.

And whether you're an expert 250-words-per-minute typing superstar or a hunt-and-pecker praying for enough money to buy voice-recognition gear for your computer, you'll find some helpful keyboard tips in this chapter.

The Complete Set of Basic Navigation Keys

Rounding out the complete set of navigation keys in Word for Windows 95 are the four arrow keys and the Home, End, Page Up, Page Down, and Tab keys. Pressed in combination with the Ctrl key, any of these navigation keys also becomes super-charged. For example, when you're pressing the right-arrow key, the cursor moves right one letter (character) in your word; pressing Ctrl+Right Arrow moves right one word in the sentence. Here's a list of the common navigation keys and their functions:

Key	Moves cursor to...	Ctrl+key moves cursor to...
Left Arrow	Left one character	Left one word
Right Arrow	Right one character	Right one word
Up Arrow	Up one line	Up one sentence or paragraph
Down Arrow	Down one line	Down one sentence or paragraph
Home	Beginning of line	Beginning of document
End	End of line	End of document
Page Up	Up one screen (previous screen, same position)	Left one screen (or previous unit, if left is not meaningful)
Page Down	Down one screen (next screen, same position)	Right one screen (or next unit, if right is not meaningful)
Tab	Next field (Shift+Tab moves in reverse order)	Next larger field

Other helpful key combinations include Ctrl+Alt+Page Up (or Down) to move page by page through your document, and the Shift+F5 keys to go back to wherever you came from. The Shift+F5 key combination is especially useful while you're learning your way around and getting lost.

Don't Forget About Our Little Mouse Friend

The mouse provides a quick and easy way to move the text cursor during your travels. After moving to a new location in your document, move the mouse pointer to where you want the text cursor to be and click the left mouse button. The cursor is instantly relocated. See Chapter 3 for more about using the mouse.

Getting Back to Where You Were

If you ever end up someplace you don't want to be, you can go back to where you started by pressing Shift+F5. This command even works after closing a document and coming back the next day. Just press **Shift+F5**, and the cursor takes you to the exact spot in your document where you were previously working.

The Go To Command

If the Ctrl+Home and Ctrl+End key combinations let you fly to the beginning and the end of a document, what do you do if you want to get off somewhere in the middle? The Go To command in Word for Windows 95 is what you need.

Go To enables you to go directly to just about anywhere in the document you want to be. To get there, press the **F5** key (or you can click the **Edit** menu and then click the **Go To** command). You will see the Go To dialog box.

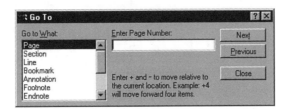

Get where you're going with Go To.

You can type a number of things in the Go To dialog box, but probably the most useful is the page number. For example, type **12** in the box and press **Enter**, and you'll be taken to page 12 in a heartbeat.

So Where Are You?

If you're interested in knowing exactly where you are in a document, look at that status bar! It gives you some valuable information about your location within a document. The status bar shows you which page you're on, which section you're in, and your exact position relative to page number, distance from the top of the current page, the line number, and finally the column. Someone out there must find this useful.

Let Your Fingers Do the Walking

The computer keyboard is the primary method of getting your thoughts on paper. You type, and your words show up on-screen. You print, and they show up on paper. It's a necessary evil, this keyboard. It was designed long before you were born, probably on a dark and stormy night. There's no order here; some keys are big, others small. None of them are lined up correctly, not to mention the alphabetical order problem. A committee probably designed the keyboard.

Here's some good news—almost all desktop computers built since 1990 have the same style keyboard. This is good because computers make much use of keys that didn't exist on the original typewriters, like Alt (Alternate), Ctrl (Control), Esc (Escape, ha!), F1-F12 (function keys), and a bunch more. Maintaining a keyboard standard means these new keys will always be where you expect them to be.

Keyboard lessons.

So What About the Weird Keys?

By themselves, they don't add anything visible to your written page, but without them, you'd be hard pressed to create a decent document. This is the scoop on those "miscellaneous" keys on your keyboard:

Enter In Word for Windows 95, you press the Enter key at the end of a paragraph, which is any grouping of words that should be treated as a unit—this includes normal paragraphs as well as single-line paragraphs (such as chapter titles, section headings, and captions for charts or other figures). This key also comes in handy with dialog boxes. One button on every dialog box is usually "selected" (has a darker border than the other buttons), and pressing enter (regardless of where your mouse pointer is) will "push" that button.

Esc Called the Escape key, Esc is used to cancel commands or to back out of an operation in Word.

Function Keys These are the keys labeled F1 through F12. They perform a function all by themselves, but each program uses them differently. Word uses F1 to mean Help, F2 means Move, and so on.

Shift Used just as it is on a typewriter, to type capital letters and special characters (such as #$%?>). In some programs, you can use the Shift key with other keys to issue commands with the keyboard. For example, in Word for Windows 95, Shift+F7 activates the Thesaurus.

Alt and Ctrl   The Alt and Ctrl key are used like the Shift key; press them with another key to issue commands with the keyboard. For example, in Word for Windows 95, Ctrl+B makes your words bold, and Alt+F opens the **File** menu.

Caps Lock   This locks in the capital letters. Unlike the "Shift Lock" on a typewriter, however, you will not get ! when you press the 1 key (even with Caps Lock on). To get ! when the Caps Lock is on, you must still press the Shift key and 1 key together. The same is true of @, #, and the rest of those top row characters (and a few others, like semicolon, period, and comma).

Backspace   Press this key to erase the letter or number to the left of the cursor. Use the Backspace key to erase all or part of a paragraph.

Arrow keys   These keys will make the cursor move in the direction of the arrow (if it is possible at the moment).

Spacebar   Use the Spacebar to insert a space between words and at the end of sentences. Documents these days include a single space between sentences, not two. In fact, it's rare to ever use two spaces in a row because other tools are better used to align text (like the Tab key, margins, or centering tools).

Tab   Use the Tab key to indent the first line of a paragraph or to line up columns in a pinch. A tab will always line things up. The Spacebar can't promise the same.

Insert (Ins)   If Insert is turned on (which is the default in Word for Windows 95), what you type is inserted between characters, beginning at the current cursor position. Press this key to switch to Overtype mode, and what you type will then replace existing characters. It's a toggle key, so pressing it once more returns to Insert.

Delete (Del)   This key deletes the character to the right of the cursor.

Home and End   Home moves the cursor to the beginning of the current line; End moves to the end of the current line.

Page Up, Page Down   Page Up displays the previous screen of text; Page Down displays the next page of text.

Num Lock   Hey, more arrows! If your keyboard has a numeric keypad built in, you'll find keys with numbers *and* arrows on them. The Num Lock key will toggle which is which. On, you get numbers; off, you get an additional set of arrow keys.

Laptop and Notebook Computers Beware

Laptop users have even more weird keys. After all, the full-sized keyboard wouldn't fit. Cut out some letters? Saw it in half? Some manufacturers chose to shrink all the keys down. People with little fingers had no problems, but the majority rebelled. No, the solution has been to sacrifice your numeric keypad or some function keys. We still wanted them, of course.

To provide the same function in a smaller space required the existing keys to work harder. Instead of the simple life of the J key, for instance, sitting around and doing nothing but creating a J, it has been assigned more work. Now it's the J key *and* the 1 key *and* the End key all at the same time (as long as you press J in combination with the Num Lock key and Alt, Ctrl, or Shift, depending on which laptop you're using). So you probably still have the numeric keypad, it's just overlapping existing keys.

Menu Commands and their Keyboard Equivalents

If you glance up at your menu bar in Word for Windows 95, you may see a peculiar trend. At least one letter in each menu is underlined. And if you open each menu, you'll find that each menu command has a single letter underlined.

These underlined letters are keyboard shortcuts. Instead of reaching out and grabbing the mouse, dragging it up to that menu, and clicking the button to open it, you can quickly click two keys and get the same results. The trick is to remember the **Alt** (Alternate) key. Try it yourself. The **File** menu has an underlined letter F. First click the **Alt** key, then click the **F** key. The menu opens! And that's faster than anyone can move and click a mouse.

If you get halfway through the process and change your mind (you pressed the Alt key but no letter) you must press the Escape key to continue.

You can expand your repertoire by using several keys in a row. The menu commands can be executed directly with the underlined letter, without using the **Alt** key. So to open a new file, you could type **Alt+F+N**.

Pay attention to any word with an underlined letter, including buttons (**Yes, No, Help**), menus, and help screens. Chances are you can execute it directly from the keyboard, and you may be more comfortable doing so.

Top Ten Keyboard Commands for Word (in No Particular Order)

So what keys do you plan to use beyond the 26 letters? Here are some of the favorites gleaned from previous generations of intense study and late-night experimenting.

Help (F1 Key)

Right there on top of the charts is the Help key, good old F1. Just like 911, it got its fame long before Word, and it's almost universally recognized as where to go for help. The Help key in Word for Windows 95 is made extra special because it's *context sensitive*, which means it looks at where your cursor is and gives a close proximity of the help you require.

Undo What I Just Did (Combination Ctrl+Z Keys)

Holding close at number two, and truly a godsend for trigger-happy folks, is **Ctrl+Z**. This magic key combination, used immediately after a screw-up, will put things back the way they were before the screw-up. You can also get to it from the **Edit** menu with the **Undo** command. And since you now understand shortcut keys, you can also use the **Alt+E+U** combination, but it's an extra letter of labor compared to **Ctrl+Z**. There is also an **Undo** button on the standard toolbar. Don't be afraid to try any new feature in Word now that you know how to repair things if it's not what you expected.

Once in a blue moon, however, (you knew this was coming) you can't undo what has just been done. It's just too hard for your computer. So always save your work often. Then you can close without saving to get rid of a screw-up. Some examples? Changing your screen view, or switching between opened documents, or printing. You have to take care of these yourself, using other methods.

If you made a mistake undoing something good and want to redo it, you can use the **Ctrl+Y** combination (or the **Edit** menu, **Redo** command; or keyboard equivalent **Alt+E+R**). There's also a **Redo** button on your standard toolbar. Think of the fun you can have trying to confuse your computer by pressing Undo and Redo at the same time.

Go Away! (Escape Key) Same as the Cancel Button

It's always safe to press the Escape key. Nothing bad will happen. Use the Escape key when you want to back out of a dialog box you don't understand or to get rid of a menu or message obstructing your view.

Save It Now! (Combination Ctrl+S Keys)

Save—after every word if your document is that important (or your memory really bad). What are you saving it from, you ask? The unknown. And since it's unknown, I can't describe it to you. But if you save often, you should have no fear of the unknown. You'll always be able to return to the state of your document at the last save.

Cut (Combination Ctrl+X Keys) but Not the Delete Key

This popular combination is used to remove selected text and store it in a temporary area called the *clipboard*. It's useful if you're trying to move something in your document. A cut is usually followed by a paste (see following sections).

The Delete key does not store the text in the clipboard, so it should be avoided unless you're really, really sure you want to get rid of something.

Cut can also be selected on the **Edit** menu with the **Cut** command. The keyboard equivalent is **Alt+E+T** when text is selected. **Cut** is also a button on the standard toolbar.

Copy (Combination Ctrl+C Keys)

Another popular function is to copy stuff around. The **Copy** command will easily copy the selected text or graphics to the clipboard, while leaving the original intact.

Copy can also be selected on the **Edit** menu with the **Copy** command. The keyboard equivalent is **Alt+E+C** when text is selected. **Copy** is also a button on the standard toolbar.

Paste (Combination Ctrl+V Keys)

Paste is usually used in conjunction with cut or copy (see preceding sections) because it pastes from the clipboard, that secret hiding place inside your computer. If nothing is in the clipboard, there is nothing to paste.

Paste can also be selected on the **Edit** menu with the **Paste** command. The keyboard equivalent is **Alt+E+P** when text is selected. **Paste** is also a button on the standard toolbar.

Do That Again! (F4 Key)

If you find yourself using the same command over and over again, no matter what it is, press the **F4** key. This key directs Word to automatically do the same thing again. It can be useful for repetitive maneuvers like adding text or symbols.

Take Me Back to Where I Was! (Combination Shift+F5 Keys)

It's easy to get lost in Word for Windows 95, especially in a large document. If you just pressed **Ctrl+End** for no apparent reason and suddenly find yourself at the end of your document, press **Shift+F5** to get back to where you were previously. This can be a real time-saver.

Print Now! (Combination Ctrl+P Keys)

Don't ask me any questions, just print the thing. Thank you. You can also find Print on the File menu, or you can use the keyboard equivalent **Alt+F+P** to do your printing. There is also the **Print** button on the standard toolbar for your convenience.

Installing Word for Windows 95

Installing Word for Windows 95 is relatively easy—easier than using it, actually. In fact, Windows 95 makes it so easy to install any product, including Word, that you don't have to understand the process at all. Just follow these steps.

1. Turn on your computer. Look for a switch on the front, back, or right side of that big box thing. You may also have to turn on your display (or monitor), which looks like a TV.

2. Windows 95 should start automatically. It looks really different than previous versions of Windows. If you don't have Windows 95, you won't be able to run Word for Windows 95.

3. If you have the CD-ROM containing Word, by all means use it. Just open your CD-ROM drive, place the CD label-side-up into the drive, and press the button to close the CD-ROM door.

4. If you have the diskette version of Word, insert the diskette labeled "SetupDisk 1" into the diskette drive on your computer. Click the **Start** button on the Windows 95 Taskbar and choose **Settings** and then **Control Panel**. Double-click the **Add/ Remove Programs** icon and then press the **Install** button.

5. During the installation process, you will be asked to type your name and company, and confirm the name of the installation folder, and you should accept the default provided.

6. Then you will see a screen that asks which type of installation you want to use. I'd recommend **Typical Installation** because it's the easiest and contains the most common options you are likely to need. If you don't have enough room on your computer, the installation program will tell you so, and then you can select **Laptop**

(Minimum) installation, which will install the minimum number of files needed to run Word for Windows 95. Avoid the Custom installation unless you are very brave or have a computer person helping.

7. The installation is fast and painless. Even though Windows 95 will let you do other things during installation, I would suggest you stay focused on the installation screen. You can read the feature billboards that appear on your screen during the installation period. They are actually helpful in pointing out the new features and describing how they can be used.

That's it! Follow any instructions you see on your screen, especially if you are installing from diskette; your computer will alert you when it's time for the next diskette. If for any reason you want to abandon the installation, you can press the **Cancel** button at any time.

Speak Like a Geek: The Complete Archive

The word processing world is like an exclusive club, complete with its own language. If you want to be accepted, you need to learn some of the lingo. This mini-glossary will help you get started.

accelerator keys   Keys which activate a command without opening the menu. Usually a function key or a key combination (such as Alt+F10) is displayed next to the menu command. To use an accelerator key, hold down the first key while you press the second key.

active document   The document you are currently working in. The active document contains the insertion point, and if more than one document window is being displayed on-screen, the active document's title bar appears darker than the other title bars.

alignment   How text in a paragraph is placed between left and right margins. For example, you may select left-aligned or centered text.

ASCII file   A file containing characters that can be used by any program on any computer. Sometimes called a text file or an ASCII text file. (ASCII is pronounced "ASK-EEE.")

border   A line placed on any (or all) four sides of a block of text, a graphic, a chart, or a table.

bulleted list   A list similar to a numbered list made up of a series of paragraphs with hanging indents, where the bullet (usually a symbol such as a dot or check mark) is placed to the left of all the other lines in the paragraph. A bulleted list is often used to display a list of items or to summarize important points.

cell   The box formed by the intersection of a row and a column in a Word table. The same term is used when describing the intersection of a row and a column in a spreadsheet. A cell may contain text, a numeric value, or a formula.

click   The single press or the release of the mouse button after you have moved the mouse pointer over an object or an icon.

clip art   A collection of prepackaged artwork whose individual pieces can be placed in a document.

Clipboard   A temporary storage area that holds text and graphics. The Cut and Copy commands put text or graphics on the Clipboard, erasing the Clipboard's previous contents. The Paste command copies Clipboard data to a document.

columns   Vertical sections of tables. See also *newspaper-style columns*.

command   An order that tells the computer what to do. In command-driven programs, you have to press a specific key or type the command to execute it. With menu-driven programs, you select the command from a menu.

cropping   The process of cutting away part of an imported graphic.

cursor   The vertical line that appears to the right of characters as you type. A cursor acts like the tip of your pencil; anything you type appears at the cursor. See also *insertion point*.

data source   A special document file that contains information (like names and addresses) that is later merged with another document to produce form letters or mailing labels.

desktop publishing   A program that allows you to combine text and graphics on the same page, and manipulate text and graphics on-screen. Desktop publishing programs are commonly used to create newsletters, brochures, flyers, resumes, and business cards.

dialog box   A special window or box that appears when the program requires additional information prior to executing a command.

disk drive   A device that writes and reads data on a magnetic disk. Think of a disk drive as a cassette recorder/player. Just as the cassette player can record sounds on a magnetic cassette tape and play back those sounds, a disk drive can record data on a magnetic disk and play back that data.

document   Any work you create using an application program and save in a file on disk. Although the term document usually refers to work created in a word processing program (such as a letter or a chapter of a book), a document is now used to refer to any work, including spreadsheets and databases.

document window   A window which frames the controls and information for the document file you are working on. You may have multiple document windows open at one time.

double-click   Pressing and releasing the mouse button twice in quick succession after you move the mouse pointer over an object or icon.

drag   Pressing and holding the mouse button when moving the mouse pointer from a starting to an ending position.

drop cap   An option used to set off the first letter in a paragraph. The letter is enlarged and set into the text of the paragraph, at its upper left corner. Word calls this letter a dropped capital.

edit   To make changes to existing information within a document. Editing in a word processor usually involves spell checking, grammar checking, and making formatting changes until the document is judged to be complete.

embedded object   An object that maintains a connection to the application that created it, so that if changes are needed, you can access that application by double-clicking on the object. An embedded object is stored within your Word document.

end mark   Mark designating the end of the document. As you enter text, this mark will move down.

field   Part of a file record containing a single piece of information (for example, a telephone number, ZIP code, or a person's name). A field is also a code inserted into a document which is updated when the document is opened, such as the Date field.

file   The computer term for your document. Anything can be placed in a file: a memo, budget report, or graphics images. Each document you create in Word for Windows 95 is stored in its own file. Files have filenames to identify them.

fixed disk drive   A disk drive that has a non-removable disk, as opposed to floppy disk drives, in which you can insert and remove disks. See also *disk drive*.

floppy disk drive   A disk drive that uses floppy disks.

floppy disks   Small, portable, plastic squares that magnetically store data (the facts, figures, and documents you enter and save). You insert the floppy disk into the floppy disk drive. See also *disk drive*.

folder   A place to store documents. Folders can exist on diskettes or hard drives, and folders can be stored inside other folders. Before Windows 95, folders were known as *directories*.

font   Any set of characters which share the same typeface (style or design). Fonts convey the mood and style of a document. Technically, font describes the combination of the typeface and point size of a character (as in Times Roman 12-point), but in common use, it describes a character's style or typeface.

footer   Text that can be reprinted at the bottom of every page within a document.

formatting   Changing the look of a character (by making it bold, underlined, and slightly larger, for example) or a paragraph (by centering it on a page, indenting it, or numbering it), or a page (changing margins, page numbers, or paper orientation).

Formatting toolbar   A set of buttons and commands arranged in a single bar that provide an easy method for changing the appearance of text within Word for Windows 95.

frames   Small boxes in which you place text or pictures so you can move them easily within your document.

function keys   The 10 or 12 F keys on the left side of the keyboard or the 12 F keys on the top of the keyboard. F keys are numbered F1, F2, F3, and so on. These keys are used to enter various commands in the Word for Windows 95 program.

Grammar Checker   A special program within Word for Windows 95 that reviews your grammar and offers suggestions on improving it.

graphic   A picture which can be imported into Word in order to illustrate a particular point.

gutter   An unused region of space that runs down the inside edges of facing pages of a document; it's the part of each page that is used when the pages of a book or a magazine are bound together.

handles   Small black squares that surround a graphic or frame after it is selected. Handles can be dragged to change the size or shape of a graphic.

hanging indent   A special kind of indent where the first line of a paragraph hangs closer to the left margin than the rest of the lines in the paragraph. Typically used for bullet or numbered lists.

hard disk   A non-removable disk drive that stores many megabytes of data. Because it is fixed in place inside the computer (see fixed disk drive), it performs more quickly and efficiently than a floppy disk.

header   Text that can be reprinted at the top of every page within a document.

header record   Storage of field names (column headings) for a data file.

I-beam   Another name for the mouse pointer in the text area of a document.

icon   A small graphic image that represents another object, such as a program or a tool.

indent   The amount of distance from the page margins to the edges of your paragraph (or the first line of a paragraph).

input   Data that goes into your computer. When you press a key or click a mouse button, you are giving your computer input. Data that your computer gives back to you (by printing it out or displaying it on the monitor) is called **output**.

Insert mode   The default typing mode for most word processors and text editors. Insert mode means that when you position your cursor and start to type, what you type is inserted at that point, and existing text is pushed to the right.

insertion point   A blinking vertical line used in Word for Windows 95 to indicate the place where any characters you type will be inserted.

intelligent field   Text within a Word document that is updated automatically as changes are made. Some intelligent fields, such as the date and time fields, are updated when the document is opened or printed.

kilobyte   A unit for measuring the amount of data. A kilobyte (KB) is equivalent to 1,024 bytes.

landscape orientation   Your document is oriented so that it is wider than it is long, as in 11-by-8$^1/_2$ inches. The opposite of landscape orientation is **portrait**.

leader   Dots or dashes that fill the spaces between tab positions in a list.

linked object   An imported object (such as a graphic) that maintains a connection to the program that created it, so that if changes are made to that object, those changes can be updated (either automatically or through a command) into your document. A linked object is stored separately from your Word document.

macro   A recorded set of instruction for a frequently used task which can be activated by pressing a specified key combination. Macros resemble small programs.

margin   An area on the left, right, top, and bottom sides of a page that is usually left blank. Text flows between the margins of a page.

megabyte   A standard unit used to measure the storage capacity of a disk and the amount of computer memory. A megabyte is 1,048,576 bytes (1,000 kilobytes). This is roughly equivalent to 500 pages of double-spaced text. Megabyte is commonly abbreviated as M, MB, or Mbyte.

memory   Electronic storage area inside the computer, used to store data or program instructions temporarily when the computer is using them.

menu   A list of commands or instructions displayed on the screen. Menus organize commands and make a program easier to use.

menu bar   Bar located at the top of the program window. This displays a list of the names of menus which contain the commands you'll use to edit documents.

merging   The process of combining information stored in a data source (like names and addresses) with a main document (like a form letter) in order to produce a series of form letters or mailing labels.

Mirror margins   An option you can use when creating magazine-like reports. When open, the pages of your report would face each other.

monitor   A television-like screen where the computer displays information.

mouse   A device that moves an arrow (or I-beam, or other point symbols) around the screen. When you move the mouse, the pointer on the screen moves in the same direction. Used instead of the keyboard to select and move items (such as text and graphics), execute commands, and perform other tasks. A mouse gets its name because it connects to your computer through a long "tail" or cord.

mouse pointer   An arrow or other symbol that moves when the mouse is moved. When the mouse pointer is over text, it changes to an I-beam. When the mouse pointer is over an element of the screen, it usually takes the shape of an arrow.

newspaper-style columns   Similar to the column style found in newspapers. Text in these columns flows between invisible boundaries down one part of the page. At the end of the page, the text continues at the top of the first column on the next page. Columns can be "interrupted" by graphics (pictures or charts) that illustrate the story being told.

numbered list   Similar to a bulleted list. A numbered list is a series of paragraphs with hanging indents, where the number is placed to the left of all other lines in the paragraph. A numbered list is often used to list the steps of a procedure in the proper order.

Overtype mode   The opposite of Insert mode that is used in word processors and text editors. Overtype mode means that when you position your cursor and start to type, what you type replaces existing characters at that point.

page break   A dotted line which marks the end of a page. A page break can be forced within a document by pressing **Ctrl+Enter**.

pane   What Word for Windows 95 calls the special boxes that you use when adding headers, footers, and annotations. In Normal view, a pane appears in the bottom half of the document window. (Since it's part of a window—rather than being a separate box like a dialog box—it's called a pane.)

paragraph   Any grouping of words that should be treated as a unit. This includes normal paragraphs as well as single-line paragraphs (such as chapter titles, section headings, and captions for charts or other figures). When you press the Enter key in Word for Windows 95, you are marking the end of a paragraph. (Note: some computers call the Enter key Return.)

passive voice   A type of sentence that states what is done by (or to) the subject, rather than what the subject does (active voice). For example, compare "The race was won by our team" (passive voice) to the same phrase in active voice: "Our team won the race."

point   To move the mouse pointer so that it is on top of a specific object on the screen.

point size   The type size of a particular character. There are 72 points in an inch. Font families usually have only certain point sizes available; if you need larger or smaller letters than your font offers, switch to a different font.

portrait orientation   Your document is oriented so that it is longer than it is wide, as in 8$^1/_2$ -by-11 inches. This is the normal orientation of most documents. The opposite of portrait orientation is **landscape.**

printer   Device connected to most computers for printing documents.

program   A software product written in the language a computer understands. Typical programs are word processors, spreadsheets, databases, and games.

pull-down menu   A type of menu containing selections for a Main menu command. Pull-down menus are activated by clicking on them, and the menu appears similar to the way a window shade can be pulled down from the top of a window frame.

readability index   A measure of the educational level a reader would need to understand easily the text in a given document. It is determined by counting the average number of words per sentence, and the average number of characters per word. A good average is about 17 words per sentence.

record   In a data file, a record is a collection of related information contained in one or more fields, such as an individual's name, address, and phone number.

Restore button   The middle button found in the Title bar located in the top right corner of all windows in Windows 95. The picture on the button (called the icon) is two small cascaded windows. When you press the Restore button, a window is restored to its previous size, and the Restore button changes into the Maximize button.

Ruler   The thin bar in Word for Windows 95 that makes it easy to set tabs, stops, indentations, and margins.

scaling   The process of resizing a graphic so it does not lose its proportions.

scroll   To change the portion of a document you are viewing on the screen. Scrolling moves text up or down, or to the right or left on the screen.

scroll bars   Bars located along the bottom and right sides of the document window. Use scroll bars to display other areas of the document. To scroll around a document, you can either click the arrow boxes on either end of the scroll bar, click on either side of the scroll box, or drag the scroll box within the scroll bar.

scroll box   The moving square in the scroll bar that tells you roughly where you are within your document. If you click on the scroll box with the left mouse button, the current page number will be displayed.

section   A part of a document that has different settings from the main document (for such things as margins, paper size, headers, footers, columns, and page numbering). A section can be any length: several pages, several paragraphs, or even a single line (such as a heading).

Selection bar   This invisible area runs along the left side of the document window. It provides a quick way for you to select a section of the text that you want to edit.

selection letters   A single letter of a menu command, such as the x in Exit, which activates the command when the menu is open and you press the key for that letter.

shading   The box of gray which is placed behind text or behind a cell in a table in order to emphasize it.

shortcut menu   A small pop-up menu that appears when you point at an object and click the right mouse button. Shortcut menus contain commands that are specific to the object you're pointing at. For example, if you point to a block of text and click the right mouse button, you'll see a shortcut menu for copying, moving, and formatting text. Shortcut menus are also referred to as **context-sensitive menus** because they sometimes change based upon what you are doing.

software   Programs that tell your computer (the hardware) what to do. There are two types of software: operating system software and application software. Operating system software (such as Windows 95) gets your computer up and running. Application software (like Word) allows you to do something useful, such as type a letter.

Spell Checker   A special program within Word for Windows 95 that assists you in correcting spelling errors within a document. In Word for Windows 95, misspelled words are underlined with a red wavy line.

Spike   A command within Word for Windows 95 that allows you to move multiple groups of text, from one or more documents, to a single location in another document.

split bar   Located on the right side of a document window; when you double-click on this bar, the window splits vertically into two smaller windows called panes.

Standard toolbar   One of the most often used toolbars because it contains the most commonly used commands (such as opening, saving, and printing a document) in button form.

status bar   Located at the bottom of the program window, the status bar displays miscellaneous information about your document, such as the page and section number, the current line and column number location of the insertion point, and the new spell checker status icon.

style   A collection of specifications for formatting text. A style may include information for the font, size, style, margins, and spacing to a section of text. When you apply a style to a block of text, you format it automatically (according to the style's specifications).

Style Area   An area that can be made to appear at the far left side of the Word for Windows 95 screen, and which displays the name for the style of every paragraph in a document.

tab   A keystroke that moves the cursor to a specified point. Tabs are used to indent paragraphs or align columns of text.

328

table   Used to organize large amounts of data in columns. Tables consist of rows (horizontal) and columns (vertical). The intersection of a row and column is called a cell.

template   Defines the Word environment, such as margin settings, page orientation, and so on. The template also controls which menu commands are available and which buttons are located on the various toolbars. Word for Windows 95 comes with over 25 additional templates you can use to create specialized documents. If you are using one of these templates, your screen may look different from the ones shown in this book. Also, you may have additional commands available on the menus.

text area   The main part of the document window. This is where the text you type will appear.

text file   A type of file that contains no special formatting (such as bold), but simply letters, numbers, and such. See also *ASCII file*.

toolbar   A bar across the screen that presents the most common Word commands in an easy-to-access form. For example, clicking on one of the buttons on the Standard toolbar saves your document.

view mode   A way of looking at a document. Word for Windows comes with several view modes: Normal, Outline, Page Layout, Print Preview, and Master Document.

widow/orphan   Typically considered unwanted in a document. A widow is the last word (or last line) of a paragraph that appears alone at the top of the next page. On the other hand, if the first line of the paragraph gets stranded at the bottom of a page, it is called an orphan.

Word for Windows 95   Brought to you by Microsoft. Word for Windows 95 is one of the most popular Windows word processing programs.

word processor   A program that lets you enter, edit, format, and print text. A word processor can be used to type letters, reports, and envelopes, and to complete other tasks you would normally use a typewriter for.

word wrapping   Causes text to remain within the margins of a document. As the text you're typing touches the right margin, it's automatically placed at the beginning of the next line. When you insert text into the middle of a paragraph, the remaining text moves down. If you delete text, the remaining text in the paragraph moves up.

Index

336

337

G

H

O

Object command (Insert menu), 223
objects
  embedded objects (defined), 323
  graphic objects
    captions, inserting, 127-128
    embedding, 129-130
    linking, 128-129
    linked objects (defined), 325
    WordArt objects, formatting, 221-223
OCR (Optical Character Recognition), 159
off-line printers, 209
OLE (graphic objects), 128-130
online help, *see* Help system
Open command (File menu), 176, 268, 282
Open dialog box, 176, 268-269, 282-286
opening
  documents (non-Word documents), 150-154
  menus, 29
  multiple documents, 176-177
Optical Character Recognition (OCR), 159
option buttons (dialog box controls), 38
Options command
  Tools menu, 60, 181, 188, 240
  View menu, 270
Options dialog box, 270
Organizer dialog box, 263
orientation (defined), 325, 327
orphans
  defined, 329
  files, 278
Outline command (View menu), 240
Outline toolbar, 107, 241

Outline view mode, 240-242
  formatting/selection tips, 242-243
  reorganizing documents, 243-244
outlines (hierarchy structure), 241-242
output (defined), 324
Overtype mode (defined), 326

P-Q

page breaks (defined), 326
Page dialog box, 203
Page Layout command (View menu), 73, 115, 117, 218, 236
Page Layout view, 116, 209, 235-236
Page Number command (Insert menu), 112
Page Numbers command (Insert menu), 108
Page Numbers dialog box, 108
Page Setup command (File menu), 102, 104-105
Page Setup dialog box, 102, 104
Page Up/Page Down keys, 313
pages
  deleting page breaks, 295
  formatting
    building subdocuments, 106-107
    centering text, 102-103
    footnotes, 115-117
    hard page breaks, inserting, 98
    margins, setting, 103-105
    section breaks, 98-101
    setting page size, 105-106
    switching/inserting number formats, 107-108

headers/footers, 110-115
  defined, 324
  editing, 115
  inserting, 110, 113-114
  intelligent fields, inserting, 113-114
  viewing, 114-115
  watermarks, inserting, 114
print problems, 304
single pages, printing, 203-204
starting, 98
switching views, 72-73
viewing page numbers, 295
Paint program, 120
panes (defined), 326
paper jams, 303
Paragraph command
  Format menu, 88
  shortcut menu, 93
Paragraph dialog box, 88, 93-94
paragraphs
  defined, 326
  formatting
    centering text, 87-88
    copying formats, 94
    flushing text, 88
    hanging indents, 89-90
    indenting, 89
    numbered/bulleted lists, 90-91
    Paragraph dialog box, 93-94
    Show/Hide button, 86
    spacing, 88-89
    tabs, setting, 91-93
  styles, 246-247
    building, 249-250
    copying, 249
    formatting, 250-253
    inserting, 248-252, 254-256
    viewing, 247-248
  troubleshooting
    AutoCorrect entries, deleting, 293
    bulleted/numbered lists, formatting, 294-295

343

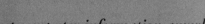

PLUG YOURSELF INTO...

THE MACMILLAN INFORMATION SUPERLIBRARY™

Free information and vast computer resources from the world's leading computer book publisher—online!

FIND THE BOOKS THAT ARE RIGHT FOR YOU!

A complete online catalog, plus sample chapters and tables of contents give you an in-depth look at *all* of our books, including hard-to-find titles. It's the best way to find the books you need!

- ● STAY INFORMED with the latest computer industry news through our online newsletter, press releases, and customized Information SuperLibrary Reports.

- ● GET FAST ANSWERS to your questions about MCP books and software.

- ● VISIT our online bookstore for the latest information and editions!

- ● COMMUNICATE with our expert authors through e-mail and conferences.

- ● DOWNLOAD SOFTWARE from the immense MCP library:
    - Source code and files from MCP books
    - The best shareware, freeware, and demos

- ● DISCOVER HOT SPOTS on other parts of the Internet.

- ● WIN BOOKS in ongoing contests and giveaways!

TO PLUG INTO MCP: ➤ WORLD WIDE WEB: **http://www.mcp.com**

GOPHER: gopher.mcp.com

FTP: ftp.mcp.com

MS END USER LICENSE AGREEMENT

END-USER LICENSE AGREEMENT FOR MICROSOFT SOFTWARE

IMPORTANT—READ CAREFULLY: This Microsoft End-User License Agreement ("EULA") is a legal agreement between you (either an individual or a single entity) and Microsoft Corporation for the Microsoft software accompanying this EULA, which includes computer software and associated media and printed materials, and may include "online" or electronic documentation ("SOFTWARE PRODUCT" or "SOFTWARE"). By opening the sealed packet(s) OR exercising your rights to make and use copies of the SOFTWARE PRODUCT, you agree to be bound by the terms of this EULA. If you do not agree to the terms of this EULA, promptly return this package to the place from which you obtained it.

SOFTWARE PRODUCT LICENSE

The SOFTWARE PRODUCT is protected by copyright laws and international copyright treaties, as well as other intellectual property laws and treaties. The SOFTWARE PRODUCT is licensed, not sold.

1. GRANT OF LICENSE. Microsoft grants to you a nonexclusive, royalty-free right to use one copy of the SOFTWARE PRODUCT. The SOFTWARE PRODUCT is licensed as a single product. Its component parts may not be separated for use on more than one computer or by more than one user at any time. The SOFTWARE PRODUCT is in "use" on a computer when it is loaded into temporary memory (i.e. RAM) or installed into permanent memory (e.g., hard disk, CD-ROM, or other storage device) of that computer.

2. COPYRIGHT. All title and copyrights in and to the SOFTWARE PRODUCT (including but not limited to any images, photographs, animations, video, audio, music, text, and "applets," incorporated into the SOFTWARE PRODUCT), the accompanying printed materials, and any copies of the SOFTWARE PRODUCT, are owned by Microsoft or its suppliers. The SOFTWARE PRODUCT is protected by copyright laws and international treaty provisions. Therefore, you must treat the SOFTWARE PRODUCT like any other copyrighted material except that you may either (a) make one copy of the SOFTWARE PRODUCT solely for backup or archival purposes, or (b) install the SOFTWARE PRODUCT on a single computer provided you keep the original solely for backup or archival purposes.

3. OTHER RESTRICTIONS. This EULA is your proof of license to exercise the rights granted herein and must be retained by you. You may not reverse engineer, decompile, or disassemble the SOFTWARE PRODUCT, except and only to the extent that such activity is expressly permitted by applicable law notwithstanding this limitation.

LIMITED WARRANTY

NO WARRANTIES. MICROSOFT AND ITS DISTRIBUTORS, INCLUDING WITHOUT LIMITATION MACMILLAN PUBLISHING USA, EXPRESSLY DISCLAIM ANY WARRANTY FOR THE SOFTWARE PRODUCT. THE SOFTWARE PRODUCT AND ANY RELATED DOCUMENTATION IS PROVIDED "AS IS" WITHOUT WARRANTY OF ANY KIND, EITHER EXPRESS OR IMPLIED, INCLUDING, WITHOUT LIMITATION, THE IMPLIED WARRANTIES OR MERCHANTABILITY, FITNESS FOR A PARTICULAR PURPOSE, OR NONINFRINGEMENT. THE ENTIRE RISK ARISING OUT OF USE OR PERFORMANCE OF THE SOFTWARE PRODUCT REMAINS WITH YOU.

NO LIABILITY FOR CONSEQUENTIAL DAMAGES. IN NO EVENT SHALL MICROSOFT OR ITS DISTRIBUTORS, INCLUDING WITHOUT LIMITATION MACMILLAN PUBLISHING USA, OR ITS SUPPLIERS BE LIABLE FOR ANY DAMAGES WHATSOEVER (INCLUDING, WITHOUT LIMITATION, DAMAGES FOR LOSS OF BUSINESS PROFITS, BUSINESS INTERRUPTION, LOSS OF BUSINESS INFORMATION, OR ANY OTHER PECUNIARY LOSS) ARISING OUT OF THE USE OF OR INABILITY TO USE THIS MICROSOFT PRODUCT, EVEN IF MICROSOFT HAS BEEN ADVISED OF THE POSSIBILITY OF SUCH DAMAGES. BECAUSE SOME STATES/ JURISDICTIONS DO NOT ALLOW THE EXCLUSION OR LIMITATION OF LIABILITY FOR CONSEQUENTIAL OR INCIDENTAL DAMAGES, THE ABOVE LIMITATION MAY NOT APPLY TO YOU.

U.S. GOVERNMENT RESTRICTED RIGHTS

The SOFTWARE PRODUCT is provided with RESTRICTED RIGHTS. Use, duplication, or disclosure by the Government is subject to restrictions as set forth in subparagraph (c)(1)(ii) of The Rights in Technical Data and Computer Software clause at DFARS 252.227-7013 or subparagraphs (c)(1) and (2) of the Commercial Computer Software—Restricted Rights at 48 CFR 52.227-19, as applicable. Manufacturer is Microsoft Corporation/One Microsoft Way/Redmond, WA 98052-6399.

If you acquired this product in the United States, this EULA is governed by the laws of the State of Washington. If this product was acquired outside the United States, then local laws may apply.

Should you have any questions concerning this EULA, or if you desire to contact Microsoft for any reason, please contact the Microsoft subsidiary serving your country, or write: Microsoft Corporation/One Microsoft Way/Redmond, WA 98052-6399.

Installing the Screen Saver

The Windows 95 package comes with a few screen savers of the not-stunning-but-hey-they're-better-than-a-kick-in-the-head variety. If you want stunning, though, you need to install the screen saver that comes on this book's disk.

Before you install the screen saver, use Explorer or My Computer to check out the contents of the disk. In particular, you want to look for two files named aviwin95 and Win95. When you find them, copy both files to your Windows folder. Crank up the Display Properties dialog box either by right-clicking on the desktop and selecting **Properties** or by selecting **Settings** from the Start menu, selecting **Control Panel**, and selecting the **Display** icon. In the Display Properties dialog box, select the **Screen Saver** tab and choose **aviwin95** from the **Screen Saver** drop-down list. Finally, click on the **Settings** button, type **win95.avi** in the **Filename** text box, and select **OK** to return to Display Properties. To give the screen saver a test drive, select the **Preview** button. Pretty cool, huh? To make this your full-time screen saver, jiggle the mouse to get the screen back and select **OK**.